"PEG BRACKEN'S *ALMANACK* DOES FOR COOKING WHAT THE PILL DOES FOR MARRIAGE: MAKES IT ENJOYABLE."

—Jessamyn West

The
I HATE TO COOK ALMANACK

A BOOK OF DAYS

Peg Bracken

A FAWCETT CREST BOOK

Fawcett Books   Greenwich, Connecticut

THE I HATE TO COOK ALMANACK

THIS BOOK CONTAINS THE COMPLETE TEXT OF
THE ORIGINAL HARDCOVER EDITION.

A Fawcett Crest Book reprinted by arrangement with
Harcourt Brace Jovanovich

Copyright © 1976 by Peg Bracken

ISBN: 0–449–23370–7

Selection of the Macmillan Book Club
Selection of the Literary Guild

Printed in the United States of America

10   9   8   7   6   5   4   3   2   1

ABOUT THE AUTHOR

For some time, Peg Bracken and cooking have been involved in an uneasy hate-love relationship. Though the course of it has never run smooth, still they can't quite leave each other alone.

When she wrote *The I Hate to Cook Book,* she wasn't aware that she was speaking for other people, too. But since the book's appearance several years ago, a great many other noncooks have come out of the kitchen closet, so to speak, fearlessly admitting that nearly anything is more rewarding than cooking is—an admission that unfortunately doesn't alter the fact that some cooking occasionally has to be done.

Hence these recipes, which are good, dependable, and mainly simple. Peg Bracken has no truck with glazes, sauces, boning things, or simmering them all day. She wants it known, too, that when she finally stands face to face with that Great Cook Up Yonder, she will be able to state unequivocally and unafraid that she never asked anyone to squeeze anything out of a pastry tube or told anyone to cover anything with a clean towel.

—The Publisher

FOR UNAUTHORIZED PERSONNEL ONLY

Before I quite finish typing it, I would like to explain some things about this book.

As I have found to my frequent distress, writing a book isn't easy, and writing even a cookbook isn't a piece of cake. It is more like a cross-country bus trip, with the writer driving. Sometimes there are more curves than straightaways, and some unexpected detours, so that driver and passengers alike may be a little uncertain of where they are going and whether they'll get there. And yet, with luck, it can be a good trip, too, sometimes brightened by new vistas and an occasional Rest Stop, and perhaps a few serendipitous dividends.

This is a Book of Days, or an Almanack, or a filled-up Calendar, or a Houseperson's Year, or quite possibly a Combination Plate. When I began it, I didn't know that so many things (besides recipes) and so many people would be trying to climb aboard. Many times I was firm and shut the door. But not always. Some kept coming back, and so I made room for them. After all, nearly anyone's Calendar, or Year, contains a fair amount of assorted this-and-that, as well as some new friends.

These people are all identified, either as they appear or else in the list at the back, except—I just noticed—for the occasional footnotes marked "Ed." This is Ed Scheidelman, who does the sidewalks and wastebaskets around the building where I was typing the manuscript. He took quite an interest, and I want to thank him. As for the words that are not attributed to anyone else, they are my own.

I thank *Family Circle* Magazine, too, for permission to use some material that originally appeared there. Some of these recipes were clipped out by its readers, who then misplaced them, and panicked, and wrote to me for help. I have recopied and sent them out more times than I care to think about, and I am glad I could include them here. Now they won't disappear so fast, for a book is harder to lose; and I won't have to copy things out any more.

Finally I want to salute all the reluctant cooks and the harried housepersons of this world who hang in there, doing as good a job as they can in the face of mountable odds. To them, with abiding respect and affection, I dedicate this book.

Peg Bracken

CONTENTS

Recipes

MARCH

APRIL

MAY

NOVEMBER

DECEMBER

"All these things heer collected, are not mine,
But diverse grapes make but one sort of wine;
So I, from many learned authors took
The various matters printed in this book.
What's not mine own by me shall not be father'd,
The most part I in fifty years have gather'd,
Some things are very good, pick out the best,
Good wits compiled them, and I wrote the rest.
If thou dost buy it, it will quit thy cost,
Read it, and all thy labour is not lost."

—JOHN TAYLOR

". . . The *Almanac* is a happy association of
astronomy, prophecy, philosophy, and poetry . . .
and a recipe for banana doughnuts. . . ."

—E. B. WHITE

January

bringeth comforting Words about Cooking & other Things, too; it considereth Matters practical & impractical & introduceth new Friends; also featureth Receipts for

  a most heartening New Year's Day Soup
  Rain-or-Shine Moose
  Aunt Henry's Eggless Raisinful War Cake
  extraordinarily good Soya Short Ribs
  a strange and easy pastry
  the Engstead Cake

. . . and divers good Victuals too numerous for mention

⋘∿∿∿∿∿∿∿∿∿∿∿∿∿∿∿∿∿∿⋙

> Weariest of trees, The Christmas, now
> (Once hung with jewels along the bough)
> Irrelevant, just stands around,
> Shedding its needles by the pound.

JANUARY 1   NOW ARRIVETH COLD JANUARY,
                   the open Gate of the Year, and through
it bloweth a keen Winde. Now sleepeth the Snaile warm under the dead Leaves & sleepeth the Houseperson late, an that
be possible. But it proveth a fitful Sleepe with tossings & turn-
ings, for this be the Start of the Year & All to do, Nothing
done. Yet looking backwards & forwards achieveth mainly
tennis-match Necke; and the wise do look hopefully to Janus,
god of January & god of Beginnyngs. For all Beginnyngs are
Adventures even though they do bear within them the sorrow-
ful Seede of Completion, New Year's Day being but 364 days
distant from Old Year's Night.

> *On this day in 1801*, Ireland became part of the
> United Kingdom of Great Britain and Ireland, to
> the considerable regret of them both ever after.

> *On this day in 1775*, the American colonies num-
> bered 2,500,000 people.

> *On this day in 1976*, the United States numbered
> 218,210,700 people and some of them weren't feel-
> ing very good.

In ancient Rome, Cato's preferred hangover cure was raw
cabbage leaves. But since the invention of ice cream, a quart
of vanilla has seemed therapeutic to many. Then some like a
Canadian Red Eye: half beer, half tomato juice. Some like
Moose Milk, a little whiskey in a lot of milk. Some swear by
vitamin B_6 pills, four on retiring, four on arising; and some
like pineapple juice in large amounts. Some take a Drama-
mine pill before going to bed, which seems to quiet the bed
down. But the hollowest leg west of the Rockies, though it
sloshed over last night, says the best remedy besides time is
the hottest-available small red or green peppers eaten with
soda crackers.

A HEARTENING NEW YEAR'S DAY SOUP
for 6 to 8

1 can tomato soup, undiluted
1 can beef or chicken bouillon
½ to ⅔ cup sherry

Stir it up, heat it, top it with sour cream, and sprinkle with chopped fresh dill or dried dill or parsley if any there be.

And on this day in 1907, President Theodore Roosevelt set the world's record for handshaking by shaking hands with 8,513 people, a remarkably friendly way to start a New Year.

JANUARY 2   Because of some problems yesterday, resolutions were postponed until today.

RESOLVED:

Not to open a new bottle of catsup till the old one is used up.

To read the newest news magazine instead of catching up with week-before-last's first, which is like always eating rotten apples.

To start a fresh rap sheet for certain people instead of adding to last year's.

To educate the kids out of the rollicking notion that just because something exists they have to have one of it.

To organize the kitchen tool drawer and keep it organized.

To hit the next person who says, "What are we having for dinner?"

". . . The man who does not at least *propose to himself* to be better *this* year than he was last, must be either very good or very bad indeed! . . . But, in fact, to propose to oneself to do well, is in some sort to *do* well, positively. . . ."
                              —*Mirror of the Months*

". . . Merely to have gotten as old as you are, and to move as far as you have in the tricky pageant of life, is reason for satisfaction—and thus respect. Just think of all the things you aren't, and

are glad you aren't, and you have another solid
ground for satisfaction, and respect of self."
                                    —Charles McCabe

". . . It's not a small thing, you know, this learning to be less of an ass, to get in there and pitch;
even to roll with the waves. And I do have limita-
tions. . . . I'm forty years old, I must accept the
small integrities of my life. You see that, don't
you?"

                                    —Anne Higgins

JANUARY 3   Now a fresh wind bringeth a fair day to
                   ponder one's life-style and see if it has
                   any.

"She's in a rut," someone said of a woman we both know.
The lady in question spends every vacation in Colorado,
reads only science fiction, and always wears navy-blue-and-
something. But I considered the judgment hasty. How dis-
tinguish between a rut and a groove and a preferred pattern?
It is the old adjective game, and we reserve the prettiest words
for ourselves. (*I'm casual; you're messy; she's a slob.*)

I know a man who has eaten cream cheese on buttered
whole-wheat toast every morning for breakfast for years.
Though he has tried cereal, bacon-and-eggs, steak-and-eggs,
bagels, and many other things, he has found that cream
cheese on buttered whole-wheat toast suits him best. So it
could be called a breakfast rut. But isn't it equally accurate
to say that he has evolved his own preferred breakfast style?

MS. AESOP'S FABLES (No. 1)

A Dog was making the rounds of the neighborhood one
morning and stopped to see his friend the Pig. The Pig was
eating peanut butter with pickles, on crackers. "If that isn't
just like a pig!" the Dog snorted, and walked on.

Next he came to the house of his friend the Ass. The Ass
was eating peanut butter with pickles, on crackers. "What an
ass he is!" the Dog exclaimed, and walked on.

Next he came to the house of his friend the Owl, who had
sold several articles on high-class cuisine to high-class magazines. The Owl was eating peanut butter with pickles, on
crackers. "H'm," the Dog thought, "must be pretty good

stuff," and he went home and tried some and liked it very much.

Moral: It's also who's doing it.

JANUARY 4   Take a raincoat and a sweater;
Weather to be cold and wetter
(Unless the weatherman's a liar
And it turneth warm and drier).

AN EXCELLENT RAIN-OR-SHINE MOOSE

1 6-ounce package semisweet chocolate bits
2 tablespoons sherry
¼ teaspoon salt
4 eggs, separated

Find the double boiler, have water simmering in its bottom, and in the top part melt the chocolate bits. Take off the pan, turn off the burner, beat in the sherry, salt, and egg yolks. Now beat the egg whites till they're stiff and fold them in. Then, if you will pour it into eight little pudding dishes or demitasse cups and refrigerate them at least four hours, the world will be a better place.

JANUARY 5   How to Make Graham Crackers and
Why

It was a raw, wintry day, a sharp wind pasting leaves to the windowpanes—a good day to stay home and do things that didn't need doing. Even the kitchen wasn't a bad place to be. So, having the ingredients as well as a mild curiosity as to whether this Graham Cracker recipe would really turn into graham crackers, I set about making some.

It wasn't long before I had a sizable supply of square, crisp, tan, faintly sweet objects you'd have recognized anywhere, which pleased me no end.

GRAHAM CRACKERS

½ cup shortening   **1 cup enriched white flour**
1 cup packed light brown sugar **1 teaspoon baking powder**
½ cup granulated sugar   **½ teaspoon baking soda**
1 teaspoon vanilla   **¼ teaspoon salt**
2 cups whole-wheat flour   **½ cup milk**

First, cream the shortening with the sugars and vanilla. Then sift the dry things and add them alternately with the milk, mixing well each time. Chill about twenty minutes in the freezer.

Now the going gets mathematical: Divide it in 4 parts and roll each part ⅛ inch thick. Trim each into a long rectangle, 5 inches by 15 inches. Cut this into 6 smaller rectangles, 2½ inches by 5 inches. And there's your classic double graham cracker, lacking only a line down the middle. So make one with a table knife, indenting lightly, and add some dimples with a fork. This is important. No dimples, and they won't look official. Then, with a spatula, put them carefully on a couple of greased cooky sheets and bake in a 350° oven for ten to twelve minutes, till the edges are brown.

This makes forty-eight single graham crackers that keep well in a tin box in the refrigerator. They are also good to eat immediately, as I did for lunch, with a glass of milk and six chapters of a book I'd been wanting to get at for some time.

. . . As to why you would ever make graham crackers when you can buy perfectly good ones cheaper, I suppose the reason is that it's rather fun if you don't have to. Fun the way a walk in the mud can be, if you're dressed for it, or the way even cleaning a closet can be, once in a blue moon when the soul's own weather is right and your mind can roam free while your hands busy themselves with a not-too-demanding operation.

Sometimes I wonder if women who hate domesticity so vocally ever award themselves a day like this. I mean a day to roam around in and cultivate, whether it comes up flowers, weeds, or graham crackers. This kind of a day is a celebration, really, of those curious freedoms you can know, at home— even in this day and age, even in the much-maligned nuclear family. They are freedoms I'd certainly hate to be wholly liberated from.

> ". . . Don't get me wrong. I do not suggest that because the difficulties of housekeeping have been grossly exaggerated by writers of both TV commercials and feminist tracts—it is therefore lots of fun. Though many women (my wife included) find some aspects of homemaking—cooking and preserving, for instance—rewarding at least part of the time, much of it is incontestably dull. Though no duller, I would wager, than working in a typing pool or on an assembly line.

"Nor can I see it as 'degrading'—at least not until someone explains to me why it is degrading for a woman to sweep a floor but not for a man to sweep a street.

"Least of all am I suggesting that woman's place is in the home; her place is wherever her tastes, talents and luck can get her.

"I do say, however, that for those who approach the home with common sense, free from the manufactured obsessions of the housekeeping mystique, there are a lot worse places a woman could be. Or a man, for that matter."

—Robert Claiborne

Now, it just so happened that the morning I read Mr. Claiborne's words was the same morning a letter came from my Aunt Henry Macadangdang.* She's worked at home and other places, and periodically she likes to sound off about it:

"Running a house is no rose garden. But it's no bramble patch either, and a lot of it's therapeutic, and you can't tell me a lot of women don't know it, whether they're holding down outside jobs or not. . . . I'll tell you something: the biggest problem people have is leisure. Anybody can handle a jampacked day. But filling an empty one with something that doesn't disgust you when you look at it tomorrow, *there's* your problem. That's why your retired men get heart attacks. They don't know how to design their own days. Women get more practice, earlier. . . ."

Here, by the way, are Aunt Henry's favorite

MANILA WAFERS

(A great little cooky, she says—no rolling out and stays crisp in a can with a good, tight lid)

¼ pound butter	½ teaspoon baking powder
1⅛ cup sugar	1¼ cups flour
1 egg	1 teaspoon vanilla
¼ teaspoon salt	

* Aunt Henry Macadangdang, nee Cafferty, is a staunch advocate of Marriage and the Home. Her fourth and present husband is Ramon Macadangdang, a handsome Filipino woodcarver she met on a package tour of the Far East in 1965. Sixty-two years old now, Aunt Henry is still a dynamo, ninety-three pounds and four-foot-ten from her shiny black topknot to the holes in her socks, though of course she doesn't wear any, there in Manila, where she has gone in heavily for stick-dancing and native crafts.

She creams the butter with the sugar till they're well acquainted, adds the unbeaten egg, then the sifted dry things and the vanilla. Then she drops them by the teaspoonful onto a greased cooky sheet and puts it on the middle rack in a 400° oven, to bake for seven or eight minutes. And watches them. When they start to brown, she says, they *brown*.

JANUARY 6   A day for some negative thinking, which is quite as good as the other kind, though most recipe books don't think so. They love to tell you to do something (usually something you don't want to do), but they don't say what not to do and why, which can be just as important.

9 KITCHEN NO-NO'S AND WHY
from Stella Trowbridge Hinky*

1

DON'T remove the blender's lid the minute you're done blending something hot unless you are looking for an excuse to scrub the ceiling.

2

DON'T freeze a stew or anything else that has potatoes in it without first removing the potatoes, for they will end up revoltingly mushy. Only professional potato-freezers know how to freeze potatoes. Ditto carrots.

3

DON'T use a metal fork for fishing something out of a plugged-in electrical appliance like a toaster, or you can end up dead with a permanent wave.

* Stella Trowbridge Hinky was graduated *summa cum laude* from Jackson College, in Hibited, N.D., in the field of Home Arts. Pompon girl, yearbook editor, straight-A student, she was one of those girls you can't fault or stand either, for very long at a time, and for a while they all called her Stinky, though she shaped up later Ms. Hinky majored in Cream Sauce and minored in Fly Spray, and whatever she says, you'd just better believe it. Now mother of three and wife of one, she is active in Consumerism; recently mounted a nationwide campaign to outlaw steri-seal plasticoat packaging of some 2,052 items including fingernail polish and garden fertilizer; is active in the movement to get catsup packed in wide-mouthed jars, so you can put some in a bowl on the table without the problem later of poking it back down that little skinny bottleneck. Author of several books, including the ever-popular college text *The Houseperson's Houseperson*, The Garlick Press.

4

DON'T whip an egg white when the egg is stone cold from the refrigerator if you can help it; you won't get the volume.

5

DON'T beat muffin batter till it's smooth or you'll have tough muffins.

6

DON'T measure anything right over the mixture you're adding it to unless you really want a half-cupful of pepper. Something or somebody's bound to jog your elbow.

7

DON'T add cream or salad dressing or nuts to a recipe without tasting them first, for these can all spoil when you're not looking and queer the whole thing.

8

DON'T store a once-opened bottle of green olives with the lid on, or green peppers with their seeds in, because they spoil faster that way.

9

DON'T think the oven is as good a place as any to store the breakfast biscuits that didn't get eaten (telling yourself that of course you'll remember to take them out before you heat the oven again, because you won't).

JANUARY 7   St. Distaff's Day.
         ". . . the Christmas holidays having ended, good housewives resume the distaff and other industrious employments."

            —The Book of Days

A good day to attack the recipe collection and separate the Sheep from the Goats from the Dogs.

THE SHEEP are the good, docile recipes that always work. They go into the card file. THE GOATS are untried recipes from friends and untried recipes clipped in a moment of euphoria under the hair dryer. They go in a heap on the table. THE DOGS are (a) so-so but not worth doing again, or (b) so complicated you know you'll never actually try them. They go in the wastebasket, eventually to be recycled into magazines containing more recipes. But don't think about that.

Now assemble thirteen manila file folders. These are for stabling the Goats. Label them

BREAD & SO ON
CAKE, CANDY, COOKIES
CASSEROLES
CHICKEN & OTHER FOWL
   THINGS
DESSERTS (misc.)
DRINKS

FISH THINGS
MEAT THINGS
ODD THINGS
PASTRY, PIES
SALADS & SALAD DRESSINGS
VEGETABLES

and one more labeled ?????? for things even odder than Odd Things. Then file each untried Goat in its proper folder. Later, should one turn into a Sheep, it graduates to the card file.

> ". . . However jumbled his desk may be, there is some distant region of the spirit where his files are clearly labeled and his papers have been written in a neat hand on one side only and are stapled into bundles with their edges straight—the great plan encompassing every particular in every pigeonhole. There is something of this, too, in all of us."
>
> —John Radar Platt

JANUARY 8   The Battle of New Orleans ended on this day in 1815. This was the last battle in the War of 1812, when Andrew Jackson's army licked the British. As it turned out, they needn't have bothered to fight this particular battle, because the war had already been over for two weeks. It was harder to run a neat war then, back in the good old days before Alexander Graham Bell and the ten o'clock news.

However, during the course of the troubles, the citizens were undoubtedly eating War Cakes. A War Cake usually means an eggless cake, for reasons that escape the present scribe. Perhaps the hens get nervous and forget to lay, or maybe the chicken farmers get nervous and drop the eggs. No matter.

AUNT HENRY'S EGGLESS RAISINFUL WAR CAKE

(Fast, easy, and easy to double in the event of a larger war)

1 cup raisins	½ teaspoon salt
2 cups water	1 teaspoon soda
½ cup margarine	½ teaspoon cinnamon
1¾ cups flour	½ teaspoon nutmeg
1 cup sugar	

First she finds her big saucepan because it's the mixing bowl too, and she boils the raisins in the water for ten minutes. Then she adds the margarine and lets it cool. Then, without sifting, she adds everything else—some chopped nuts are good too but not essential—mixes it up, and bakes it in a greased ten-by-ten-inch pan for thirty-five minutes in a 350° oven. If you'd rather use a loaf pan, bake it fifty-five minutes to an hour, same temperature, and test it with a broom straw.

JANUARY 9   "'. . . You still don't understand nostalgia, do you?' he said with a sigh. 'Yesterday's kick in the head becomes today's treasured memory.'"

—Ralph Schoenstein

THE GOOD OLD DAYS

"In 1872 we used over 250,000 pounds of opium. . . . The habit of opium-eating seems to prevail chiefly among women. The fact may explain the great percentage of farmers' wives in lunatic asylums.

". . . The prevalence of the habit among women is probably explained by the unhappiness of most of them, the mental stagnation, the liability to nervous depression, and, in the country, the seclusion and grinding physical work. Moreover, women are excluded by public opinion from the beerhall and the dram-shop, and stimulants must be secret. Opium, in its various forms of laudanum, paregoric, and sulphate of morphia, can be taken readily in private and without interruption of duty. . . ."

—*Frank Leslie's Illustrated Almanac, 1875*

These people who want to get back to the womb! Maybe it wasn't so great in there. Maybe you're bored silly, and the food has a dreadful sameness, but there you are. It is just as well that we forget it, along with teething, which must have been a miserable business too, and diaper rash.

JANUARY 10   On this evening in 1976, Mrs. James (Muriel) ("Mumu") Harbottle, of 52 Oak Trees, Illinois, discovered at her buffet supper for ten that only three people ate the lettuce that was under their Waldorf salads. So, the next day, she telephoned Stella Trowbridge Hinky, long distance, to ask her if it would be okay if she didn't put lettuce under it any more—just stuck a sprig of watercress into it, or something, and Ms. Hinky said Yes, that would be okay.

JANUARY 11   New Words for a New Year!

ANTIPESTO	Italian roach powder.
BLANDWICH	Hamburger without any onions.
CANAPEW	A small, dank toast square smeared with curry mayonnaise or shrimp paste, served before dinner to spoil people's appetites.
CAVIAR EMPTOR	It's only some kind of fish eggs.
EATNIK	Health-food buff who won't touch it if it isn't enriched with granular kelp and blackstrap molasses.
HORSE D'OEUVRE	Steak Tartare made with finely ground horsemeat.
HUNTER-STYLE	Descriptive term for the dish you must hunt around for things to stretch it with. For example, Creamed Chicken Hunter-Style means padded with a cupful of sautéed chopped celery, several sliced hardboiled eggs, and nine sliced stuffed olives.
NECHO	(Etymologically related to the small boy who said he had three things for lunch that started with N—a Negg, a Norange, and a Napple.) A Necho is (1) a variation on a familiar theme, like last night's rice fried with onion and bits of leftover meat or (2) a simple rerun of last night's dinner: the roast, cold-sliced, and the rest of the mashed potatoes in potato cakes. "What are we having for dinner, Mommie?" "A Necho, dear, and shut up."
PIASCO	What you're involved in when the pastry comes apart.
SCRUFFULOUS	How the house looks when it's in good enough shape that you don't feel like

doing anything about it but not good enough that you're dying to have anybody drop in.

STEWP Any mixture thinner than stew and thicker than soup.

SWALLUP The extra bonus of cake frosting left in the pan for somebody to lick.

JANUARY 12 A perfect day for celebrating Horatio Alger's birthday! Born in January in 1834, Horatio Alger wrote 120 books, after he grew up, all with invigorating titles like *Luck and Pluck, Work and Win, Strive and Succeed,* his thrust being that there is always a way. That is where he was wrong. He had probably never been inside a kitchen, where you can strive all you like but there is still no way to unburn the beans. There are only exceptions that prove the rule.

". . . Take Hollandaise sauce, for instance: nothing curdles more easily, and nothing is easier to fix with a tablespoon of boiling water and a bit of stirring."

—Mimi Sheraton

". . . Making a custard sauce, one memorable morning, I noticed to my considerable dismay that it had separated—indeed, looked rather like buttermilk. However, with that swiftness of reaction-*cum*-action that has long distinguished my every move in the kitchen, I tossed in a few marshmallows, stirred them a moment, and—Presto! Smooth as cream! . . . But even though the outcome isn't that happy, it must be remembered that every wife in the course of a wifetime has cooked things that had only one fault: they didn't taste good. It simply happens, occasionally, like hangnails and moles in the garden and other small unpleasantnesses which, taken in stride, are quickly forgotten."

—Stella Trowbridge Hinky

". . . In most recipes there are encouragingly few pitfalls. One mustn't go berserk with the thought, but a quarter cup of liquid, a tablespoon more or less of butter, five minutes or so of cooking time are all variable and the sooner the beginning cook learns it the better the food will be."

—Craig Claiborne

JANUARY 13   *A cold rotten day.*

Now doth the harried houseperson put plastic sacks over the sick-looking house plants to humidify their individual atmospheres, for this doth often bring the invalid back to green-growing health but not always.

"We've got to accept the idea that plants just up and die for no apparent reason."

—Lynn and Joel Rapp

JANUARY 14   This is St. Hilary's Day, known to be the coldest of the year.

". . . a day to retreat and regroup as the sleet lashed the windows and the wind whistled. I went to bed with a stack of books and a bottle. But, presently, with a nod toward the rugged life, I turned the electric blanket down to Medium. . . ."

—Albert Wooky*

As Mr. Wooky remarked recently on bringing some cookies to a hospitalized friend just back from skiing at Stowe, "It's cheaper and more fun to set fire to a few hundred-dollar bills, lock yourself in the freezer, and break both ankles with a tire iron."

* Bachelor, amateur chef, and essayist (author of *Regrets Only*), Albert Wooky was the first in Pittsburgh to know his Social Security number by heart and own a crêpe pan. He likes his lamb pink, his olives wrinkled, his mushrooms raw, and his telephone silent. He also believes in whole-grain cereals and General Utilities (Common Stock), of which he owns a small but tender fraction. A former newspaperman, Mr. Wooky still spends nine hours a day at his desk, covers the local bistro scene for the evening paper, hasn't had a cold or a headache or a hiccup in forty-eight years, and credits his excellent health to total avoidance of vigorous exercise. People over thirty who play tennis, he believes, should see a psychiatrist; and people who ski, once they have their second teeth are certifiable.

THE WOOKY COOKY

(Singularly crisp and buttery)

1 cup butter	½ cup chopped nuts
1 cup sugar	½ cup Rice Krispies (not
1½ cups flour	crushed)
½ teaspoon baking soda	1 teaspoon vanilla
½ teaspoon baking powder	

Deftly he creams the first two ingredients together. Then without sifting anything, he adds all the rest and mixes it well. After cooling it in the refrigerator long enough to write a short review of a bum restaurant, he shapes it into balls, presses them firmly with a fork on a greased baking sheet, and bakes them at 325° for ten to fifteen minutes.

Aspects also favorable today for conceiving a female child if one be female. Aspects poor for cleaning the house, however, except for dusting. Science has now finished counting and reports that there are 250,000 dust particles in the average room. One room is sufficient.

JANUARY 15   STRANGE AND EASY PASTRY!

"... This is the only recipe my mother ever saw fit to hand down to me. She kept a lovely home and set a good table, but she absolutely refused to teach the art of housecraft to her daughters, other than requiring us to keep our rooms picked up so we could find the beds.

"It's for piecrust. There are three ingredients: flour, shortening, water. There is one formula: use half as much shortening as flour, and half as much water as shortening. These proportions never vary.

"For a two-crust pie I generally start with a cup of flour. Then I have a little extra dough left to cut in strips, sprinkle with sugar and cinnamon and bake briefly till browned. My kids love them, and I feel like a Traditional American Mom.

"Okay. Dump 1 cup of flour in the bowl. Then add half as much shortening—hence, ½ cup. Cut in the shortening till it looks like a bowlful of small pebbles. Now add ½ as much water as shortening, so—¼ cup, cold, warm, or luke, as long as it's wet. Pour it all in at once and mix it with your hands. Apparently something about the heat of your bare hands has a magic effect on the dough, and it also provides the same sort of tensional release I'm told gardeners have when they dig in The Good Earth. Anyway, it's great therapy, and I can generally use some. . . ."

—Sarah Willett

Presently then, Mrs. Willett continues, when it is a sticky ball, you quit kneading, wash your hands, take half, and start rolling it out. "Use lots of flour," she says, "scattering it freely in all directions. Keep rolling from the middle, and don't go over the edge every time or the edge gets too thin. When it's the size you want, slap it into the pie pan and that's it. It's delicious every time, and it makes potpies and so forth very simple: even the scroungiest leftover is enhanced. . . ."

And so I tried it, adding a teaspoon of salt to that first cupful of flour, for luck, and found the piecrust to be just as good as Mrs. Willett said. She's right about using plenty of flour. I used another ¾ cup anyway, possibly more. But no-measuring is part of its charm. And the big virtue is handle-ability. No tearing and patching, and still it's a tender, flaky crust. I don't understand it at all.

JANUARY 16   Emmett Neitzelgrinder, M.D.,* was
                    born sixty years ago today. An excep-
tionally busy man, his patients requiring as much counseling
these days as they do medicine, Dr. Neitzelgrinder still finds
time to cook on weekends. Here are four of his favorite
recipes.

DR. N.'s
FRENCH-FRIED POTATO SKINS

baking potatoes
vegetable oil
salt

---

* Dr. Neitzelgrinder, a graduate of Northwestern Med School, first practiced in a small southern Illinois town—practiced very hard indeed, till
he felt he was finally good enough for a bigger place. After moving to
Chicago, an interest in cooking and nutrition led him to invent and
patent several helps for housepersons. Among them is a heavy-duty twin-
bladed cleaver for people who have trouble cutting the mustard; and for
the cholesterol-minded, his ever-popular STIFFO, a special butter that
won't melt in your mouth. Author of the best-selling *The Truth about
Peanut Butter*, he is currently at work on another nutrition book, *Get
Away from Me with Those Soybean Cupcakes*.

He bakes some big Idaho potatoes as usual, then cuts them lengthwise in quarters and scoops out the pulp. (What he does with it depends on how he feels; maybe throws it out, maybe saves it for potato cakes sometime.)

Then he heats some vegetable oil to 365° and fries the skins till they are golden-brown. About two minutes. Then he drains them on brown paper sacks, salts them, and serves them forth.

Good plain, he says, or with sour cream or applesauce. They'll stay crisp a good while, too, on a warm platter in a preheated 200° oven.

> "The test of a good cook is if you can't taste the vitamins."
>
> —Dr. Neitzelgrinder

DR. N.'s GOOD SOYA SHORT RIBS

First he makes the sauce—mixes

1 8-ounce-can tomato sauce	2 tablespoons vinegar
¾ cup water	4 tablespoons soy sauce
2 teaspoons sugar	

Then he puts about three pounds of lean short ribs in a brown paper sack with a little flour and gives them a good shake. Next he puts them in a heavy iron skillet with a tight-fitting lid. On top he puts plenty of sliced onions—two good-sized ones, anyway—pours the sauce on top, puts the lid on, and bakes for three hours at 300°.

When Dr. Neitzelgrinder goes fishing, he usually comes back with a couple of big ones. His wife perfected the following recipe for leftover fish, though he generally takes the credit for it; and that's all right with her, so long as he cooks it. Which he often does, even when there isn't any leftover fish, because it is remarkably good with canned salmon too.

DR. N.'s RICH FISH TURNOVERS

½ cup raw rice	½ teaspoon powdered dill
3 eggs	½ teaspoon powdered thyme
enough pastry for a 1-crust pie	chopped parsley, fresh or dried
1 can browned-in-butter mushrooms	1 teaspoon salt
	½ teaspoon pepper
2 cups flaked cooked fish, any kind	another egg, beaten

First, the good doctor cooks the rice. It makes about a cup and a half, cooked. He also hard-cooks the eggs and eventually slices them.

Then he rolls out some pastry, generally from a ready-mix, into a dinner-plate-size circle about ⅜ inch thick, to put on a cooky sheet.

Next, he opens the can of mushrooms, drains them, and puts them where he won't forget them, because he did, once, and the thing wasn't as good.

Concentrating hard now, he seasons the cooked fish with all those seasonings, and then starts layering it all on ½ the circle: rice, mushrooms, egg slices dotted with butter, fish, and then he repeats it. Finally he folds the dough over, crimps the edges, brushes with the beaten egg, gashes the crust to let the steam out, and bakes at 450° for fifteen to twenty minutes.

In the meantime, Mrs. Neitzelgrinder is usually melting a cube of butter and adding some lemon juice to taste, plus some more chopped parsley, for a sauce. As she says, it's the least she can do, and that was her intention.

THE NEITZEL GRINDER*

(Tony Romagna, who owns a small bakery, paid off the doctor in bread for delivering his children. As the kids and the bread started to pile up, Dr. N. felt impelled to do something, at least about the bread. So he got into the habit of making a bunch of Grinders at one time, foil-wrapping and freezing them, so they're always on hand for a fast supper or a poker party.)

He takes small loaves of Italian (or French) bread, or cuts big loaves into ten-inch chunks. Cuts them in half the long way. Brushes both cut sides with garlicky olive oil; he keeps a cut garlic clove marinating in a bottle of olive oil for this very purpose.

What he puts on them depends on what is on hand. The last one is always different from the first one, because (as the good doctor has noticed) ingredients never run out simultaneously. Sometimes he arranges, sandwich-style, MOZZARELLA CHEESE, ANCHOVY FILLETS, SLICED BOLOGNA, or SA-

---

* The Grinder is also known as the Submarine, the Hoagie, the Hero, the Po'Boy, the Torpedo, the Rocket, the Cuban, and the Bomber.

LAMI. Or maybe it's JACK or SWISS CHEESE, stuffed OLIVES, PIMENTOS, HAM, or LIVERWURST, or SARDINES, or plain sliced COLD BEEF . . . whatever is there. The important thing is NO MAYONNAISE if he's going to freeze them, as he generally does.† Then he'll heat these, frozen and still foil-wrapped, in a 350° oven for about half an hour, and he generally inserts a few fresh tomato slices when people are ready to eat.

JANUARY 17   Mary, Mary, quite contrary,
How goes the world in January?

Please, ma'am, it seems a desolate place,
Hardly snugger than Outer Space;
The weather hasn't improved a bit,
And every letter says "Please remit."
Now chill the dawns, and still the birds. . . .
Do you have, by chance, some heartening words?

RIGHT HERE:

". . . Fortunately we don't need to know how bad the age is. There is something we can always be doing without reference to how good or bad the age is. There is at least so much good in the world that it admits of form and the making of form. . . . Fortunately, too, no forms are more engrossing, gratifying, comforting, staying than those lesser ones we throw off, like vortex rings of smoke, all our individual enterprise and needing nobody's cooperation; a basket, a letter, a garden, a room, an idea, a picture, a poem. For these we haven't to get a team together before we can play."

—Robert Frost

". . . The Buddha, the Godhead, resides quite as comfortably in the circuits of a digital computer or the gears of a cycle transmission as he does at the top of a mountain or in the petals of a flower. To think otherwise is to demean the Buddha—which is to demean oneself."

—Robert Pirsig

† He should look up the cooked salad dressing that freezes, on page 195.—Ed.

JANUARY 18   On this day in 1976, Albert Wooky
                      somewhat reduced his postholiday ten-
sions by writing a forthright note to the retarded computer
that has billed him four times now for the alpaca sweater he
paid for three months ago. He explained with anatomical
precision what it could do with the bill, and, always a prudent
man, he wrote it in invisible ink—a drop of salad oil in a
teaspoon of household ammonia. It will be legible when it is
dipped in water, but Mr. Wooky didn't believe the computer
would think of that; and he hoped it developed a good pain
in the circuitry.

JANUARY 19   On this day in 1976, and in consider-
                      able distress, Mumu Harbottle visited
her friendly family physician.

"I just can't help worrying about what I'm feeding the
family, Dr. Neitzelgrinder," she said, sitting on her hands
because she had resumed her nail-biting after reading the
latest news release from the Food & Drug Administration.
"Like MSG. They say it causes brain damage in infant mice."

"Do you have some infant mice?" the good doctor asked,
with interest. "With my kids it was mostly hamsters." (He is
a big, comfortable man with a shiny pink bald head. Sometimes he paints a cheerful sun face on it for his younger
patients.)

"No," said Mumu. "I'm raising children, not mice, but it
makes me wonder."

Dr. Neitzelgrinder nodded. "Kwok's disease," he said.

"What?" said Mumu.

"Kwok's disease. The Chinese Restaurant Syndrome," the
doctor said. "This Chinese doctor—a Dr. Robert Ho Man
Kwok—found that certain people are allergic to MSG, and
some Chinese cooks use it like there was no tomorrow. You
use a whole lot of it, Mumu?"

"Well, no," she said. "I just sort of sprinkle it on eggs and
things when I think of it. Only I'm scared of eggs now, all
that cholesterol. But then—well, like cyclamates, remember
them? In the diet soft drinks. They had me really worried.
They said it gave rats cancer of the bladder."

Dr. Neitzelgrinder nodded sympathetically. "It's tough on
the lab animals," he said. "Massive doses, you know, direct
injection. It's a good question all right, mice or men? Does
mankind have a right to—"

"Yes, it certainly is," Mumu said hastily. Let him get started and you'd be there all night. "But then they took cyclamates off the market and went back to saccharin and found that *it* wasn't so hot, and then they came up with something else—"

"Aspartame," supplied Dr. N., gently removing three fingers of Mumu's left hand from her mouth.

"That's right," she said, "and *it* wasn't so good either, and how are you supposed to know where you're *at?*—Organic things. What about that? I keep reading—"

"Hold it a minute," the doctor interrupted. "I'm going to give you a prescription." He reached for his pad and scribbled, then leaned back.

"All right, here's the thing, Mumu: there hasn't been a safe century for the world since the place opened. And we're all going to die of having lived, right? In the time and country we happened to land in, right? In some other century, in some other place, you'd have had your choice of childbed fever, ditchwater typhoid, mastoiditis, beriberi, the scurvy, the scrofula, the Black Plague, and the measles, not to mention spoiled pork and dirty milk. Listen, did you know they used to put red lead in cheese as a matter of course to give it a good rich color?" he said, really warming up. "And prussic acid in your port wine?" And Mumu thought, *O, my, there's no stopping him now.*

"Yes, but—" she began. He held up a finger.

"Use your head, Mumu, and you can eat better and live better than anybody ever did since the world began. You can also die of malnutrition from going macrobiotic or high-protein, or you can die of doctoring. Pills, pills, pills, a drug here and a shot there. *Moderation,* Mumu, that's the ticket. Listen: too many vitamins can kill you. Onions can give you anemia. Nutmeg can be poisonous. Spinach and rhubarb build kidney stones. Too many carrots and you get jaundice, too much cabbage can start a goiter. Yes, and before they're done they'll find that parsnips make your nose grow and mashed potatoes make your feet itch. But meanwhile, Mumu, moderation is the word. Moderation," he repeated firmly. "Moderation in all things," he was saying, as Mumu backed out the door.

"Including moderation," he murmured, reaching into his middle desk drawer for his second Chocolate Wallop bar of the afternoon. It contained hydrogenated palm kernel oils, propylene glycol monostearate, hydroxylated lecithin, acetylated monoglycerides, and several other things, and it tasted darned good.

When Mumu finally deciphered the scrawl on the prescription blank, she found that it said, *Quit reading the paper.*

". . . This epitomizes the lack of sensitivity and intelligence of most plants; they don't even know the source of their food supply—whether they are fertilized by 'natural' (organic) or 'unnatural' (chemical—synthesized—made by man) materials. When the nutrients are broken down into their inorganic ions, *plants cannot tell their source of origin —whether they came from nature or factory.* And it really doesn't matter; an ion is an ion.

"And the same thing applies to 'natural' versus 'synthetic' vitamins. The two are identical. The absorptive site in the small intestine simply could not care less about the pedigree of the vitamin. It recognizes that the vitamin is a vitamin. They are identical in every way—except for price."
                                        —Robert H. Moser, M.D.

"Drive far from us, O Most Bountiful, all creatures of air and darkness; cast out the demons that possess us; deliver us from the fear of calories and the bondage of nutrition; and set us free once more in our own land, where we shall serve thee as thou has blest us—with the dew of heaven, the fatness of the earth, and plenty of corn and wine. Amen."
                                        —Robert Farrar Capon

JANUARY 20   Now beginneth the sign of dry
                  AQUARIUS (controlling the Legs)
which continueth through February 18, all this time being the time to
    prune a cherry tree
    shear a sheep
    buy new boots
    set herbs and teas in low oven for ten minutes to discourage mildew
    reparaffin weeping jelly jars
    wean a baby.

But the sociable Aquarian postponeth all these things and throweth a party.

JANUARY 21   Bringeth Interesting Medical Information!

"People consume too much carbonaceous food—as fats, oil, butter, lard, sugar, pork, fritters, doughnuts, greasy griddle-cakes, pies and pastry. Carbon dwarfs the soul."

—*Frank Leslie's Illustrated*
Family Almanac, 1872

JANUARY 22   ". . . The wise houseperson, cooking delicacies for the Christmas holidays, will set aside and hide a special hoard of them for personal enjoyment later in January; for it is seldom that she can enjoy the fruits of her labors during chaotic December, when the mere sight of a Christmas cooky is enough to turn her stomach. . . ."

—Stella Trowbridge Hinky

But if the houseperson didn't do this, today is a good day to make

ELEGANT SOUTHERN PRALINES

(*Ms. Hinky points out that they are Elegant Northern Pralines if they are made with walnuts instead of pecans.*)

2 cups granulated sugar	2 tablespoons butter
1 cup buttermilk	2 cups nuts, halved or coarsely
1 teaspoon baking soda	chopped
a pinch of salt	1 teaspoon vanilla

Pick a BIG saucepan, she advises. (The buttermilk and soda will foam with an exuberance that can shortly have you cleaning the whole stove.) In it, put everything except the butter, and nuts, and vanilla, and bring to a boil over medium-high heat. Keep right on stirring till the candy thermometer says 210°. (And don't be afraid you'll end up with white pralines. Somehow it all turns a beautiful dark gold.) Now add the butter and nuts, lower the heat a little, and keep cooking till the thermometer says 230°. If you haven't a thermometer, test it: the syrup should form at least a two-inch thread without breaking, when you tilt the spoon.

Take it off the heat, add the vanilla, and let it sit till it quiets down. Beat it till it loses its gloss, and drop it by spoonfuls on waxed paper. When they've cooled, wrap them individually in waxed paper squares and hide them in an unpleasant-looking used shortening can in the back of the refrigerator.

JANUARY 23   A Day for an Easy and Extraordinarily Good Cake.

My friend John mentioned a recipe for a chestnut cake he had acquired years ago from someone glamorous, I can't remember who. It was possibly, he said, the richest, most elegant, and best cake he had ever tasted.

In a rash moment, I volunteered to help him make one, and so, one sunny Saturday morning, we put it together with no trouble, hoping it would be only half as good as he remembered. Considering the ingredients, it would have to be at least adequate, I thought, despite Crumpacker's dependable 11th Law: *The quality of a dish decreases in inverse ratio to one's expectations.*

And so we baked it, frosted it, refrigerated it, and forgot it till desserttime, then brought it out. It looked handsome, cut superbly, and was by all means the richest, most elegant, best cake anyone there had ever tasted, including one man who was weaned on Sacher tortes as a little boy in Vienna.

I hardly knew what to think. Like discovering there really is a Tooth Fairy, a thing like this can reshape your world and restore your confidence. I always think of it as the day I had my faith lifted.

THE ENGSTEAD CAKE

¾ cup butter	2 cups chestnuts (shelled, cooked till tender, then ground fine)
1 cup sugar	
4 eggs	
1 tablespoon rum	¼ cup grated almonds
	1 cup whipping cream

more almonds for decoration
plus ½ pound of bitter chocolate
and ½ cup of butter for frosting

Cream the butter, gradually beat in the sugar, then add the

well-beaten egg yolks and the rum. Now add the ground chestnuts and grated almonds, beating thoroughly, and fold in the stiffly beaten egg whites. Pour it into two cake pans greased with Crisco and sprinkled lightly with graham-cracker crumbs. Bake them forty-five minutes at 350° and cool.

Put the two layers together with whipped cream: Whip a cup of whipping cream, add the merest minimum of sugar—say, a teaspoon or two—and spread it on one layer. Set the other layer neatly on top.

Now cover with chocolate frosting: Melt the ½ pound of Swiss bitter chocolate with ½ cup butter, in the top of a double boiler. Beat it till it's thick enough to spread. Then do so.

JANUARY 24   "Whatever Miss T. eats
                      Turns into Miss T."
                         —Walter de la Mare

JANUARY 25   "The Guts uphold the Heart, and not
                      the Heart the Guts."
                         —Thomas Fuller

JANUARY 26   A night to bundle up warmly, go outside, stand quietly, and see if it is possible to detect the Chandler Wobble.

The Chandler Wobble (not to be confused with the Lindy Hop or the Shrimp Wiggle) is the earth's wobble on its axis. It was invented by the American astronomer Seth Carlo Chandler, who thought it would be more interesting if the earth would wobble a little, not just keep steadily turning in the same dull, dependable way. Now that laser beams can be reflected off the moon, it may be possible for Science to predict changes in the Wobble which, for reasons not entirely clear to the present scribe, may be helpful in predicting earthquakes.

JANUARY 27   A cold, forbidding day. Scudding clouds and charcoal skies and old snow like dirty laundry filling the gutters. Wet. Raw. Chill Factor: −10. But a bright fire. Stay indoors and curl up with a good friend. Or if that isn't convenient, a good book.

JANUARY 28 How the Houseperson can set little children to amusing themselves on a sleety weekend:

LET THEM MAKE AND BAKE THEIR OWN ZOO

Mix 1½ cups flour with 1½ cups salt, and enough water to make it the consistency of a firm clay . . . start with ½ cup water and add more by cautious spoonfuls. Divide it in several sections and tint with food coloring.

Now the little children can mold some blue puppies and green roosters and pink unicorns and bake them for an hour at 350°. These are remarkably sturdy. In fact, you will have time to get good and sick of seeing them around, because they last and last.

JANUARY 29 W. C. Fields was born Claude William Dukenfield on this day in 1880. In his memory, take all those cute little animals away from the kids and then insult the dog.

JANUARY 30 Proper tides should neatly ebb and flow,
Like proper housewives, cleaning as they go.

But this one—see it now?—doth flow and ebb,
And leaveth all its trash behind for Feb.

JANUARY 31 And yet flowers come in stony places, as Masefield observed, and kind deeds are done by men with ugly faces. The elevator boy is getting over his sinus condition, and the couple in Apt. 24B made up again, and this morning's sunrise was a glorious full-color shout, audible and even visible, now that they've raised the emission standards over at the asbestos plant.

". . . At Sagamore Hill, Theodore Roosevelt and I used to play a little game together. After an evening of talk, we would go out on the lawn and search the skies until we found the faint spot of light-mist beyond the lower left-hand corner of the Great Square of Pegasus. Then one or the other of us would recite:

" 'That is the Spiral Galaxy in Andromeda. It is as large as our Milky Way.'

" 'It is one of a hundred million galaxies.'

" 'It consists of one hundred billion suns, each larger than our sun.'

"Then Roosevelt would grin and say: 'Now I think we are small enough! Let's go to bed.' "

—William Beebe

February

bringeth cold & storm & a garland of birth-days; considereth a rare Miscellanie of Topicks; also delivereth a purposeful Bevy of Delectable Breads: a Bread that

> *encourageth the novice*
> *or filleth the lunch-bucket*
> *or repaireth the health*
> *or saveth the energy*
> *or useth the milk gone sour*
> *or scrimpeth on calories*
> *or impresseth the neighbors*
> *or gladdeneth the ego & the stomach*

or even performeth these many tasks at once!

~~~~~~

"... I went and did some baking, as it all seemed beyond me and I felt frightened."
—Florida Scott-Maxwell
(age 82)

FEBRUARY 1   NOW IT IS BLEAK FEBRUARY,
                    poor bobtailed February, robbed twice
of a Day by arrogant Emperors; yet with what cool Revenge
doth the shortest Month contrive to seem the longest! Now
the pedestrian's Ankles congeal & the Chill Factor increaseth
betwixt Apartment-dweller & Maintenance Engineer, while
the Houseperson mendeth the frozen Pipe. In the north Countrie do small shivering Birds take cover from the piercing
Ayre & the Snowmobiles; while in the south Countrie do
Residents take cover & Traveler's Cheques from the Visiting
Tourist. And yet there be small Stirrings below ground &
Trees do a little begin to bud. And the reluctant Cook
vieweth with Envie the early Robin feeding its Familie on
raw Worms, while the harried Houseperson ignoreth with
gallantry the Muddle upon the coat-closet Floor.

An Excellent Cure for Feminine Melancholie
    "If any lady be sick of the sullens,* she knows not where,
let her take a handful of simples, I know not what,
and use them, I know not how, applying them to the place
grieved, I know not which, and shee shall be cured, I know
not when."

             —Sir Thomas Overbury, an
        English poet, imprisoned in the Tower
        in 1613 and slowly poisoned with blue
        vitriol by Lady Essex's agents, pos-
        sibly for writing lines like these

    But for a better cure, a kind of Shakespearean Lydia Pink-
ham's, let her try

HIPPOCRAS

    "Take about three quarts of the best White-Wine, a pound
and a half of Sugar, and an Ounce of Cinnamon, two or three
tops of Sweet Marjoram, and a little whole pepper; let these
run through a Filtering Bag with a grain of Musk; add the
juice of a large Limon, and when it has taken a gentle heat
over the Fire, and stood for the space of three or four days
close covered, put it in Bottles, and keep it close stopt, as an
Excellent and Generous Wine, as also a very Curious Cordial

---

* The sullens happen in months that do or do not have an *r* in them,
and are generally preceded or followed by a case of the stupids.

to refresh and enliven the Spirits. It easeth the Palpitations and Tremblings of the Heart and removes the Causes of Panick Fears, Frights, and Startings; it giveth Rest to weary Limbs and heats the cold Stomach."

—William Salmon, circa 1680

In This Month, in 1858, Galoshes Were Patented.

And it is remarkable that it took so long. February has always been a poor excuse for a month, so much so that some ancient Pollyanna turned its dependably foul weather into a pie-in-the-sky superstition, out of self-defense: the worse you've got it now, the better you'll have it later. And vice versa. Hence the old English proverb

"The Welshman would rather see his dam on her bier
Than see a fair Februeer."

Or, as the Scotsman put it,

"A' the months o' the yeer
Curse a fair Februeer."

(It took nearly as many years for the world to learn how to spell February as it did for it to learn how to keep its feet dry.)

However, galoshes eventually came along. And how merrily then they flopped and flapped when open! How snug they buckled against the elements, around the britches and the ankles! —Until the world regrettably regressed again to boots —boots that zipped or unzipped, if the zippers felt like it, or boots that fitted like skin and were just as painful to pull off.

In Bloomington, Indiana, this stormy day in 1974, a schoolteacher was helping a small boy tug a pair of tight boots over his wet shoes. It was a traumatic time for them both, and, finally, as she tugged the last tug, he offered helpfully, "These aren't my boots."

"Not *yours*!" Grimly she pried them off, and reeling back, panting, the boots finally free in her hand, demanded, "Why didn't you *say* so?" And he explained, "They're my brother's, but I have to wear them; they don't fit him any more."

February can be like that.

FEBRUARY 2   MS. AESOP'S FABLES (No. 2)
          One day early in February, an elderly groundhog decided it was time to teach his son the family

business from the ground up. So he said, "Elwell, get on up there and look around, and if you see your shadow, hurry home."

Elwell took off. But when he saw his shadow, he thought, *My, what a nice day to stay up here and play in the sunshine!* Which he did. Meanwhile, a bulldozer came along and bulldozed his old home into eternity right along with his parents, to make room for a parking lot.

> *Moral:* If you ever manage to get out of the hole, stay out.

FEBRUARY 3   A Dissertation on Homemade Bread

My trouble was that I captured, some years ago, the all-state amateur title for baking bread that wouldn't do what it was supposed to. Mainly, it wouldn't rise. And so, after some dazzling flops, I assumed that breadmaking required a special talent, like limbo dancing, and I abandoned the whole idea.

Or thought I had. But apparently I had only set it away in a warm place in my subconscious, where it finally rose, doubled in bulk, and surfaced one random morning when I found myself making a last gallant try, which worked. Either the yeast had improved in the long interim or I had. Possibly both. At any rate, I have been baking bread ever since when I'm not doing anything else, which is most of the time.

In my own mind, bread-baking and cooking have little in common. It isn't inconsistent to like one and hate the other. You *have* to cook, at least a little. But you don't have to bake bread, and electives are always more fun than requireds. Moreover, dinner doesn't keep, but bread does, for long, luxurious months in the freezer. I know jams and pickles last too, at least longer than dinner does. But they are trimmings, not fundamentals.

> *Perhaps it is this fundamental aspect of bread-baking that makes it therapeutic: comforting in worried times, like reading Wodehouse; and—if not stimulating—at least good for the morale in becalmed periods: at least there is something to show for the day. . . . There is no such thing, by the way, as a totally hopeless homebaked loaf. If it isn't even good toasted, it will still make good crumbs (in the*

*blender) for meat loaf; and if worst comes to abso-
lute worst, it is an adequate doorstop. Shellac it.*

. . . Now, it is a shame that all the experts have been busy
recently making bread-baking so perfectly clear that it becomes unclear. Like sex, it has developed a mystique and
an enormous literature all its own. The casual observer from
another planet would conclude that both endeavors require a
Ph.D., at the least, to get any pleasurable results. But of
course this isn't true. Also, it isn't my intention to add to the
literature. I only want to put down some points I wish I'd
known sooner.

1. Any bread recipe in any standard cookbook will probably turn out fine. Just don't let them scare you with their
nit-picking.

2. The world contains more bread recipes than the world
needs. Still, they have their little differences. When you make
an especially good one, write down the doubled proportions
to one side (but don't quite double the salt). There is no point
making less than two loaves of bread, and four is better, and
there's nothing the matter with eight or ten. Some recipes,
doubled, would nearly fill the bathtub, once the dough doubles
in bulk, and maybe the bathtub is already occupied. So divide
it and use two bowls, or even three, for the rising. Then borrow another oven to bake in.

3. Baking bread doesn't take much of your own working
time. Mainly it is the yeast that works. (You'll notice that
some recipes say, *Let the dough rest.* The dough, not you.)
It generally takes fifteen to twenty minutes to mix up a batch
for the first rising. Then it is only a matter of hanging around
the place while it rises the second time and, finally, bakes.

*The houseperson who thinks ahead will see to it that
everyone else who is customarily or occasionally
around the house—husband, wife, daughter, son,
elevator boy—is familiar with the rising-punching-
down-rising again-and-baking process, so the houseperson can mix it, knead it, and split.*

4. Before you start a batch, put a medium-size cellophane
sack by the telephone to slip your telephone hand into. At the
start of the kneading process, there is usually a point where
your hands look like the hoofs of some large, pathetic animal
stuck in a clay bank; and if the telephone is going to ring
once all day, this is the time.

5. Any kind of flour is all right except cake flour. Purists

scream at the notion of using anything but unbleached. But purists will be purists.

6. Whatever amount of flour the recipe calls for, measure it all out first, in a separate bowl. That way you'll be sure to put in the right amount, regardless of absent-minded lapses.

7. Any homemade bread is even better for you if you add 1 tablespoon soy flour, 1 tablespoon powdered skim milk, and 1 teaspoon wheat germ, per cup of flour. This considerably increases the protein content in some mysterious fashion the nutritionists understand, and let's just take their word for it.

8. About kneading: most basic cookbooks tell how, and some have pictures. But just in case—

> When the dough seems reasonably manageable, turn it out onto a floured board or kitchen counter, and sprinkle a little more flour on top. Now knead: press it down and away from you with the heels of your hands. Give it a quarter-turn, then pick up the opposite edge, bringing it toward you, then press it down and away from you again as you did before. Keep doing it. Set the timer if the recipe specifies a certain number of minutes—and add flour as necessary, till the dough is smooth and satiny. No pussyfooting, no delicate handling. Use muscle.

This matter of adding more flour, by the way, doesn't come naturally to pastry cooks, who have been taught the more flour, the tougher the product. Not so, with bread, if it's thoroughly kneaded in. Moreover, in hot, humid weather, you'll often need as much as a cupful more than the recipe says. So add it, knead it hard, and don't worry about it.

9. If you're alone and have to leave it for an hour or so while you're kneading, it doesn't matter. If it's during the rising—first or second—punch it down before you go, and let it rise again. When you get back, take a good look at it, if it's the second rising. You don't want it too high: it may use up the moxie it needs for the final surge as it bakes. Then your bread will be flatter: still good but not as handsome. So punch it back down and let it rise yet again, but not so high.

> If you're suspicious of this day before it starts, and think you may be in and out like the tides, it's a good precaution to double the amount of yeast called for. Then, once the dough is shaped into loaves in the pans, refrigerate them to bake that night or the next

*day. Take them out, let them set ten minutes, and
bake.*

10. The one time you'd better stick close, or see that
someone does, is while it bakes. Shift the pans around at
least once during the baking time, so they will bake more
evenly.

11. The handiest breadmaking tool for my dough costs less
than a dollar in the kitchenware department. It is a rectangular metal scraper, about three inches by four inches, with a
wooden handle down one side. At the sticky stage, it neatens
things no end, besides doing a fast job of scraping the bread-
board when you're done.

12. It's best to settle on one place for letting the dough
rise, rather than schlep it around different places on different
days. A dependable spot is the middle rack of a closed oven,
with only the pilot light on (if it's a gas oven), or the oven
light on if it's electric. Try that. If it takes longer to rise than
the recipe predicts, next time use the pan-of-water system.
Set a pan of it, hot and steaming from the faucet, on the
oven floor, with the covered bread dough directly above it,
and leave the oven door open a crack. Dough rises more
slowly on humid days, and by using the pan of water, you're
creating a humid day in your oven.

13. It is hard to hurt dough. If your mind wanders and
you add things in the wrong sequence, it seldom matters. The
bread may be a little different, that's all. Once I entirely
forgot to add the last cup of flour to a batch of sour dough.
It turned out odd-looking—rough-textured, dampish, and
large-pored, like a real problem complexion. But toasted, it
was crumpetlike—a chewy, muscular crust, and big holes that
soaked up the butter. Very good, and I plan to do it again
someday.

14. In fact, your bread may be different even if you make
it exactly the way you did last time. That is one of its interesting features. Weather matters, and so does the flour, as
well as—I strongly suspect—your state of mind. A recipe
you've made a dozen times will, this time, be lighter, or
firmer, or richer, or spongier. But nearly always good.

15. And you can make it different on purpose without
undue risk. If the recipe says butter, you can almost always
substitute lard, vegetable shortening, bacon fat, margarine,
or cooking oil. Or change the liquid from water to bouillon
to vegetable juice to beer or wine, if you want to experiment.

Or add chopped nuts or cheese or raisins or grated lemon peel. It will still be bread . . . maybe flatter, or yellower, or moister, or lighter, or holier . . . and possibly quite delicious. Also, many breads taste better and look prettier with sesame or poppy or caraway seeds or cracked wheat sprinkled on top before baking and after you've brushed them with egg white, melted butter, or water.

16. You can omit the salt from any bread recipe for people on salt-free diets. People who aren't can salt their toast or bread before they butter it. It won't be as good, but it won't be bad.

17. If bread calls for potato water, you don't have to boil potatoes to get it. Use three teaspoons of instant potatoes per ½ cup of water.

18. Any bread dough made with molasses or honey will be stickier, so add more flour if you have to. (Or substitute the same amount of brown or white sugar if you like, though you'd lose the distinctive taste of the molasses or honey, which may be what the recipe is all about.) Also, molasses gives bread a good color. Once when I substituted sugar for the molasses, the bread was the color of gray flannel underwear, though it tasted fine if you shut your eyes.

19. It is handy to have your own informal temperature gauge for the water the yeast goes into. A few degrees cooler than I like a hot bath works fine for me with dry yeast (the only kind I use, because it's least temperamental). Until you develop the feel for it, the deep-fat or candy thermometer should read 110° to 125°. (For cake yeast it's cooler— 80° to 90°.) It's good to rinse the mixing bowl with hot water before you start. A cold bowl can chill the contents considerably.

20. To cover the rising dough, waxed paper is easiest. Don't use a dry cloth. The dough will eventually push against it, like a fat lady in slacks, and the sticky dough is a nuisance to wash out.

21. If it isn't brown enough once it's out of the oven, you can bake it another five or ten minutes till it is.

22. If it bulges fatly over the top when it is done, let it steam in the pan five minutes before putting it on the rack to cool. It will come out more neatly.

23. Any bread freezes and refreezes fine, sliced or unsliced. No need to bother with freezer tape, paper, and so on. Use aluminum foil or thick Pliofilm sacks. Just be sure the air is squeezed out.

24. As for keeping it, Bernard Clayton writes, in *The Complete Book of Breads:*

"In several studies by the flour companies, the most surprising finding was that bread stored in the refrigerator stales *faster* than bread at room temperature. Ideally, bread should be stored in a clean dry place at room temperature. There is nothing better than the traditional bread box or bread drawer. Bread in a plastic bag will be equally fresh but moist. Bread stored in the box (without wrapping) will better retain its crispness. Nevertheless, a loaf to be held for a long period should go into the refrigerator to prevent mold from forming."

FEBRUARY 4   "I really dug this bread thing because you don't have to sift the flour, you know? But I wasn't about to buy any bread pans till I found out if I could make the stuff. So I started out with the coffee-can kind. . . ."

—Shirley Shimmelfenner,*
My Kitchen & Welcome to It, vol. 8

SHIMMELFENNER'S COFFEE-CAN BREAD

(Good-textured, and only rises once. Makes neat round slices that just fit the large-size baloney for a really well-tailored sandwich.)

First find some empty coffee cans that still have their plastic lids—one two-pound size or two one-pounders. Grease their interiors. Now assemble

1 tablespoon dry yeast	1 teaspoon salt
½ cup warm water	2 tablespoons salad oil
⅛ teaspoon ground ginger	4 or 4½ cups flour
3 tablespoons sugar	a little butter or margarine
1 can (13 ounces) evaporated milk	

* Details of Shirley Shimmelfenner's life would be redundant here, for she has revealed them in her many books, starting with *I Was a Teen-Age Drudge* (1955) to *Shirley Shimmelfenner Rides Again* (1976), The Bar Nothing Press. Indeed, one wonders how, with her vast autobiographical output ("makes Anaïs Nin look tongue-tied," as one critic remarked), she finds time to do anything to write about. But find it she does, and at last reports was hard at work on a definitive study of the psychological aspects of deep-fat cookery, *Fear of Frying.*

In a big bowl dissolve the yeast in the water. Then add the ginger and one tablespoon of the sugar. Let it set about fifteen minutes while you do likewise. Have another cup of coffee. By then the yeast will be foaming like a stein of good beer and you'll know you're in business.

Now add the rest of the sugar, plus the milk, salt, and salad oil. Add the flour gradually till the dough is heavy, stiff, and reasonably unsticky. Knead it, five minutes by the timer, then put it into your greased can or cans and put their lids on.

Let them rise till the lids pop off—say one to 1½ hours. Put the lids somewhere safe for next time and bake the bread in a 350° oven—forty-five minutes for one-pound loaves, sixty minutes for a two-pounder. The crust will be quite brown. Brush it with butter if you remember to. They'll look like tall chefs' hats, and you'll feel pretty good about it.

Also on this fourth day of February in 1976, Mumu Harbottle made her first successful loaf of bread.

Mumu was positive that her bread wouldn't rise for her, the way it does for other people. Even though Jimbo kept urging her to try it, she kept putting it off. Finally, however, she gathered her nerve and made some. Sure enough, the dough didn't rise an inch.

When she told Dr. Neitzelgrinder about this, he suggested that she fish out of the kitchen wastebasket her used yeast envelope and check the expiration date. She did this, and learned to her considerable chagrin that she had dillydallied so long that the yeast was four months too old. And so she got some new yeast and double-checked the date and single-handedly produced two beautiful loaves of

AMIABLE WHITE BREAD

(Fine-textured, good-flavored, and easy to handle)

3 packages active dry yeast   8 to 9 cups white flour
3 cups very warm water   5 teaspoons salt
¼ cup sugar or honey   5 tablespoons vegetable oil

In a good big bowl combine the yeast, water, and sugar (or honey). Stir it till the yeast dissolves. Add four cups of the flour, and the salt. Beat hard for a few minutes. Add the rest of the flour. When you have a fairly cohesive ball of dough, pour the oil over it and knead it in the bowl another two minutes. The dough will absorb most of the oil. Now cover the bowl and let the dough rise till doubled—about forty-five minutes. Punch it down, knead it slightly, then shape into two large loaves in two one-pound loaf pans, greased. Cover and let it rise again, about thirty minutes. Bake at 400° for thirty to thirty-five minutes. Then take them out of the pans and let them cool on a wire rack.

A Little-known Fact!

You can deep-fry small balls of any basic bread dough—like this one—after the second rising, for good little DOUGHNUT-CRULLERS. When the hot-fat thermometer says 350° to 375°, drop them in it for a minute, drain them, and roll them in cinnamon and sugar. Or have them for breakfast with honey or jam.

FEBRUARY 5   "Tomato seedlings and window sills go together."—Grace Firth

This is an auspicious day to start some, in eggshell halves filled with sandy dirt.

FEBRUARY 6   Precisely on this day, winter is half over. To help get you through the other half, make four rousing good loaves of

WHOLE-WHEAT TIGER BREAD

(One slice and you can move a piano. Two slices and you can play it.)

2 tablespoons dry yeast	1 cup cracked wheat
½ cup warm water	2½ cups whole-wheat flour
3 cups hot water	½ cup wheat germ
⅔ cup brown sugar	6 cups white flour (and maybe
4 teaspoons salt	a little more)
6 tablespoons shortening	

Soften the yeast in the ½ cup of warm water. In a big bowl, combine the three cups of hot water with the sugar, salt, and shortening. Cool it to lukewarm. Then stir in the cracked wheat, the whole-wheat flour, the wheat germ, and about two cups of the white flour. Beat it well, stir in the softened yeast, and add the rest of the white flour.

Knead it ten minutes by the timer, shape it into a ball, and put it in a big, greased bowl, turning it over once so the top surface is oiled too. Let it rise, covered, till doubled—about 1½ hours. Punch it down, divide it into four equal parts, let it rest ten minutes. Then shape it into round balls or loaf-shaped loaves, put it in greased pans, cover them, and let them rise again for an hour. Finally, bake at 375° about forty-five minutes. In half an hour, take a look, and if they're browning too fast, lay a piece of aluminum foil across the top.

FEBRUARY 7   ". . . Your proper Almanac deals in time: sidereal time, or clock-time, or sun-time. . . ."

—Figgins

And if it also deals in bread, it should mention Meantime, which is one of the pleasantest kinds . . . time to do something else in too. There is ample Meantime in breadmaking: time to take a walk or a bath or a flute lesson or a sounding of the general situation. (But never trust a yeast-bread recipe that mentions jigtime. Even the no-knead kind takes rising time and oven time, and two hours is a long jig.)

FEBRUARY 8   Let us consecrate this day to James Payn, whose birthday it was, in 1830.

Later, Mr. Payn wrote voluminously and hard. He wrote *Carlyon's Year, Another's Burden, Lost Sir Massingberd,* and many another fat novel you never hear about or curl up with. All, all were swallowed without a trace by time's treacherous quicksand; so of his writing, only four short lines are alive and well:

> "I never had a piece of toast
> Particularly long and wide
> But fell upon the sanded floor
> And always on the buttered side."

And yet, a wistful quatrain is better than nothing. It is just as good as being remembered as the man who broke the bank or threw the overalls, and it is considerably better than being remembered as the man who dropped the ball or dropped the bomb.

Apologia pro Sua Vita
"Little I said was very astute;
Little I wrote was deep or profound.
The gods gave me only a tiny flute
But some folks liked the sound."
　　　　　　　—Morris Ryskind

FEBRUARY 9　　　*A Cheerful Day.*
　　　　　　　　　　It is possibly Shrove Tuesday, too, a day for forgiveness and pancakes. Or, at the very least, for good homemade bread, toasted.

A Capital Joke!
　"Mama," said the little boy, drying a towel in front of the fire, "is it done when it's brown?"
　The little stupe. But this is a good question with bread, and the answer is: Not always.

　". . . So I finally learned, if the bread begins to smell great right after I put it in, to ask myself if it was supposed to smell that great that soon. Then I'd go turn off the broiler."
　　　　　　　—Shirley Shimmelfenner (*Ibid.*)

If the oven was on BROIL, to heat faster, you get broiled bread dough. Precautions should be taken. Place an unlikely object like a tennis shoe on the stove top at the same time, to flag your attention as you put the bread in, and remind you to turn BROIL off and BAKE on.

FEBRUARY 10　　　Now the provident houseperson grates fine all the random ends of bread in the refrigerator and saves the crumbs in a refrigerated jar for some future need. The improvident houseperson doesn't do this, having learned from experience that when the future need arises, the i. h. forgets they're there and goes and buys some.

FEBRUARY 11　　　The Annual Pancake Race was held in Olney, England, on this day in 1975.

But it was never reported which pancake ran the fastest. More likely, they all just rolled, which must have been something to see, all right, though not much to eat. *A rolling pancake gathers no syrup.*

Biscuits roll better, and the following biscuits have other merits too. In 1974, they were voted most likely to get eaten before anything else was, at a school cafeteria in Decatur, Illinois, where they are served every Friday to take the curse off the creamed fish.

McGUFFEY BISCUITS

4 cups flour	½ teaspoon salt
¾ cup dry milk powder	1¼ stick butter
2 tablespoons baking powder	1¼ stick margarine
⅓ cup sugar	1¼ cup water

5 drops of yellow coloring;
makes them look lovely and rich

First mix the dry ingredients together, then cut in the shortening with a pastry cutter till it's all tiny lumps, like small peas. Put the yellow coloring into the water, then add it to the first mix, stirring just enough to moisten all the flour. Drop them by the tablespoonful (or the ice-cream scoopful) on a greased baking sheet and bake at 425° for twenty minutes.

This makes a lot of nice big biscuits that freeze well. Reheat them at 425° for ten to twelve minutes.

FEBBUARY 12   A good day for making Dr. Neitzel-grinder's

TENNIS-ELBOW BREAD

(No kneading. An honest man, the good doctor points out that it still must be beaten. So use your other elbow, he suggests, or hand it to the man who comes to read the meter. A good bread, with a hearty coarse texture and a staunch French-bread sort of crust.)

In a big bowl combine	In a little bowl stir together
1 tablespoon dry yeast	1¼ cups hot water
1 cup unsifted flour	1 tablespoon sugar
	½ teaspoon salt

until the sugar is dissolved. Add this to the flour and yeast you already put in the big bowl, and stir it up.

Beat it for three minutes and stir in *two more cups of flour*. Put the dough in a greased bowl, turning it over once, then cover and let it rise for an hour. Punch it down, cover, let it rest ten minutes, and grease a round casserole dish. (Or use a loaf pan, but the doctor says it tastes better round.) Sprinkle it generously with corn meal, put the dough in, sprinkle more corn meal on top, and let'er rise forty-five minutes. Bake at 400° about forty minutes.

FEBRUARY 13   America's Oldest Public School Opened in Boston on This Day in 1635.

Almost immediately, then, the third-grade class went to work on America's first Valentine Box, the box they would need on the following day. It was a tasteful arrangement in red crepe paper and lopsided red construction-paper hearts. At the same time, some basic rules were formulated: everyone draws a name to give a paper Valentine to, and thus every child receives a Valentine.

Except that it never worked out that way, in 1635 or any year since, because some little blonde girl always gets seventeen plus a chocolate marshmallow heart. There will always be a little blonde girl.

FEBRUARY 14   With a truly deplorable lack of Aloha spirit, some hot, cross Hawaiian natives killed Captain Cook on this day in 1779. His widow, Elizabeth Cook, who was born Batts, survived him fifty-six years.

Also on this day, in 1842, Juliet Corson was born.

She opened the New York School of Cookery in 1876 and is generally considered to be the founding mother of Domestic Science. But just why she called it Science, no one has been able to figure out, inasmuch as its only underlying scientific principle is Heisenberg's Law of the Unexpected; and, always, the more scientific it gets, the less domestic it is.

> ". . . Of the home economists we have met in our lifetime, all had one trait in common: not one of them was at home."   —E. B. White

FEBRUARY 15   A good day to bake bread in honor of Susan B. Anthony, who was born on this day in 1820 and headed the National Woman Suffrage Association from 1892 to 1900.

SUSAN'S LUNCH-BOX BREAD

(The basic recipe makes five loaves, to slice and freeze ahead for sandwiches. It's easy to double, too, and that's a lot of bread, girls. Use a washtub.)

5 tablespoons sugar	18 cups flour
4 cups lukewarm water	2 cups scalded milk
2 packages dry yeast (or 2 tablespoons)	3 tablespoons melted shortening
	4 teaspoons salt

Dissolve the sugar in the warm water. Next, stir in the yeast, add six cups of the flour, beat it well, and put it aside for a little. (That's a sponge you just made, and it's a good term to drop into breadbaking conversations.) Meanwhile, scald the milk, add the shortening and salt, and let it cool. It will be lukewarm by the time the sponge is ready. And when it is— when it's pretty puffy—add the lukewarm milk to it and mix it, then enough of the flour to make an easily handled dough. Knead it till it's smooth and elastic, then grease some big bowls, the number depending on whether you doubled it. If not, two are enough. Divide the dough in half, turn it over once in the bowl, cover, let rise till doubled, about 1½ hours. Then shape it into five loaves, cover, let rise again about fifty minutes. Bake at 425° for fifteen minutes, then at 350° for thirty.

FEBRUARY 16   Andrew ("One-Hoss") Shea* was born on this day in 1906.

A perennial bachelor, One-Hoss has always cooked for himself, and he really knows his way around the kitchen except late some Saturday nights, when he tends to bump into the refrigerator.

---

* Author of *I Remember Mama, Daddy, Grammaw, Aunt Pert, and a Lot of Other People* (© 1968, The Grape Press), first printing five hundred copies at a cost to Mr. Shea of $2,000, and as soon as he sells the other 483 copies he'll break even. Born in Boston, Mr. Shea eventually worked his way west to Surrey, Oklahoma, where he went to work in a buggy factory. The pay was minimal, and he'd have quit sooner if it hadn't been for the fringe benefits.

Most of One-Hoss's recipes involve some alcohol, one kind or another, except for his granola (p. 110), and who knows what he pours over it. A distinct fondness for spirits has run in the family, ever since his great-granddaddy brought the first batch of fermented potato mash across the plains in a covered flagon.

One-Hoss also affirms that gin is the absodamlutely best eyeglass-polisher he ever ran into. Unless he's in too much of a hurry when he's pouring himself one, he puts a drop of gin on each lens, and for a while he sees a lot better. Also, in most bars, he reports, they give you paper napkins just the right size to polish them with.

ONE-HOSS BEER BREAD

(Fine texture, good taste. One-Hoss says people who don't like licorice can use dill or caraway seeds instead of fennel, but it would be a real shame.)

¼ cup warm water
2 tablespoons dry yeast
1¾ cups beer, which finishes a small bottle; One-Hoss points out
    that if you open a quart, you've got some to finish yourself

¼ cup melted shortening	1 tablespoon fennel seeds
¼ cup molasses	3½ cups rye flour
1 teaspoon salt	2 to 2½ cups white flour

First he puts the warm water in a cup and stirs in the yeast, then heats the beer and shortening together in a little saucepan till they're warm. He pours this into the big bowl with the red roses on it that used to be the washbowl in Grammaw's bedroom, then adds the molasses, salt, seeds, and the yeast mix.

After he's stirred it some, he starts in on the flour—adds all the rye, beats it good, adds enough white flour so he can handle it, and kneads it ten minutes. Good for the biceps and the bread too.

Next, he puts it in a warm, greased bowl, covers it, lets it rise an hour, punches it down, and lets it rise again for forty minutes. Then he shapes a round loaf to put in a greased casserole dish, and a long skinny loaf to put on a greased cooky sheet, and bakes them at 400°. The skinny one is done in about thirty-five minutes; the round loaf takes about an hour.

FEBRUARY 17   *A Great Day for Banana Bread* in honor of Aunt Henry Macadang-dang's husband, Ramon, whose natal day it is.

After Aunt Henry and Ramon got settled in Manila, we thought we'd never hear from her again. But she kept those cards and letters rolling in, especially at monsoon season. Her Banana Letter was especially memorable, and parts of it are included here.

". . . Anyway you won't believe what I learned today. At least I didn't till I tried it. You know how you grew up not putting bananas in the refrigerator. I mean, you just didn't *do* it any more than you'd cut the tag off a mattress. Well, any time you're overbananaed, freeze them. That's right, wrap them separately in aluminum foil and they'll keep for weeks without the skins turning black, and, frozen, they taste exactly like banana ice cream."

Then she included her Fast Banana Bread recipe, and, for good measure, her Easy Banana Jam.

AUNT HENRY'S FAST BANANA BREAD

(Rich and cakelike; fine toasted)

1 egg, beaten	1 cup mashed ripe bananas
½ cup milk	1 cup sugar
3 cups biscuit mix	¾ cup chopped nuts

Beat the egg, add the milk, then add everything else. Mix it up, pour it into a good-sized greased loaf pan, and bake for an hour at 350°. Or use two smaller pans and bake for forty-five minutes.

How to Use Up Brown Splotchy Bananas, or

AUNT HENRY'S EASY BANANA JAM

(Good on toast or ice cream, or in peanut butter sandwiches)

> 6 very ripe bananas, mashed
> juice of 6 lemons

Now add a cup of sugar to every cup of the banana-juice mixture and set it on low heat. Cook it about an hour, stirring frequently. If it starts turning pink, don't be upset; it depends on what kind of bananas they are. Maybe it will, maybe it won't. Anyway, skim off the froth as the jam cooks. Then refrigerate it if you're going to eat it pretty soon, as you probably will. Or pour it into sterilized jars and seal it with paraffin.

"Bread without jam ain't bread." —One-Hoss

"He who covers good bread with jam
would mix Grand Marnier with 7-Up."
—Albert Wooky

FEBRUARY 18   Ollie, a Guernsey cow, was the first cow to fly in an airplane, on this day in 1930.

For reasons thus far unfathomed by your scribe, Ollie was milked during the flight, the milk being then sealed in paper containers and parachuted over St. Louis.

But flying never became really popular with cows, and understandably. When she got home again Ollie was probably able to hold her enthusiasm down to a reasonable level. *Nothing to moo about, girls. No scenery to speak of—couldn't see a thing, actually—but you know the way it goes, business as usual, here comes old Icy Fingers. Wonder it didn't curdle my milk.*

SOUR-MILK BREAD

(Otherwise known as Irish soda bread. Good to know about if you're out of yeast and the milk's gone west. This is a good, dependable loaf. If the milk isn't sour yet, add a good spoonful of vinegar to sweet milk and use that. Or use a mixture of yoghurt and sweet milk. You can also use all white flour, if you like, or all whole-wheat, though a mixture of both is better.)

1½ cups white all-purpose flour	1 teaspoon salt
1½ cups whole-wheat flour	3 tablespoons butter
1 teaspoon baking soda	1½ cups sour milk

Mix well till it's a soft and not-too-wet dough, then put it in a greased loaf tin (making a little trough down the middle so it will rise evenly) or put it in a round heap on a baking sheet. Bake at 375° to 400° for about an hour.

". . . As for my average Bookham day, there is not much to tell. Breakfast at 8:00, where I am glad to see good Irish soda bread on the table, begins the day. . . ."

—C. S. Lewis

FEBRUARY 19   Now beginneth the moist, earthy sign of PISCES (controlling the Feet) that continueth through March 20, each one of these days favorable for

setting seeds in sunny window sills
catching fish
mending the porch
writing a poem
baking a good brown loaf

though the watery Piscean doth too often stopple both ears when Duty calleth, and sit, and cry.

FEBRUARY 20   On This Day of 1962, in the Spacecraft *Friendship 7*, John Herschel Glenn, Jr., Orbited the World Three Times.

FEBRUARY 21   *The New Yorker* Magazine was born on this day in 1925. Also on This Day in 1846, Sarah Bagley Became the First Woman Telegrapher.

History doesn't tell us what were the first words she telegraphed, and that is probably just as well. In all likelihood they were "Now is the time . . ." or "The quick brown fox. . . ." Unless a speaker gets a chance to sharpen up his historic first words before history gets hold of them, they usually don't amount to much. Like Thomas Stafford's remark when he learned that his Gemini 9 mission was finally, after great suspense, postponed. "Aw, shucks," he said, and unfortunately a man with a microphone was there to record it for posterity.

It is another matter, though, when you are warned in advance that some good First Words will be expected. The "one small step" remark on the moon had a nice professional polish to it. So did the alleged Hillary-Tenzing "because it's there" remark after they climbed Everest, although this one has a small but vocal group of detractors. Smart-ass, they say. "Why did you eat up all the cake, Junior?" "Because it was there." Whap. You'd belt him one. Hillary's actual first words when he finally made it to the top are better. *"Done* the old bitch!" he puffed. But this is an exception, so far as spontaneous First Words go.*

Come to that, one should be skeptical about famous Last Words too. It is surely a remarkable coincidence when a last remark is worth writing down. Even if you had a dandy all ready, the timing would probably be wrong. You'd come out with it just before heaving what you expected to be your final breath, but turns out it isn't. You live some more.

Well, you can't say it again now; that would be like repeating the tag line of a joke. So you have to think of something else, and meanwhile you're saying a number of unmemorable things, like Ouch, or Please pass the Kleenex. The law of averages says that one of these will be your exit line.

Perhaps the best solution is to have a well-intentioned biographer at the bedside at the critical time—someone with a keen editorial ear and a pencil handy; someone who will select the best thing among several, and write it down.

Some Good Last Words:

> JOHN LOCKE, the English philosopher: "Cease now." (He said this to Lady Marsham, who had been reading him the Psalms.)
>
> ALBRECHT VON HALLER, the Swiss anatomist: "The artery ceases to beat."
>
> GEORGE GORDON, LORD BYRON, the English poet: "I must sleep now."
>
> MADAME DE POMPADOUR: *"Un moment, Monsieur le Curé, nous nous en irons ensemble."* (She said this to the curé, who had called to see her and was taking his leave.)
>
> CHARLES II of England: "Don't let poor Nellie starve." (He meant his mistress, Nell Gwynne.)
>
> TITUS OATES of the Scott Expedition (sick and unwilling to be a drag on his teammates) as he walked out into the blizzard to die: "I am just going outside and may be some time."

---

* It is also not 100 percent certain that these *were* his first words. Another equally reliable source says that when he staggered down the summit, he announced to his waiting teammates, "Well, we knocked the bastard off!" Perhaps he said both. Perhaps he said neither. Perhaps we'll never really know.

FEBRUARY 22   On this day in 1976, Mrs. Charles ("Edie") Grumwalt* finally divulged her easy Hot Roll recipe to a reporter for the local paper, and it was all over but the baking. Now she has to think up something else.

EDIE'S EASY BUTTERY HOT ROLLS

(Mainly she likes to shape these like croissants. But sometimes she uses a little less sugar and shapes them into hamburger-size buns, or smaller round buns, which she makes into rare-beef or ham sandwiches, for hearty canapés.)

1 tablespoon yeast	**4 tablespoons sugar**
1 teaspoon salt	**1 egg, beaten**
1½ tablespoons shortening	**3½ cups flour**

Soften the yeast in two tablespoons warm water. Then, in a big bowl, put one cup of hot water and add the salt, shortening, and sugar. Cool it. Add the yeast and the egg, and beat in the flour, and add a trifle more if it seems really necessary. Let this rise till it's double in bulk. Then roll it out, as for piecrust. (It's easier to divide the dough in half first.) Cut in wedges, brush with melted butter, and roll up, for croissants. Let them rise, about thirty minutes, and bake ten minutes at 425°.

FEBRUARY 23   Samuel Pepys was born on this day in 1632, and John Keats died on this day in 1821.

There seemeth no logical connection between these facts and Dill Cottage Cheese Bread, but that is the way the ball sometimes bounceth.

* "Chuck" and "Edie" Grumwalt are the acknowledged leaders of the Mervyn Meadows (Calif.) in-group. First on the block to have a bidet and a compost heap, first to join an encounter group and first to get out of it, they entertain frequently at their solar-heated beach cottage, formerly called "Laffalot" but rechristened "There" after they started meditating transcendentally.

DILL COTTAGE CHEESE BREAD

(A crusty savory loaf. Makes a big round one to serve with hearty soups and stews, or two smaller loaf-shaped loaves for sandwiches.)

1 cup (8 ounces) cream-style cottage cheese	2 teaspoons dill seed
1 tablespoon dry yeast	1 teaspoon salt
¼ cup very warm water	¼ teaspoon baking soda
¼ cup butter or shortening	1 well-beaten egg
2 tablespoons sugar	2¼ to 2½ cups all-purpose flour
1 tablespoon minced onion	

some melted butter and extra dill seed

In a little saucepan, heat the cottage cheese to lukewarm; and in a big bowl, soften the yeast in the water.

Now add the shortening, sugar, onion, dill seed, salt, and baking soda to the lukewarm cheese in the little pan. Add all this to the yeast-water mix, and beat in the egg. Add the flour a bit at a time, stirring to make a soft dough. Knead it for five minutes. Put in a greased bowl, cover it, let it rise till doubled—about an hour and twenty minutes. Punch it down, rest it ten minutes, then shape into two loaves for loaf pans or one big round loaf for a casserole dish, being sure to butter those pans first. Cover and let rise again about forty minutes, then bake at 350° for forty minutes.

FEBRUARY 24   There's Nothing Hard about Home-made FRENCH BREAD except the Crust.

Now, then. It's a good feeling, better than money in the bank, to have eight baguette-size loaves of French bread on hand. Money doesn't keep so well now; it shrinks in the bank. But this bread keeps fine in the freezer for at least a year, though chances are small that it will be allowed to, because the reluctant cook will start depending on it for so many meals, especially dinner. The knowledge of its comfortable thereness makes the thought of dinnertime more bearable: you can dispense with potatoes or pasta and have something much better besides. It also solves the problem of the small hostess gift, if you're plagued with small hostesses. A foil-wrapped baguette indeed solves many perplexities.

But first it's best to get some pans to bake it in. While heavy aluminum foil can be shaped into long narrow troughs (like gutters on a house) to use as baguette pans, it doesn't work as well as the ones Clyde Brooks developed after he left Paris. An air-force man, Mr. Brooks went to Paris in the early fifties.

". . . when all the fresh food passed through Les Halles and the street markets, and bread came from your neighborhood boulangerie. Everyone walked to his local bakery twice a day, and in the afternoon—if you were early—you waited till your baker opened after his long lunch break. The bread came in several diameters and lengths, and each was named, but the one enjoyed by most Parisians [and Mr. Brooks] is the baguette. . . ."

He became, in a word, converted; and so he learned all he could from his own little *boulangerie* in Paris. Finally, back in the United States, he devised and is now making his PARIS X Baguette Pans, which make eight loaves, for $9.90, shipping costs included. His address is 5000 Independence Avenue, S.E., Washington, D.C. 20003.

Along with the pans, he includes a set of crystal-clear instructions for the tyro, as foolproof as anything can be in this imperfect world. Boiled down, the recipe is this:

> 5 cups warm water
> 2 tablespoons dry yeast
> 4 tablespoons sugar
> 2 tablespoons salt

1. Stir till dissolved.
2. Add fourteen cups white flour.
3. Knead ten minutes.
4. Raise till doubled.
5. Punch down, knead three or four times to remove air. Divide into eight equal pieces.
6. Shape into loaves, place in well-greased pans, and *slash*.
7. Brush with egg whites.
8. Raise.
9. Bake fifteen minutes in preheated oven at 450°, thirty minutes at 350°.
10. Remove from pans and cool.
11. Wrap in foil and freeze.
12. To serve, warm in foil twenty minutes at 350°, open, and cool.

"P.S. Try these: Cut ½-inch slices of bread, pan-fry in butter, and serve under a small broiled steak. You will be hard put to tell which is better—the bread or the meat—but the combination is unbeatable. ALSO: Split a half loaf of bread the long way, spread with butter and broil in the oven for the best toast you ever ate. And for a super breakfast treat spread with cream cheese and fruit jam."

—Clyde Brooks

FEBRUARY 25   This is my birthday, and a funny thing about your birthday is, no matter where you are on it or what you're doing, you feel somehow impelled to tell someone. Not how many birthdays you've had, necessarily, just the fact that it's your birthday. A number of other people were born on this day, too. I want to send them my greetings and earnest hopes that they have found it all, so far, worth the trouble.

FEBRUARY 26   Buffalo Bill was born on this day in 1846. And Dr. William Kitchiner died on this day, 1827, after a hearty supper and a most pleasant evening.

Dr. Kitchiner of London was a jolly M.D. and writer of cookbooks, as well as other books, with titles like *The Art of Invigorating and Prolonging Life* (though he died, himself, at the age of fifty) and *The Pleasures of Making a Will.*

Dr. K. was a popular host. Every Tuesday evening he gave a *conversazione*, at which he brought together people he considered interesting, for good talk and supper. On his mantelpiece, he kept a placard inscribed COME AT SEVEN, GO AT ELEVEN. On one occasion, a brash young guest found a chance to insert the word "it" between "go" and "at," which was considered by the guests to be a real kneeslapper, though it leaveth the present scribe unmoved.

The good doctor's menus were simple: a cold roast, a lobster salad, and ales and wines ready on the sideboard. He probably had bread or muffins there too, and he would undoubtedly have appreciated the many merits of

6-WEEK MUFFINS
Makes about 7 dozen

1. v. wholesome 2. v. good 3. makes a lot 4. batter keeps in the fridge for six weeks 5. sweet enough to serve as dessert when there isn't any

2 cups boiling water	5 cups flour
5 teaspoons baking soda	1 tablespoon salt
1 cup shortening	4 cups All-Bran
2 cups sugar	2 cups 40% Bran Flakes
4 eggs	2 cups chopped dates
1 quart buttermilk	1 cup chopped walnuts

Add the soda to the boiling water and cool it. In another pan, cream the shortening and sugar, then add the unbeaten eggs one at a time. Stir in the buttermilk, flour, and salt. Add the water and soda. In a *big* bowl now, mix the All-Bran, Bran Flakes, dates, and nuts together, then add the first mixture. Store it covered in the refrigerator. When you want to bake some, don't stir it—just spoon it into well-greased muffin tins, about ⅔ full. Bake them at 375° for twenty minutes.

FEBRUARY 27   On this day, Stephanie ("Fats") Stumflug went to consult Dr. Neitzelgrinder about her overweight problem.

"I've been baking bread till I doubled in bulk," she reported, "and now I've sworn off for keeps."

Dr. Neitzelgrinder explained to her, tactfully, that it wasn't the bread's fault. She was also (he pointed out) the sort of person who couldn't eat one chocolate, but must finish the box at a sitting. One slice of bread has only sixty-three calories, he continued, and if it's good enough bread, it needs nothing on it at all.

> ". . . Indeed, bread can be an important element in common-sense weight reduction and control, as demonstrated at the University of Nebraska where a group of students lost an average of 19.2 pounds in 8 weeks on a calorie-controlled diet containing large amounts of bread."
>
> —Bernard Clayton, Jr. (*Ibid.*)

And then Dr. Neitzelgrinder gave her his recipe for the flat, crisp Armenian bread called *lahvash*. Kept frozen, then briefly toasted and spread minimally with butter, a book-size piece of it has the dieter feeling loved—feeling that all is not lost but considerable may be, yet, and possibly even in the right places.

Lahvash must be made (the doctor explained) on a leisurely day with a mind at ease, or what passes for it, these troubled times. A fire to read by, or someone to play Scrabble with, is helpful, though not essential. The doctor admits that one June morning he delivered triplets, did a vasectomy, and played nine holes of golf before he came back to rolling it out. Much can be done in three hours.

LAHVASH

1½ teaspoons dry yeast	3 tablespoons sesame seeds,
½ teaspoon white sugar	untoasted
2 tablespoons warm water	1 cup very warm water
¼ cup butter	1½ teaspoons salt
2½ cups all-purpose white flour	another teaspoon sugar
1 cup whole-wheat flour	

1. In a small bowl put the yeast, ½ teaspoon sugar, and the 2 tablespoons warm water. Don't stir it.

2. Put the butter in a little pan over low heat to melt. Look out the window or go water the cactus. Come back and stir the yeast mix.

3. In a big bowl put both flours and the sesame seeds. Stir it a bit, then shape it into a pyramid and poke a deep well down the center. Into this, pour the yeast mixture, the cup of very warm water, the melted butter, the salt, and the teaspoon of sugar.

> (The Armenian rug peddler who gave this recipe to Dr. N. didn't explain the reason for this well routine, and Dr. N. freely admits he can't see the point of it. The minute the water goes in, it looks like the day the dam busted. But be that as it may.)

4. Stir it with a big spoon till everything is well blended, and then knead it, in the bowl or on a flat, floured surface. If necessary—it probably won't be—add a little more flour. Five minutes' kneading is enough.

5. Shape it into a ball, put it in a greased bowl, turn it over once, cover it with waxed paper, and let it rise. Now both of you get a three-hour recess, ample time for a walk and a little TM or the matinee at the Bijou.

6. After three hours, punch the dough down and take it out of the bowl.

7. Divide it into fourteen equal chunks. On a floured surface, roll each one out to its absolute paper-thin limit—an area of about ten by six inches.

> Dr. N. says the shape doesn't matter. Circles are

fine if circles come natural, but inasmuch as the pieces are customarily broken into chunks before serving, it's up to you. He says his rolled-out pieces generally resemble undiscovered continents, though once he got such a good map of South America he could pinpoint Buenos Aires.

8. Put these on a lightly greased cooky sheet—one cooky sheet will hold two pieces. Prick with a fork.

9. Bake at 450° about six minutes, till partly gold and crisp.

They keep well, covered, in a dry place, and a year or more if they're antimoisture-wrapped, in the freezer. At breakfast-time, thirty seconds in a hot toaster is all they'll need. (This is good with a piece of cheese in the afternoon as a dieter's snack, too.) It is exceptionally good with soups, salads, and stews, on almost any occasion except possibly just after you've had a couple of teeth pulled, in which case, Dr. Neitzelgrinder says, dunk it.

FEBRUARY 28   As the day lengthens so the cold strengthens.

FEBRUARY 29   There may be one of these and then again there may not; but it is a short-sighted Almanack indeed that doesn't allow for it.

On the last day of the month say Bunny Bunny. Next morning, first thing, say Rabbit Rabbit. This makes for extraordinarily good luck the whole day long, according to a third-grader who knows all about these things.

March

doth find us in that turbulent Body of Water called Financial Straits & eating our Boot Tops in a high Winde as the Rain descendeth, indicating that mayhap the Rainbowe's Ende discloseth no Pot of Gold but a Pot of Beans; featureth

> 7-Happiness Beef and Rice
> home-roasted soybeans
> cookies for when they're kicking sand
>   in your face
> Fancy Fishwiches
> some truly remarkable doughnuts

and divers other good cheap things

~~~~~~

lean month
mean month
branch all bare,
rag month
hag month
curlers in her hair

MARCH 1   NOW IT IS MARCH-MANY-WEATH-
                 ERS & Spring engageth olde Winter in
mortal Combat & winneth always, yet always it seemeth
touch-and-go, sun & cloud, wet & winde, save us, Father, we
have Sinned. The baby Lamb bleateth & with good Reason;
the Skunk Cabbage flowereth, yet this lifteth not up the
Heart. And in the Citie nerves do jangle, & everywhere do
the reluctant Cook & the harried Houseperson feel hard-
pressed, nay, Penniless, for always the long long month out-
lasteth the Money.

And it was in March that the charter was granted for the
first Savings Bank, in the City of New York, in 1816, though
it didn't open for business until July, for it takes time to chain
all those desk pens down.

But it is a good thing that the Savings Bank was finally
invented. Back in the good old bad old days, people used to
keep their savings under the mattress, and this was the first
place burglars looked. Or else they taped it to the bottom of
a dresser drawer, which was the second. Or they buried it in
the yard, where the dog dug it out and ate it. Or they hid it
in the oven, where it got burned up.

Then, with the advent of the freezer, certain shrewd folk
started keeping their extra cash in a frozen-vegetable carton
tucked between the Frozen Baby Onions in Cream Sauce
and the Chopped Spinach, which proved safe enough. But still
these frozen assets gathered only frost crystals, whereas in
the Savings Bank they grew at least a little, enough to pay
for the shoe leather it took to get them down there. And
every little bit helps in March, the cold month, the broke
month, the worried old windy month, with wind from all
quarters.

ONE MAN'S BEANS
6 servings

*(This is Dr. Neitzelgrinder's recipe, given to him by
a grateful patient. Some doctors get boats and digital
wristwatches from grateful patients, but Dr. N.'s are
never quite that grateful. He doesn't complain, though,
because they've never sued him either.)*

First he assembles, with ceremony, the ingredients:

1½ pounds ground beef
1 package dehydrated onion-soup mix
several cans of beans: red kidney beans or pinto beans and
    some canned navy beans in tomato sauce, to total about
    6 cupfuls
1½ cups water
½ cup chili sauce

In a skillet he browns the crumbled beef. Then, parking his pipe with considerable care in a Limoges saucer, he opens the onion-soup package and all those bean cans, stirs them into the meat, adds the water and chili sauce, and lets it simmer half an hour (and longer won't hurt). If he thinks to do it, and sometimes he doesn't, he pours it all into a casserole dish and grates some cheese on top to melt under the broiler. Then he settles down and eats quite a lot of it.

> "Shake a Leicestershire yeoman by the collar
> And you shall hear the beans rattle in his belly."

> "Shake a Leicestershire woman by the petticoat
> And the beans will rattle in her throat."
> —Old sayings from Leicestershire,
>   a great place for beans

MARCH 2   St. Chad Died on This March Day, A.D. 672

It was St. Chad who introduced Christianity to the east Saxons. When he wasn't preaching, it was his habit to stand naked, praying, in a spring of cold water, probably praying that he wouldn't catch cold. And as it turned out, he didn't, though he did die, eventually, of the plague.

PARSLEY is nearly as good as prayer for preventing colds, because it is so full of vitamins A and C. This would be a good day for a

SPRING TONIC SALAD

Wash and dry a big bunch of parsley. Remove the coarser stems and chop the parsley somewhat. To it, add any likely spring vegetables, chopped or sliced: green onions, cucumber, celery, a little tomato and some black olives, sliced. For a dressing, mix olive oil and lemon juice together, 2 to 1. Pour it over the greenery, mix it well, and stop sneezing. *Gesundheit.*

MARCH 3   On this day in 1605, Edmund Waller was born.

When he grew up, he wrote a lovely poem to a rose, requesting that it go tell his shy lady to quit keeping her charms to herself, and requesting further that the rose then die, to show his lady "how small a part of time they share/That are so wondrous sweet and fair." In that day, swains seemed to be no less dogged in pursuit, but they were more lyrical about it.

On this day also, in 1847, Alexander Graham Bell was born.

To commemorate his birthday, make a nice cheap little cake, good enough and quick enough to call up Mother about, although if you do, there go your savings unless she lives in the same town. Better think twice and write home about it.

LETTER CAKE

   a package of golden-yellow cake mix, enough for a
       one-layer cake
   2 egg whites
   1 cup brown sugar
   as many chopped nuts as you can spare

Put the cake together according to its directions, and pour the batter into a greased and floured eight-inch square pan. Now beat the egg whites till stiff, and gradually add the sugar. Spoon it onto the batter, sprinkle the nut meats on top, and bake at 350° for forty minutes.

MARCH 4   Mothering Sunday
                     was celebrated every March about this time, a couple of centuries ago in England. (The conscientious Almanack-person has trouble pinning celebration dates down with any exactness from year to year because they tend to slide around. But this is approximately it.)

On Mothering Sunday, the great-great-grandmother of Mother's Day, it was customary to visit the female parent on the mid-Sunday of Lent and take her a game or a trinket. Whoever did this was said to "go a-mothering." And then Mother, not to be outdone, would prepare a special dainty called *frumenty,* a dish of wheat grains boiled in sweet milk, sugared, and spiced, probably the great-great-grandmother of Rice Pudding.

It **is** too bad that any of this happened, but we can't fight history.

MARCH 5   On this day in 1976, Mumu Harbottle thoughtfully examined her hoard of 5¢-Off-Regular-Price coupons for things like the Large Family Size Plastic Pudding, and her BIG INTRODUCTORY OFFER coupons for items she didn't really want to be introduced to. After asking Dr. Neitzelgrinder if it would be okay, she then made a nice fire of them and sprinkled the ashes around her rosebushes.

". . . When my children ask for a new food product they see on TV, I always buy it once. I say, 'Let's see if this really tastes like on TV. Look in the mirror as you eat. Does your face look as smiling and as happy when you eat as the little girl in the TV?' They say, 'No, mommy,' and that's the end of that."   —Sita Byrne

". . . and I got to wondering who they think they're kidding, whoever writes those articles about cutting your food bills. Have a Gourmet Binge on a Budget! Throw a Pork Liver Party! They never face facts. To cut your food bills

"1. Go on a diet.
"2. Don't have company.
"3. When you're real hungry go visit somebody.
"4. Send the kids to the neighbors on weekends.
"5. Serve what nobody likes; it'll go farther.
"6. Put the dog on a diet."
                    —Shirley Shimmelfenner,
                    How Gray Were My Dishtowels, vol. 4

MARCH 6   Everyone should be allowed three things he won't eat, according to Aunt Henry Macadangdang.

But she admits that if there are five in the family and everyone chooses three different things not to eat, you've got trouble. Prima donnas (she amended hastily) must go.

MARCH 7   Luther Burbank was born on this day in 1849.

He was first to introduce a California dewberry to a Siberian raspberry and come up with a Primus Berry. Not one to rest on his laurels, he went on to mate a California dewberry with a Cuthbert raspberry to get a Phenomenal Berry, and a Japanese plum with an apricot for a Plumcot.

It is too bad he didn't think of introducing the sugar cane to the rhubarb, for a self-sweetening Subarb, or of applying his talents to certain vegetables that can't go anywhere but up. A fruitabaga would be nice, and so would a turnipeach.

> ". . . Looking back, of course I made a few mistakes. Giraffes. It was a good thought, but it really didn't work out. Avocados—on that I made the pit too big. Then there are things that worked out pretty good. Photosynthesis is a big favorite of mine. Spring is nice. Tomatoes are cute. Also raccoons."
>
> —God, as quoted by Avery Corman

MARCH 8   Frugal Day

> ". . . If there are bits of butter left on the plates, free from specks, let them be put away carefully for greasing tins. As butter is used with the knife only, and the knife never touches the lips, this piece of economy will shock no one."
>
> —Elisabeth S. Miller

Stella Trowbridge Hinky's Miserable Mean-spirited Penny Pinchers Which Are Nevertheless Very Sensible:

For a week, live off your hump; off the food that's already in the house. This will probably produce some picturesque menus, but it will save some cash, polish off some impulse buys, use up some items before they go west, and show the family you mean business. See that everyone substitutes a cheaper eating habit for a frill: protein-enriched toast (p.

53) for fancy cereals; instant coffee, black, for percolated with cream; water instead of soda in the highball. Or, instead of chips and salted nuts,

HOME-ROASTED SOYBEANS

(Which aren't as good as salted peanuts, but then, few things are. At least the soybeans have less fat and more status.)

> soybeans
> butter
> salt

Soak a cup of dry soybeans in four cups of water in the refrigerator overnight. Next day, strain them, dry between paper towels, spread out on a baking sheet, and roast at about 200° for two hours, mussing them around once in a while. Then turn on the broiler and stir them frequently till the soybeans are a pretty shade of brown. Shake them up in a paper sack with a touch of salt and a little butter.

Set aside a refrigerator shelf for leftovers and print LOOK BEFORE YOU COOK on the door and then do it.

When a recipe calls for anything perishable that comes only in some quantity, figure ahead how you'll use it all before you get it.

Stay out of stores as much as possible.

When the butcher marks down the meat because it turned maroon, buy it. It was the fluorescent lights that changed the color, but they didn't hurt the meat any.

With meat, think for two nights instead of one, and steal some from the first night's before cooking it—*i.e.*, get a slightly larger steak and cut off strips for tomorrow's Stroganoff.

Praise the Lord and pass the peanut butter. Two and one-quarter tablespoons of dry milk powder mixed with six tablespoons of peanut butter and spread on enriched bread is a powerhouse protein combination. Use it for stuffing celery stalks.

As insurance against future bored or weary times when you'll want to eat out or send out for something, cook and freeze ahead in periods of energy and virtue.

Buy things together with a neighbor—turkey, ham, canned goods by the case, or flour by the big sackful—if they're cheaper that way.

Powdered milk is cheaper than bottled; frozen orange juice is cheaper than fresh or bottled; canned peas are cheaper than fresh or frozen. Buy brands you never heard of, if they cost less.

When you open a can of pimentos, put them separately in small plastic bags to freeze, so you eventually use them all instead of watching the rest grow whiskers. Or tomato paste. When a recipe calls for only a tablespoon, cover the top of the can with foil and freeze it. Next time, thaw it enough to take out what you want, then freeze it again.

Try hard not to burn things up. If you often pan-fry in butter, clarify a pound of it so it won't scorch so fast, and keep it cold in a labeled jar. *To clarify butter:* Put it in a deep saucepan and melt it over low heat so the foam disappears and there is a light-brown sediment in the bottom. The butter part should be clear and golden. Pour it off into a jar with a bit of nylon stocking stretched over its mouth to strain it.

Remember that the oven and the stove burners cost the most to cook with. When you can, use the electric skillet, the slow cooker, the pressure cooker, the toaster-oven, or the microwave oven—whichever you have.

Remember that it costs more to make things hot than to make things whiz around: seven times more to dry a load of clothes than wash them, a lot more to heat an oven than run a mixer, a lot more to dry the dishes in a dishwasher than wash them in it. Turn the machine OFF before it hits DRY, and open the dishwasher door.

Set the thermostat at 60° when you plan to be away for more than a day.

MARCH 9   But You Can Be Frugal for Only So Long
    And if they don't stop kicking sand in your face, all your aggressions will come to the fore. That is the time to make

AGGRESSION COOKIES

(A fine cheap crisp cooky that makes quantities. This came via the Community Mental Health Center at St. Lawrence Hospital in Lansing, Michigan. They printed and mailed it out in the hope of channeling some energies away from throwing bricks. The more you knead, mash, and squeeze, the better you feel and the better the cookies. Makes fifteen dozen.)

3 cups firmly packed brown sugar
3 cups butter (or half butter-flavored margarine)
6 cups oatmeal, uncooked
1 tablespoon baking soda
3 cups all-purpose flour

Put all this in a big bowl and knead, mash, squeeze. Then form the dough into small balls and put them on ungreased baking sheets. Butter the bottom of a small glass, dip it in granulated sugar, then mash the balls flat. Bake at 350° for ten to twelve minutes. Let them cool a few minutes, then remove them with a spatula onto paper towels or brown grocery sacks. Put them in cans with good tight lids when the cookies are thoroughly cooled and crisp.

MARCH 10   March Hare Day
    No one is quite sure what March hares are mad about, unless it is because we eat them and simultaneously make a big fuss over the twinkle-nosed Easter bunny, which does seem a little hypocritical.

The man who butchers the rabbits at the supermarket says he can taste the difference between a rabbit killed this morning and one killed this afternoon, but then he is a hare-splitter. Still, some people are supersensitive about chickens too, and they want a chicken that squawked its last squawk approximately six minutes before they buy it. This is getting harder to achieve. But sometimes these people bribe the butcher with a jug of his favorite tipple to tell them the Chicken Code. (In big markets, where packaged chicken is often coded as to which day of the week it came in, the butcher—the little dickens—is likely to spread out the stale chicken on top.)

MARCH 11   On this day in 1847, Johnny Appleseed died, after roaming for years about the Ohio River Valley, planting apple trees.

> A toast to Johnny now, a very
> Special kind of missionary
> Who roamed the hills and vernal glade
>   By early Spring enchanted,
> Who did his praying with a spade
>   And never preached, but planted.

And on the very next day, MARCH 12, in 1912, the U.S. Girl Scouts were founded, and the Girl Scout Cooky was invented the very same afternoon. In honor of them both, make

APPLE BROWNIES

First, cream together	Sift together and add
a stick of butter	1 cup flour
1 cup sugar	½ teaspoon each soda
Add	baking powder
1 beaten egg	cinnamon
2 medium-sized chopped apples	
½ cup chopped nuts	

Pour it into a greased brownie-sized pan—eight by eight inches or seven by eleven inches—and bake at 350° about forty minutes. Cool it in the pan and cut in squares.

MARCH 13   A day of delicate sunshine and breeze nearly lyrical. Undoubtedly the weather is practicing up for an early springtime.

A Day for Flower Salad: Make it of nasturtium leaves, including some blossoms, plus the leaves of wild violets, "sweeter than the lids of Juno's eyes," as well as rich in vitamins A and C, a fact that Shakespeare probably didn't know or he would have mentioned it. Wild violets are usually found on sunny banks half-protected by hedges, or in woodsy vacant lots if you get there before the bulldozer does.

MARCH 14 On this day in 1879, Albert Einstein was born.

Many people are unaware that if he hadn't discovered the theory of photoelectric effect in 1905, we probably wouldn't have television yet. And if we didn't, the houseperson wouldn't be able to watch—among many other things—those exquisite feminine fingers whisk the charred sludge out of a skillet with touch of Magic *Voilà!*, which gives her hands a beauty treatment.

> Harken, friend and gentle neighbor,
> To a truth I know for sure:
> Manual—er—personual labor
> Never helped a personicure.

Baking soda is cheaper than *Voilà!* and two tablespoons of it in a cup of water, boiled for ten minutes or so in the burned skillet, will make the stuff easier to remove.

MARCH 15 Died, on this day in 1655, Theodore Turquet de Mayerne, a famous physician, doctor, and cook. In his cookbook, *Archimagirus Anglo-Gallicus*, a catchy title for those days, the chef-d'oeuvre is "A City of London Pie," which called for—among other things—eighteen sparrows, a peck of oysters, forty chestnuts, a pound of dates. . . . And this wasn't a particularly expensive recipe then, because both oysters and chestnuts were plentiful, and sparrows were free.

Times change. Today, ground beef is the stand-by, and the next three ground beef dishes will feed six or eight, cheaply.

7-HAPPINESS BEEF AND RICE

1. It is meat and starch combined.
2. Neither has to be cooked first.
3. Everything goes together at once.
4. Very young people and very old people like it, and the others don't mind it much.

5. The amount of meat depends on what's there.
6. Odds-and-ends of vegetables can go into it.
7. Though it looks like dog food when it goes into the oven, it doesn't when it comes out.

¼ cup salad oil	1 teaspoon salt, pepper, paprika
1 cup uncooked rice	1 medium onion, chopped
½ to 1½ pounds ground beef	2 cups V-8 or tomato juice
small bottle of stuffed olives, sliced	2 cups boiling water
	grated cheese to spread on top

Crumble the raw beef in a big bowl. Add everything but the cheese and mix it up. Pour it into a nine-by-thirteen-inch baking pan and bake for an hour at 350°. Then reduce the heat and bake an hour longer. Half an hour before serving time, sprinkle the grated cheese on, and finish baking.

4-HAPPINESS SPAGHETTI

1. People with hearty, uncritical appetites like it and eat it—little kids, football players, and guests who had a third Martini.
2. It is quickly put together ahead of time.
3. It doesn't cost much.
4. It will sit in a 200° oven for an hour or longer without being noticeably affected.

2 pounds ground beef crumbled and browned in a little oil
2 large onions, chopped and sautéed till transparent
2 cans Franco-American or similar spaghetti
1 or 2 cans drained mushrooms, the more the merrier
8½-ounce can of petite peas, the petiter the better
½ pound sharp cheese
1 cup tomato juice (or enough that it cames about halfway up through the food)

Layer these things in this order: beef, onion, spaghetti, mushrooms, peas. Sprinkle it well with garlic salt and pepper, plus several squirts of Worcestershire sauce. Put the cheese on top and pour on the tomato juice. Freeze it if you like, or keep it in the refrigerator as long as thirty-six hours. (Either way, warm it to room temperature before you cook it.) Or bake it immediately, covered, in a 325° oven, at least an hour.

ITALIAN CHOP SUEY

(or Chinese Macaroni)

1½ pounds ground beef, lean   1 6-ounce tomato paste
2 medium onions   ¼ cup soy sauce
2 green peppers   1 pound small shell macaroni
5 stalks of celery

Pan-fry the ground beef in a little oil till it loses its pinkness. Then add the sliced vegetables and let them simmer thoughtfully for ten minutes. Then add the tomato paste plus two or three cans of water (some like it wetter, some like it dryer) and the soy sauce. Simmer it, covered, forty-five minutes. Finally, cook the shell macaroni the way it says to on the package, drain it, add it, and serve.

MARCH 16   On this day last week, Mumu Harbottle started rubbing expensive French Turtle Butter into her face because her skin was rough enough to sand floors with. Now she says it would only sand smaller objects like footstools and birdhouses.

". . . It makes little sense to skimp on groceries, only to spend the savings on cosmetics, when such splendid beauty aids are already in the pantry or the refrigerator. *Mayonnaise* is literally a cold cream that cleanses and protects—a real boon to sensitive skins. *Corn meal* sprinkled on a soapy cloth cleanses deep-down. *Egg white*, lightly beaten and allowed to dry on the face, is a mask that tones, stimulates, beautifies. . . ."   —Stella Trowbridge Hinky (*Ibid.*)

A Powder to Make the Teeth Sweet!
    "Take the powder of Sage the Shavings of ivory put them amongft ye juice of lemons & every evening and morning rub your teeth therewith & it will make them both white & fweet."   —*Toilet of Flora*
       (15th century)

MARCH 17   Now the Length of the Day Exactly Equals the Length of the Night.
And St. Patrick was born on this day, A.D. 464.

"GOD KEEP US AND SAVE US!"
CRIED OLD MRS. DAVIS

"God love and presarve us!"
Cried old Mrs. Jarvis

"You're making me nervous,"
Said young Mrs. Purvis

Not everyone knows that St. Patrick rid the Emerald Isle of Druids as well as snakes, but nevertheless it is the absolute Irish truth. Pursuing the accepted modern policy of curing a country if it kills it, he cursed the fertile Irish lands so they became dreary bogs, cursed the rivers so they produced no fish, and cursed their very kettles so that no amount of fire and patience could make them boil. Finally—why didn't he think of it in the first place?—he cursed the Druids themselves, so that the earth opened up and swallowed them.

Indeed, St. Patrick had quite a way of doing bad while he was doing good, though presumably he didn't mean to. Once when the venerable saint had finally converted a stubborn Irish chief, he baptized him while leaning heavily on his crozier, unaware that the point of it was resting on the chief's big toe. It must have hurt like billy-be-damned, for the blood gushed forth. But the poor chief thought this was part of the act and never even said Ow. The place where this happened is called Struthfhuil (pronounced *Struill*).

GREEN PANCAKES
(pronounced *Frittaten*)

4 cups grated raw zucchini	salt and pepper
1 cup flour	½ teaspoon thyme
2 teaspoons baking powder	butter for frying
2 eggs, well beaten	

Put the grated zucchini in a bowl. Sift the flour and baking powder together and beat the mixture into the vegetable. Then beat in the eggs, salt, pepper, and thyme. Blend it till it's a thick pancake batter, then drop by the spoonful into a skillet containing some good hot butter. What you're aiming for is pancakes about three inches wide. The British find them good accompaniment for the Sunday joint.*

---

* English families like to go out for Sunday-night supper, to some one special pub, which is called "the Sunday joint."—Ed.

MARCH 18   This was the day Noah and his wife entered the Ark. Legend has taken more liberties with Noah's wife than Noah probably ever did, because no would would dare take any with an old battle-ax like that. She not only sneered at Noah for being so gullible as to build the Ark in the first place, she refused to enter it when it was built. Then, when it really started to rain hard, she jumped into it and then jumped on *him*, beating him with her fists.

But we must look at her side of it. Perhaps Noah's track record wasn't so good. Perhaps he had tried and failed at many a darn-fool thing, and to Noah's wife this may have looked like just one more. Then too, as she watched all those animals filing in, she probably saw clearly who would get to play janitor, and it wasn't Noah; he'd be at the helm.

Worst of all must have been her swift realization after it started to rain that he was right, after all. She would never hear the end of his I-told-you-so's if she lived to be a thousand. It's no wonder she beat him up.

MARCH 19   This is the day when the swallows fly back to Capistrano, and if they don't always hit the date precisely, they come twittering in on some other day, sometimes after a journey of ten thousand miles, to the considerable relief of the Capistrano Chamber of Commerce.

This particular Capistrano swallow is the cliff swallow, *Petrochelidon pyrrohonta*, with a square tail and a light-brown patch on his rump. (A bird's tail is not synonymous with his rump; see any Bird Book.) The reason they fly back to Capistrano is that ten thousand miles is too far to walk. Swallows are noted for their strong wings and weak feet.

MARCH 20   Heigh-ho Spring-time,
Pretty pretty ring-time!
Sun-time! Dance-time!
Aphids in the plants time!

". . . Chives will keep aphids away from roses; most of the aromatic herbs—such as borage, lav-

ender, sage, parsley, or dill—will repel great num-
bers of garden pests, while marigolds seem to
protect almost any garden from almost anything!"
            —*The Mother Earth News Almanac*

". . . Garden chores for March are numerous and
unpleasant but, as Dostoevsky pointed out, happiness is earned through suffering. . . ."
            —Grace Firth

MARCH 21   Now beginneth the sign of ARIES (con-
                   trolling the Head) that lasteth through
April 19, all days mightily auspicious for
    planting early peas
    playing poker for large stakes
    killing weeds in the gravel
    conceiving children
and the enterprising energetic Arien doth hop to it with a
right good will.

". . . When one's work gloves are temporarily mislaid,
soapy lather is a fair substitute. Before gardening or garage
work, I often soap my hands, working the lather well into
and around the nails, then letting it dry. Grease and dirt will
wash off easily then. I have always been rather proud of
my hands. . . ."

            —Albert Wooky (*Ibid.*)

MARCH 22   On this day in 1976 in Duluth, Minne-
                   sota, Dorothea Hoenig for the twenty-
eighth time cremated a final cooky-sheetful of Nut Nuggets
because she forgot to slip the timer into her pocket when she
went into the other room to answer the phone. She estimated
that it was a 42-cent mistake, not including the cost of the
electricity.

MS. AESOP'S FABLES (No. 3)

A Stick and a Stone were of some small service to a Hindu
holy man, and in gratitude he said he would transform them
into any other Object they desired to be. The solid Stone said
he would like to become a Strongbox, to protect the holy

man's Sacred Relics, but the vain Stick said it wanted to become a beautiful Hindu Robe.

Thus it came to pass: the Stone became a Strongbox and the Stick became a Robe. But on that night, a terrible fire ravaged the village, burning down the holy man's hut, burning up the Robe, but leaving the Strongbox untouched.

> *Moral:* Better be Safe than Sari.

MARCH 23   On this day in 1769, William Smith was born. He is known as the Father of English Geology. And on this day in 1975, Mumu Harbottle visited her local Board of Environmental Control to try to get some things clear in her head.

"What can I do for you, Mrs. Harbottle?" said Firman Fuller, the head of the board.

"Well, I saw the cutest idea in a magazine," Mumu said.

"Yes?" said Mr. Fuller.

"About table settings," Mumu elaborated.

"Yes?" said Mr. Fuller, looking polite but restive.

"Well, and I wanted sort of an Environmental Impact Statement on it," said Mumu. "This article said to use little terry-cloth guest towels in napkin rings, instead of paper napkins. To save paper and, you know, like trees?"

"A sound idea," said Mr. Fuller. "And?"

"So I thought, fine," said Mumu. "And I bought some napkin rings, and then I got my little guest towels out of the drawer—you know how guests always sneak a corner of a big bath towel anyway; they don't want to mess up one of those little things—"

"Yes," said Mr. Fuller. "And?"

"And so I put them on the table, and that night my husband said, What's this? And I said it was his napkin. And he said, Are we having spareribs? And I said, No, it's your napkin, and you'll get a clean one next week."

Mr. Fuller nodded approvingly.

"So then the next night," Mumu continued, "Jimbo—my husband—said he'd rather have a clean paper napkin. And I said, But look at the trees we're saving!"

"That's right!" said Mr. Fuller. "It takes seventeen trees to make a ton of paper."

"Yes," Mumu said. "But Jimbo is an accountant, and he figured it out—so much detergent per wash-load, so much water, so much spray-and-wash for the bad stains, out of one of those aerosol cans. And then so much energy per dryer-load because I can't dry outside, it's so wet now. And actually the paper napkins are biodegradable, and . . ." She trailed off, unhappily.

"Well . . ." Mr. Fuller said judiciously, placing his fingertips neatly together, tent-fashion. "Your husband has an interesting point there, a ve-e-ry interesting point."

Fortunately his secretary came in then to tell him he had a long-distance call, and, taking the telephone, he waved Mumu away. She backed out, mouthing her earnest thanks.

> ". . . It's no wonder we spend so much of our daily life saving one another's faces. It's the least we can do."
>
> —Peter de Vries

MARCH 24   Conger T. Hatt Day

". . . We are bemused and befogged with trivia, so that we don't see the big issue. If most Americans—that is, the affluent among them—would say, once and for all, 'Okay: we'll settle for one car, one house, one bicycle, and we'll share appliances and quit keeping an eye on the Joneses . . .' maybe the Joneses would wither from insufficient attention. Then *all* Americans and a greater part of the world could live quite comfortably with less work, while honestly pursuing those goals to which, so far, they have given only lip-service."
          —Conger T. Hatt

> "Who's first?"
>
> —Shirley Shimmelfenner,
> *Crack-Up!*, vol. 13

MARCH 25   Frogs haven't appeared yet in most places, which is just as well for them.

". . . As part of his fishing gear, my grandfather carried an empty beer bucket (a half-gallon container with a tight lid) in which he laid the cleaned frogs' legs for Grandma to fry like chicken when we got home.

"He liked to clean his meat or fish on the creek bank,

because throwing the offal back into the water helped to sustain the balance of wildlife. 'I trade with the creek,' he declared. 'Other creatures' food for frogs' legs.' He believed that the earth was a gigantic balance, that when you used one resource you were obligated to trade back to the earth in another way. . . . 'You got to have something to trade, either with the earth or with other people,' he told me over and over."

—Grace Firth (*Ibid.*)

MARCH 26   On this very day a few decades ago, Adhesive Plaster was patented by Dr. Day and Dr. Shecut.

> "Hooray for us!" cried Dr. S.
>   "Now bandages will stick!
> For hospitals, and such, I guess
>   The stuff will do the trick!"

> "You're right, it's swell!" said Dr. D.,
>   "For First Aid—sea or land aid—
> But dammit, think how rich we'd be
>   If it had been The Band-Aid!"

MARCH 27   And Now a Fine Cheap Way to Fill Up Chinks! One-Hoss, who never feels too hard up if there's something around that he likes to munch on, occasionally makes himself a fast batch of

GOOD PHONY DOUGHNUTS

He buys a loaf of soft, spongy white store-bread, cuts the crusts off eight slices, and cuts them in quarters. Then, whistling gently through his teeth, he mixes up

1½ cups biscuit mix	1 beaten egg
1 tablespoon sugar	¾ cup milk
1 teaspoon baking powder	¼ teaspoon nutmeg

and some grated lemon peel if he can find the lemon. He also heats some oil in a saucepan—a few inches of it—till it's hot enough to brown a small cube of bread in about fifty seconds (or about 370° on a deep-fat thermometer, which he doesn't have). With a two-tined fork, he dips the bread quarters into the batter, drops them into the fat, and cooks them. Then he lets them drain on an old grocery sack before he rolls them in granulated sugar.

Somebody told him that if he'd make jam sandwiches* to quarter and dip the same way, he'd have some Jam Doughnuts. It sounded logical, and he's thinking seriously about it for next time.

Dear Aloise,

These experts that tell you to go buy some cheesecloth to strain your hot fat through make me laugh! Don't they know you can use old nylons? Or paper towels?

L. C.

Dear L.C.,

You're tops! I tried it and it works! What would we do without folks like you? I love you!

Aloise

MARCH 28   And Now a Good Reasonably Cheap
                  Way to Fill Guests, if they can't be
headed off:

FANCY FISHWICHES

Thaw four frozen fillets of sole and cut each one in half. Spread four of the halves with this filling:

4 tablespoons mushrooms sautéed briefly in butter
2 tablespoons chopped onion
a little salt, pepper, tarragon

Top each one with the remaining fish halves and put the resultant Fishwiches in a buttered baking dish. Salt and pepper them lightly, and brush them with melted butter OR heavy cream. Finally, sprinkle them with fine cracker crumbs and bake at 500° about ten minutes—no need to turn them over. Garnish with plenty of parsley and quartered lemons.

MARCH 29   Vera Cruz Surrendered on This Day in
                  1847.

* Jam is better for this than jelly, which tends to run too much.

She was a pretty little thing, born of Mexican parents, and you know how strict they can be. But Pedro had been after her hammer and tongs for more than a year, and a girl's only human, after all. However, he married her and everything worked out fine.

Vera turned out to be a good cook, of the economical sort, and Pedro really went for

VERA'S CLAM FRITTERS

She'd open two cans of minced clams and drain them. Then she'd combine them with

- 2 well-beaten egg yolks
- 1 cup fine-toasted bread crumbs
- ½ teaspoon chopped chives and parsley
- 1 teaspoon salt
- ⅓ cup milk (approximately; she didn't want it too thin)

Then she'd whip the two egg whites till she was stiff and so were they, and she'd gently fold them into the first mix. Then she'd drop the batter by the tablespoon into clarified butter in the skillet, and presently they would turn into the prettiest little golden-brown clam fritters you ever saw.

MARCH 30   The Eiffel Tower Was Opened on This Day in 1889.

The French way of preserving eggs is to dissolve beeswax, mix a little olive oil with it, and use it to paint the eggs all over. If they are kept cool and unjostled, they will stay good for two years, which is probably true of most of us. Then the price of eggs will probably be cheaper than it was when you put them away, because that is how things usually work out. Still it is a good thing to know.

MARCH 31   is one of the Borrowed Days, borrowed by March from April. It is unlucky. John Donne died on this day in 1631. Beethoven died on this day in 1827. It is best to do nothing at all on this day besides wait for April.

April

bringeth Floods, Muds & Buds, with Puns & Riddles & suchlike Drolleries, yet introduceth the Houseperson's best Friend, plus eggstra-ordinary Receipts including

> a Shakel Egg Supper
> a Wagon-Wheel Cooky
> a Rootin-Tootin Sundae
> a Dazzleberry Pie

. . . and Easy Easter Buns, courtesy the Yeaster Bunny!

~~~~~~~~~~~~~~~~~~~~~~~~~~~~~~~~~~

How to Remember Something:
If you will wear your left shoe on your right foot and your right shoe on your left foot, it will remind you to switch them back again pretty soon so they won't feel so funny.

APRIL 1   NOW IT IS MERRIE APRIL that was
                 named for Aphrilis, well rooted in the Greek
name for Venus, though Lovers in the Parke love it not as the
vertical Dewe descendeth; and mayhap it was named for the
Latin *aperio*, "I open," for so do the Heavens & the smalle
winking Flowers & the Wallet as the Tax Man cometh. Now
the Bee goeth abroad for Honey while the Physitian doth
minister to a poor sniffling World, two Aspiryns & bed-reste.
Yet Hope punctually appeareth, in the shape of an Egge; and
appeareth too the merrie April Fool, who seeketh the left-
handed Monkey-wrench and dutifully returneth the telephone
call to a certain Mr. Lion at the Zoo.

Q. And why doth little Egbert cry so hard on Easter
   morning?

A. He hates to set the Easter Egg dye.

Q. And why is little Egglantine telephoning the
   Chinese restaurant?

A. She wants to know what time the Egg Rolls.

On this day in 1974, U.S. Mailmen were first allowed to wear
shorts, and a good thing, too. It must have been awfully
scratchy without them, under those hot wool pants.

Now look to thy summer crop of scarecrows and plant thy
scaraway seeds!

Bet you didn't expect to meet a turkey on April 1!

But it is now ninety-nine days since you looked the Christmas turkey in the cavity, and a good day to roast

THE BIRD UNSTUFFED

Get a big one. If it is frozen, thaw it in the refrigerator two
or three days for a twelve-to-twenty pounder. Or leave it in
a pan at room temperature for about half that long. Smear
it lightly with mayonnaise, all over. Put it in a roasting pan.
Tie the drumsticks together, and tie a string around the bird
if you want to, to keep the wings flat. If you don't want to,
the turkey will look unusually relaxed when it is done, but
it will taste all right.

Now, then: turn him on his side for half the cooking time, and on the other side for the rest of it. When he is done, turn off the oven and turn him breast down for twenty minutes.

". . . Almost all cookbooks tell you to roast chickens, turkeys, pheasants and other birds breast up. This is quite wrong, for the following reasons. The breast and wings of a bird cook quicker than its other parts, and furthermore, the upper part of the oven is the hottest. Ergo, when a chicken is cooked breast up, the breast cooks more quickly and will be overcooked when the legs and other parts are done. And the juices produced by cooking will drain from the breast into the back, which is not eaten."

—Nika Hazelton

Before you start him to roasting, bend a piece of aluminum foil loosely over him. (Take it off half an hour before the turkey is done so the bird will brown.) And figure the cooking time twenty minutes per pound at 325° for sixteen pounds or less, and fifteen minutes per pound for a larger bird.

That's about it. Now you have pounds of turkey meat, to serve plain as long as they'll let you. ("Think of all the people in this world who'd just love to eat turkey every day!")

When this no longer works, freeze the rest, sliced, in bundles about the size of a box of kitchen matches. Represent it pretty soon as turkey sandwiches, club sandwiches, or turkey salad: chopped turkey, celery, onion, lemon juice, and mayonnaise. You could add a touch of curry if you like. Or seedless white grapes. Or chopped nuts.

APRIL 2   "So we went to this fancy turkey dinner but
               the bird had been arrested!"
               "How come?"
               "He was a peeping Tom!"

APRIL 3   Learn to Observe & Predict!

Spiders make larger webs as rain approaches.
Swallows fly low when rain is coming.
Insects bite harder when rain is near.
People scratch harder when insects are near.

APRIL 4   The Happy Book Cook!
          Now take the wet, soggy book you left on
the lawn, pop it into a microwave oven, and Presto—it's as
dry as your old *Elementary Principles of Economics,* according to James M. Flink, assistant professor of food-processing
at MIT, and no harm done.

The way to tear a telephone book in two and amaze your
friends is to bake it first in a 350° oven for three hours.

APRIL 5   Some Almighty Olde-Tyme Jests!

          A traveler, stopping for dinner at a roadside
inn, found on the table nothing but a mackerel and a pot
of mustard. When he inquired if that's all there was, the landlord said, "Why, there's enough mackerel there for six."
     "But I don't like mackerel," the traveler said. And the
landlord said, "Then help yourself to the mustard."

Mark Twain reports this one in *Overland Stagecoaching.*
It was old in his great-granddaddy's day and in his great-
granddaddy's day before that.
     However, for the real vintage yuk, the fifteenth-century
gutbuster, we look to a gentleman named Wynken de Worde,
who shows us what they were laughing at in 1511, in his
riddle book entitled *Demands Joyous:*

Demand	How many calves' tails would it take to reach from the earth to the sky?
Response	No more than one, if it be long enough.
Dem.	What is the distance from the surface of the sea to the deepest part thereof?
Res.	Only a stone's throw.
Dem.	What is it that never was and never will be?
Res.	A mouse's nest in a cat's ear.
Dem.	Why doth a cow lie down?
Res.	Because it cannot sit.

Dem. Who killed the fourth part of all the people in the world?

Res. Cain when he killed Abel.

APRIL 6 Two Siamese kittens joined by a single caudal appendage were born on this day, 1944, to Mrs. Tabitha Katt (of the Cheshire Katts). See *Annals of Obstetrics & Gynecology, Felis domestica*, vol. 2, p. 366, "A Tail of Two Kitties."

APRIL 7 Hodag Day

The hodag (*biggus mammalis hodaggus*, habitat North America) is a large, rough-skinned, bucktoothed, short-legged, and spiny-backed animal who mainly sits around and weeps copiously because he is so ugly.

Take a hodag to lunch today. They don't eat a great deal because of snuffling so much, and they're pretty nice once you get to know them. Presently you will find that some of your best friends are hodags.

APRIL 8 National Laugh Week ended today, and not a moment too soon.

"Its purpose: to promote a national sense of humor and a national sense of happiness."

—Chases' Calendar

"I'm glad my legs are broken—glad, glad, GLAD!"

—Pollyanna

"And so we went to this fancy Chinese dinner but the main course was in jail!"

"How come?"

"It was a Peking Duck!"

APRIL 9 And now in the village of East Whapping is held the merrie Dazzleberry Festival as men compete to grow the greatest Dazzleberry and little children do eat a bellyful and ladies do make

DAZZLEBERRY PIE

(If the dazzleberries aren't ripe yet, use canned cherry pie filling. Actually, canned cherry pie filling is much better in this particular pie, which is more of a cake or pudding anyway, and very good.)

Into a nine-inch pie pan pour a can of cherry pie filling (or apple or any other kind if the birds got all the canned cherries too). Sprinkle a one-layer box of golden-yellow cake mix over it, fairly evenly. Sprinkle a cup of coarsely chopped nutmeats over that. Now dot the whole thing with plenty of butter— a good third of a cupful—and bake it at 350° for forty-five minutes.

APRIL 10   On this important day in the annals of personkind and babykind did a certain Walter Hunt patent the safety pin in 1849.

> How promptly we commemorate
> With reverence each bloody date:
> Battles, wars and Lizzie Borden,
> Slaughter by the River Jordan!
> While the gun still belches hot
>   And ere the sound of carnage ceases,
> We raise the stone to honor not
>   The Man of Peace but man in pieces.
> So let us praise abundantly
>   A friend for every time and weather
> Whose gentle ingenuity
>   Has kept us—so far—pinned together.

APRIL 11   "... The uncertain glory of an April day."
    —William Shakespeare

"... Holsom as the Aprile showr fallyng on the herbes newe."   —John Lydgate

Why is it that *Bartlett* bulges with quotations by men? Why is it that they outnumber ten to one the quotations by women, when women (as men are the first to point out) do all the talking?

It is because whenever a man said anything, there was usually an admiring little woman around to exclaim, "I say! That's jolly good! *Awfully* good! I'll write it down!"

But now that men and women are done role-playing, the action changes.

SCENE:

A stormy night in Philadelphia. Benjamin and Mrs. Franklin are at home, warming their toes at the Franklin stove, and reading. Ben sighs, then looks up from his copy of *The Saturday Evening Post*.

BEN: I don't like the way things are going, Deb. Not a bit.

MS. F: What things?

BEN: The country. I mean the colonies. I see but little evidence of that essential underlying unanimity of purpose that alone can make of all these disparate fibers a strong rope.

MS. F: (*absently, still reading*): Hmmmmmm . . .

BEN: I feel it strongly. We must indeed all hang together, or most assuredly we shall all hang separately.

MS. F: (*still reading*): Hmmmmm.

BEN: Say, Debby, that wasn't bad.

MS. F: (*looking up*): What wasn't?

BEN: What I just said. Or didn't you hear me? "We must indeed all hang together, or most assuredly we shall all hang separately." Might be good for the Almanac.

MS. F: I don't know, Ben. . . . I guess it's all right. (*Back to her book.*)

BEN: What do you mean, "all right"? It's damn good. Or maybe you don't get it. First I use "hang" in the sense of "stick"—*stick* together. Then I—

MS. F: (*impatiently*): Oh, I get it, all right. It's just—well, it strikes me as wordy. Long-winded. Needs sharpening. Actually, Ben—and I've been meaning to mention this— you've been getting away with some pretty sloppy stuff lately. Last issue, wasn't it, you had something about "a penny saved is a penny got." Now *honestly!* What are you trying to say? If you save a penny, you'll have a penny? So what? And that one about patience—how did it go—"He that can have patience can have what he will." That's not a bit catchy, Ben, and, furthermore, it's a crock, and you know it. Sit in the same old office for fifty years and what do you get? Retired with a gold watch and a cheap dinner. Patience, my foot. What about the Pilgrims? Where'd we be if *they'd* been all that patient?

BEN: God defend me from a literal-minded woman.

MS. F: Yes, and another thing. You'd better knock off the sex stuff if you don't want to go down in history as the original male chauvinist pig.

BEN: (*reddening a little*): You mean . . . uh . . .

MS. F: I mean advising that young man to take an old mistress "because they're so grateful." . . . Well, I have to admit it, a mature woman does find a young man a delightful change from wattles and potbellies and skinny shanks and toot-toot-puff-puff, the little old engine that couldn't. . . . Say, that's sort of cute, don't you think? Maybe I can use it somewhere. Will you pass me the quill pen, dear?

"Are women books? says Hodge, then would mine were
An Almanack, to change her every year."
                              —Poor Richard

"But not vice versa, dear," quoth Deb to Ben.
"At least, I know there *is* no changing men."
                              —Poor Peggie

APRIL 12   Shad running.

APRIL 13   Geese flying; things are picking up.

APRIL 14   Item from the Mervyn Meadows *Evening Clarion* Society Section, this day in 1976:
"At a pre-income-tax-day luncheon for the girls ('Come and eat cheap,' said the invitations, scrawled on brown paper!), Mrs. Charles ("Edie") Grumwalt got absolute raves on her delectable Tuna French Loaves, served with plenty

of white *vin du pays,* which (she explained) was Safeway's cheapest. . . ."

TUNA LOAFWICH GRUMWALT
for 6

large loaf of French bread	½ cup mayonnaise
butter	¼ cup chopped parsley
⅓ to ½ pound Swiss cheese	½ teaspoon garlic salt
2 7-ounce cans flaked tuna	1 tablespoon lemon juice
¼ cup sour cream	

Cut the bread in half lengthwise, butter both halves, and pave each half with thin slices of Swiss cheese. Then put them on a baking pan, mix up everything else and spread it on, with more cheese on top if some is left. Bake at 350° for about twenty-five minutes and cut in chunks.

APRIL 15   ". . . They did things better in old Egypt. Tax delinquent citizens took a beating, and the longer they stood it, the less they had to pay. But we just take one while paying and we've stood it for years. . . ."
                                    —Albert Wooky (*Ibid.*)

To sweeten the day, practice up on some

EASY EASTER-MORNING SWEET BUNS

Get an eight-ounce package of refrigerator Parkerhouse Rolls. Find enough muffin-tin pans to make twelve buns. Then, in a saucepan, mix

> 3 generous tablespoons brown sugar
> ⅓ cup light corn syrup
> 2 tablespoons butter
> a dash of salt

Cook it over low heat and let it bubble placidly for a minute. Then add

> ½ cup coarsely chopped nuts

Cool it a little while. Then put a good spoonful into each muffin cup, put a roll in, and bake for fifteen minutes at 400°. Let them cool. Then turn them out onto a wire rack so they won't get soggy.

APRIL 16   How doth the hard-cooked Easter Egg
                      Improve the April scenery,
                  A-gleam behind the table leg,
                      A-twinkle' midst the greenery,
                  'Midst tender pansy-plant and pink,
                      And gentle pussy-willow,
                  But oh, that little chocolate fink
                      Behind the sofa pillow!

". . . melted chocolate Easter Eggs (sludgies) are a real pain. You have to act fast. First, find out what jackass left one there and belt him one. Then scrape off the chocolate. Then read the label on the spray spot remover. If it claims to remove chocolate, give it a whirl. If it doesn't, and you've got a washable sofa, sponge it with cold water. Several times. Add some detergent the fourth time. If it's still a mess, and this is the day after the thing was dry-cleaned, as it usually is, put the pillow back where it was and wait till you have the job done again. People have no business prying behind the pillows on other people's sofas.

—Shirley Shimmelfenner,
*Everything You Never Wanted to
Know About Housekeeping,* vol. 2

EGG-PLANT

Plant a hard-boiled egg in a claybank for a couple of months. Then dig it up and quarter it and eat it. This is how the modern Chinese achieve their allegedly 100-year-old eggs. Yours will be just as good as theirs and they couldn't possibly be any worse.

APRIL 17   Hard-cooked eggery:

1. Wash not thine egg before cooking-time.
2. Let not the water boil for it will toughen the egg therein.
3. A pinprick through the rounded end preventeth cracking.
4. The hard-to-peel egg spoileth the morning. But the egg started in cold water that simmered ten minutes and was peeled hot brighteneth the day.
5. A handy crayon to mark the Hard-cooked from the

Raw preventeth profanity. Mark them T for 'Tis cooked, and T for 'Tain't cooked.

6. Water in which the egg hath cooked doth revitalize green-growing house planth.

Poached eggery:
The tattered poached egg, how to avoid
A. Walk around it.
B. Let it sit ten minutes in very hot water in a cup before cracking it into a dish and slipping it gently into the simmering water.

APRIL 18   Ms. AESOP'S FABLES (No. 4)

The White Egg & the Brown Egg

A White Egg in the refrigerator told a Brown Egg, "I am better than you are," and the Brown Egg replied, "I am better than you are." Then a Scientist came along and, overhearing the argument, said, "Shut up, both of you, and I will find out who is right." So he took them both to his Laboratory, where he tested them, and finding no difference at all, scrambled them up for breakfast over his Bunsen burner.

Moral: You have no idea the silly talk that goes on inside the refrigerator once the light goes out.

As the hard-cooked eggs start piling up, have a

SHAKEL EGG SUPPER

Alternate layers of cooked broccoli with sliced hard-cooked eggs, pour cheese sauce over it, and bake at 350° for thirty minutes. (If you have no canned cream sauce, make your own: stir 2 tablespoons flour into 2 tablespoons melted butter in a saucepan, then add a cup of milk and ½ cup grated sharp cheese, and keep stirring till it's thick.)

APRIL 19   And as they keep rolling out, make a traditional

PETER ABBOTT SALAD

(*To serve on a lettuce leaf or in sandwiches*)

Slice about ten hard-cooked eggs. Then slice thinly, on the

diagonal, about 1½ cups of celery. Drop it in boiling water for about a minute and drain. Cut half a green pepper in thin strips. Then mix together

> a green onion, chopped
> ½ cup mayonnaise
> 1 tablespoon Dijon mustard
> 1 tablespoon vinegar

and combine everything. Decorate it if you like with more green pepper strips or pimento, chopped stuffed olives, sliced black olives . . . whatever is handiest.

APRIL 20   Now beginneth the sign of stubborn TAURUS (controlling the Necke) that continueth through May 20, this being a faire good time to
> plant potatoes
> paint the house
> shear a sheep
> slaughter a pig.

And the methodical Taurian doeth the first three (at his own slow pace) but leaveth the pig alive & well, for Taurus is tenderhearted.

APRIL 21   ". . . It is pleasant to see a great bed of tall dandelions on a windy April day shaking all their golden heads together; and common as it may appear, it is a beautiful compound flower. . . . How beautifully, too, the leaves are cut! and when bleached, who does not know that it is the most wholesome herb that ever gave flavor to a salad? . . ."

—R. Chambers

A SALAD BOTH PRETTIE & CHEAP
IF YOU GROW YOUR OWN DANDELIONS

They must be very young light-green dandelions—the plants, not the flowers. Wash them thoroughly and dry them thoroughly. Then sprinkle and toss them with salt, pepper, lemon juice (or vinegar if you have no lemon juice) and twice as much olive oil as lemon juice. Very good with crisp crumbled bacon and finely chopped cucumbers too.

Q. Why did little Eggbert wear his asbestos suit
to the produce market?

A. He didn't want to get chard.

Q. What hath a round face and ticks and strikes?

A. A fat California lettuce-picker who got lost in
a weed patch and never got his overtime.

APRIL 22   Prof. Arlo Crumpacker, Inventor (Ph.D.,
B.S.), was born forty-five years ago today.*

It is his collection of Household Laws that made him na-
tionally famous. Crumpacker is to the daily household round
as Newton was to the Fig, except that he formulated more
laws.

Some of Crumpacker's Laws of Household Management:

1. It's in the other handbag.
2. No matter what the paint can says, the job will need
   another coat.
3. Whichever traverse-curtain cord you pull is the wrong
   one.
4. In making a three-egg meringue with the last three
   eggs in the house, it is the third egg yolk that oozes
   into the whites.
5. A level cupful of liquid cocoa becomes a quart of
   liquid cocoa when a child spills it on a white rug
   (Crumpacker's Law of Liquid Expansion).
6. If a fresh double-bed sheet is desired, it is a single-
   bed sheet that is unfolded.
7. Throwing the remaining mitten irretrievably out causes
   the missing mitten to reappear.
8. The missing red wool sock can always be located without difficulty in the wash load of white tennis clothes.

---

* Prof. Crumpacker's original field was Population Control, or Family
Planning. However, he soon realized that he could do even more for the
mental health of the home in other ways. Among his many popular in-
ventions is a kitchen drawer that won't open, for keeping the vacuum
cleaner's paint-spraying attachment in. Equally well received was the
smartly tailored paper sack he designed for putting over a lady's head to
cure her hiccups after reading what the magazines expect her to serve
for an impromptu Springtime Brunch. At last reports, Prof. Crumpacker
was hard at work on a ham that self-destructs on the morning of the
fifth day.

9. Any recipe calling itself foolproof isn't.
10. If you put on a pair of clean socks every morning, in a few days you won't be able to get your shoes on.

APRIL 23   ROOTIN-TOOTIN SUNDAE
             A LA ONE-HOSS

First, make about a quart of Coffee Liquer and let 'er mellow. A month should do it.

1 2-quart jar of instant coffee	1 pint brandy or vodka
4 cups sugar	a vanilla bean, cut in little
2 cups boiling water	pieces

Stir up the coffee and sugar in the boiling water till it is dissolved. Cool it. Add your brandy and vanilla bits, and pour it into some jars with tight lids. After a month in the icebox, it's ready to strain and pour over your ice cream—Mocha, Chocolate, Almond, Vanilla—and hot diggety.

APRIL 24   A good thing to have with it, or have anyway, is one of his

BIG WAGON-WHEEL COOKIES

(*Crisp, buttery, and, One-Hoss says, the bigger the better*)

Sift	Cream
½ teaspoon baking soda	1 cup butter
4 cups flour	2 cups sugar
1 teaspoon salt	

Beat
    1 egg
    ½ cup milk

Add the dry stuff alternately with the wet stuff to the sugar-butter mix. Roll out, cut out, bake on a greased cooky sheet about fifteen minutes at 375°.

APRIL 25   ". . . Acronyms fill an increasingly important place in the superjet age. And naturally, for they save not only time but breath, energy, and paper."
                              —Conger T. Hatt

NATO, UNICEF, SNAFU, RADAR, SONAR. And SASE, Stamped

And Self-addressed Envelope. And AKA, Also Known As. And ASAP, As Soon As Possible. Then there are abbreviations, like VIP and TGIF. And FYI, For Your Information, and FBI, for the government's information. Take an abbreviation to lunch today, say a PB&J or a BLT.

Apparently, the first real acronym to hit the top of the charts happened when an English police clerk booked a sailor for deflowering one of the village maidens. Scratching his head over how to record the change with suitable decorum, he finally settled on For Unlawful Carnal Knowledge,* which was later boiled down for convenience when the rest of the fleet hit port. And a good thing, too. Otherwise, literature would probably never have reached its present remarkable state of lucidity, and our armed forces personnel wouldn't be able to communicate at all.

After that, there was no stopping the acronym. Via the mails, on the backs of envelopes—MALAYA, My Anxious Lips Await Your Arrival, NELLY, No one Ever Loved Like You, POLAND, Please Open Lovingly And Never Destroy, SWAK, Sealed With A Kiss, BOLTOP, Better On Lips Than On Paper, HOLLAND, Hope Our Love Lives And Never Dies, and ITALY, I Trust And Love You.

And then the airlines—TWA, Try Walking Across. PIA, Please Inform Allah. ALITALIA, Always Late In Takeoff, Always Late In Arriving. BEA, Britain's Excuse for an Airline, undoubtedly full of the bellhop's GDT's, the Goddam Tourists.

Then there is the English teacher's handy NEASWAP, Never End A Sentence With A Preposition, an admonition we'd better not forget about. Nor can we afford to overlook the Organization Man's personnel approach—his WIGO, What Is Going On?, and his DFI, Damn Fool Idea, and his KITA, Kick In The Ass, all equally applicable in the domestic arena too.

When will the acronym hit the cookbooks? PIP, SLAM, POP. Put In Pan, Stir Like A Maniac, Pour Over Pie.

APRIL 26   ". . . If you've ever tried to scour a sink with Parmesan cheese, you know the wisdom of reading labels first. . . ."
                                        —Dereck Williamson
This is especially vital with magical products named

---

* Sometimes confused with "Frigg" or "Frigga," the goddess of marriage in Norse mythology.

WHIFFO or JIFFO or CREAMO or DREAMO, which is a drain-cleaner if it isn't a spot-remover or a cake-frosting.

But as for the operating instructions that come with house-hold appliances, reading them isn't necessary, because it wouldn't do any good. Mumu Harbottle didn't know this when she went to see Dr. Neitzelgrinder the other day with a sheaf of How to Operate manuals in her hand.

"I'm afraid something is the matter with my head, Doctor," she said. "Look. For my new vertical broiler. It says, 'Failure in adjustment of extruded Part A may support combustion. . . .' At first I thought they meant if I didn't tighten the knob, it would start a fire. But if they meant that, they'd have said it, wouldn't they?"

"No, Mumu," said the doctor sadly. "Not necessarily."

"And then it goes on," Mumu said, " '. . . in which eventuality, suppression of conflagration may be effected by prompt application of sodium chloride.' "

Listening intently, Dr. Neitzelgrinder nodded. "Means if a fire starts, throw salt on it."

"Oh. Well, then, Doctor, this one, for the garbage grinder in the sink, it says, 'Do not introduce fibrous material to sink disposer unit.' Mrs. Sink Disposer Unit, may I present Mr. Fibrous Material? What are they talking about?"

"Artichoke leaves," said Neitzelgrinder. "Jerusalem artichokes. Celery. Stringy stringbeans. Stuff like that . . . By the way, Mumu, how old is your little girl now?"

"Two and a half," Mumu said.

"Just wait," said the doctor. "You think you've got trouble now, wait till you read the directions for putting your first Barbie Doll Dreamhouse together. You should see my waiting room the day after Christmas. This is the Acorn Academy."

Then he explained to Mumu that manufacturers spend so much money on TV time that they have to leave all instruction-writing to the President of the Board's nephew, who smiles a lot and collects tin foil and learned at Stupid School never to use a two-syllable word if a four-syllable word can be found.

Mumu gradually felt better as the doctor talked on, sooth-ingly, about the millennium sure to come, some day, when expert instruction-writers will write instructions, and pack-agers will quit using triple-thick where triple-thin tissue would do the job, and there won't be an aerosol can left in the world or a Barbie Doll either, and the lion will lie down with the lamb and have a pleasant conversation, clearly understood by both parties.

We must learn to communicate with clarity, and if we can't, we must learn to shut up.

"Mrs. Jones," said the doctor, frowning, "I don't like the way your husband looks."
"I don't either," said Mrs. Jones, "but he's good to the kids."

Now let us stand for a reading of the Twenty-third Psalm.
". . . The Lord is my external-internal integrative mechanism. I shall not be deprived of gratification for my viscerogenic hungers or my need-dispositions. He motivates me to orient myself toward a non-social object with effective significance. . . ."

—*Time* Magazine, in an
article about jargon

APRIL 27   Mrs. Andreyev Taloff of Cleveland, Ohio, had an identity crisis today.

The Coffee Shop waitress asked her, poised with a plate held high, "Are you the lamb chop?" And when she gave the attendant her claim check at the parking lot, he said, "You the blue Volks?" And at the City Hall, where she works, the messenger boy said, "You Traffic Control?" And to her dentist she is the Twisted Lateral, and to her doctor she is the Postnasal Drip, and to Macy's Alterations she is the Polyester Flares. And to her children she is Ma and to her husband she's Hon, and she says that sometimes she can't help feeling like considerably less than the sum of her parts.

APRIL 28   NOW!! More Jolly Breakfast Foolery from the Same Fun-filled Folks Who Brought You Chocolate Sugar-coated Krunchy-Nut Num-Nums!

This morning, in 1976, Stephanie ("Fats") Stumflug found she had granolaed herself right out of her caftan. Couldn't pry it on with a shoehorn.

The trouble—she explained to anyone who would listen—

was that the side of the granola box said only 125 calories
per ounce, but the pretty picture showed a generous bowlful . . . actually about five ounces, if she'd ever weighed a
generous bowlful, but she never did.

"I might have known," she said bitterly. "You can't trust
anything that tastes good."

". . . We've compiled information on more than 78 cold
cereals of all types, and found that on a cup-for-cup basis
most of the new 'naturals' contain four to seven times as
many calories as other cereals—even the sugared 'kid stuff'
cereals."

> —Barbara Gibbons
> San Francisco *Chronicle*

But for those who can trust themselves with a measuring
cup and for those who don't care, One-Hoss recommends his

GRANNY'S DATE GRANOLA
(You add the dates the last thing)

In a big bowl mix

4 cups quick-cooking oats	½ cup sesame seeds
1 cup finely chopped nuts	¾ teaspoons salt
½ cup shredded coconut	1 teaspoon cinnamon

Add

⅓ cup vegetable oil	½ teaspoon vanilla
½ cup honey	

and mix it up good. Use your hands. Then spread it out on
a couple of baking sheets and bake it at 325° for twenty-five
minutes and stick around. Stir anyway every five. Then take
it out, pour it into a big bowl, add

a cup of chopped dates

and let 'er cool. Then stir it around till it's crumbly and
store it in jars.

APRIL 29   *A Capital Idea!*
        ". . . Dr. Strabismus (Whom God Preserve)
of Utrecht has invented a small circular spoon, with a hole
in the middle. Through this hole the cook can look at whatever she is about to stir.

"The spoon has no handle, so that when she is looking at, say, porridge, through the hole, the cook must hold the spoon by the rim of the circle. When the actual stirring is to begin, a handle can be fitted to the spoon, or else an ordinary spoon can be used."

—J. B. Morton

APRIL 30   And now be very wary.
                 This is Walpurgis Night, the Witches' Sabbath, and all hell busts loose in the Hartz Mountains.

Q. What is the difference between a deer that's trying to escape a hunter, and an undersized witch?

A. One is a hunted stag and I forget what the other one is.

May

openeth Buds, Windows & Bureau Drawers;
pondereth the Order of Things (& lack of it);
bringeth indispensable Receipts including a
cowcumber Cure for Pimples & Pumples as
well as

> *a skinny fish dish for all seasons*
> *the fastest chocolate-chip cooky*
> *a most delicate noodle*
> *the handiest freeze-ahead casserole*
> *the easiest nonthinking dinner this*
> > *side of raw*

and still other choice Viands!

O see the busy chickadee
  With agile cunning stop
The bugs that buzz the cherry tree
  From ruining the crop!

Then watch him, gloriously drunk
  On song and self and sun,
Devour the lot, the little shtunk,
  Before you've picked a one!

MAY 1   NOW IT IS MIRTHFUL MAY, with gossa-
              mer Aire in remote Places to delight the
Senses and beckon to city Folke who perforce increase its
carbon monoxide content in driving thither; and it is a Time
for May baskets, May wine, May-pole syrup!

Now behold the Moon in Taurus, all moist and earthy,
as Countrie Mouse diggeth out his Wheelbarrow & Citie
Mouse shifteth the potted Begonia to catch the sweete Sunne.
This month marketh the Birthday of the great Linnaeus, who
brought Order to a disorderly World. And so doth the harried
Houseperson desire to neaten all Fuzz-and-Tousle made evi-
dent now by the clear & gentle Light of the lengthened Daye.

> "I ponder with misgiving in
>   My rounds with broom and shovel
> That it doesn't take much living in
>   A house to make a hovel."
>   —Edwina Guest

MAY 2   A likely day to neaten things up. Shirley Shim-
              melfenner once tried to.

". . . So I got this old two-drawer file and some file folders,
and labeled one drawer DULL and the other drawer INTEREST-
ING. In DULL I put tax stuff and appliance manuals and inocu-
lation records and so on. In INTERESTING I put plans for the
guest room and like that. But it didn't work. Nothing ever
stayed Dull or Interesting. I mean, the dog's rabies record got
pretty interesting after he bit the delivery boy in the pants.
And the piece about growing bonsai trees that I put in INTER-
ESTING wasn't very. Or I'd of done something about it.

"So then I went alphabetical—Anchovy Dressing, Appliances, Assessments. But I'd think 'salad,' not 'Anchovy
dressing,' or I'd think 'dishwasher,' not 'Appliance.' . . .

"Then I decided on special headings. CAR THINGS. TAX
THINGS. BANK BUSINESS. But everything belonged under two
headings, maybe three. Like the letter from the lawyer about
my insurance policies, and the payments we made to the
bank on the car.

"So then I put it all in a grocery carton on the closet floor.
Now I use the top file drawer for sweaters and the bottom
one for underwear. . . ."
                       —Shirley Shimmelfenner, *A Day
                       in the Life of . . .*, vol. 5

"There are boxes in the mind with labels on them: To study on a favorable occasion; never to be thought about; useless to go into further; Contents unexamined; Pointless business; Urgent; Dangerous; Delicate; Impossible; Abandon; Reserved; For others; My forte; etc."   —Paul Valéry

MAY 3   On this day in 1975, Mumu Harbottle calculated that if she divided the number of ballpoint pens (in the desk drawer) that didn't work by the number of jar lids (in the pantry) that didn't fit anything, and multiplied that by the number of old lipsticks (in the dresser drawer) that she didn't like the color of and subtracted her Social Security number, she would still have quite a heap on her hands.

> ". . . Nobody should have to clean up anybody else's mess in this world. It is terribly bad for both parties, but probably worse for the one receiving the service."   —Tennessee Williams

But this is not precisely so. The truth is, everyone should clean up someone else's detritus, because he isn't emotionally attached to it.

MS. AESOP'S FABLES (No. 5)

One day a Nanny-goat made her annual social call on her friend the Sow. As they settled down to a nice snack of slops and vegetable parings, the Nanny-goat noticed, leaning against the trough, the same old rusty hunk of radiator hood that had been there last year.

"I thought you were going to turn that into a planter," she said to the Sow. "Yes," the Sow said comfortably, "that'll make me a nice planter one of these days."

The following week, returning the call, the Sow was settling down with the Nanny-goat to a light lunch of mulberry branches and old gym socks when she noticed on the porch the same old corroded battery case that had been there last year.

"I thought you were going to have that wired for a lamp," she said. "Yes," said the Nanny-goat comfortably, "that'll make me a nice lamp one of these days."

Moral: It's a wise girl who knows her own garbage.

MAY 4 Pack Rats Anonymous was founded on this day, 1958.

Recently I attended an evening meeting of the group with my old friend Lester Chester. They met in a big bare room in an old house downtown . . . about twenty dedicated men and women from all walks of life.

Presently the Chairman called the meeting to order. "Attention, ladies and gentlemen. Before we get to the testimonials, will someone put the questions?"

A short, balding man called from the back of the room, "Sure. Got some flotsam?"

At his words, the women dumped their open handbags onto the floor and the men emptied their pockets. Then they all picked various items out of the litter and carried them to the fast-growing heap in the fireplace. Crumpled Kleenex, empty film boxes, broken key chains, old grocery lists, sticky swizzle sticks . . . Finally the Chairman tossed in a match, and by the light of the cheerful blaze I could read, for the first time, the words on the two big placards on the wall. ANY WOMAN CAN. ANY MAN CAN TOO.

At a nod from the Chair, Lester stood up.

"My name is Les, and I'm a pack rat," he said quietly. Then, shoulders erect, voice steady, he gave a moving account of his past fifteen years, before he finally found PRA. Of the time he first began to realize that he couldn't pass up a reusable container. Or throw one out. Of how quickly he became unable to throw out a nonreusable container either. Of how he found himself retrieving it when anybody else threw one out, along with defunct flashlight batteries, torn shower caps, old third-class mail, and corks that didn't fit anything.

In harrowing detail he described the untold mental anguish of his wife and family as his condition deteriorated, till that final terrible Sunday afternoon, two years ago. Thinking to take a nap in his study, he couldn't find the couch under the pile of old tarps, magazines, paper sacks, gallon jugs, undershirts, car rags, empty Flit cans, check stubs dating back to 1949, a Hula Hoop, and nine unopened bottles of men's cologne, and had to sleep standing up.

The others listened with understanding. They had all been there. Indeed, some had been even farther, and when Lester finished, several told their stories too. One woman's was specially poignant. A guest had mistakenly opened the wrong dresser drawer and found a ruptured bicycle pump, 107 small aluminum-foil pans that formerly contained chicken pie, and an old girdle stuffed in a corn flakes box.

At meeting's end, heartened by sharing and comparing, they all stood up to repeat in unison the organization's motto: "Every day I'll throw something away, and I'll soon feel better and better." Then, after subdued good nights, they wended their separate ways home.

It was a memorable occasion. Never will I forget the courage and quiet resolve I had seen that evening, and I told Lester so as we stopped for a beer on the way home.

"I'm paying," he said, fishing in his pocket for change, which he finally dredged up along with some old dog-track tickets, a pair of dime-store sunglasses missing a lens, three Band-Aids that had lost their stickum, and a couple of outsize toggle bolts.

The bar was dark, though not so dark I couldn't see Lester flush as he put the objects back in his pocket. But he didn't mention them, and of course I didn't either.

"... There are telltale signs of a really ordered life. Sooner or later every visitor walks into a cupboard in mistake for a room, and either is or isn't showered with fir-cones and old pingpong nets."
                                        —Katharine Whitehorn

"... Twice a year, probably, things should come up for review, like prisoners. Some need a halfway house to stay in while you develop the mental starch necessary for getting them out of your life: clothes, books you outgrew or never grew up to, one-claw hammers, funny pictures from the bulletin board that aren't funny any more, the comical apron that never was. A big moving carton is a good halfway house. Then, after six months, don't look into it. Just move it."   —Stella Trowbridge Hinky (*Ibid.*)

MAY 5   An auspicious day for making fast, easy cookies. This is especially good for those times when the children threaten to turn into mean little misfits because of not enough home cooking.

SHUTTEMUP COOKIES

(The fastest chocolate-chip cooky)

Cream together

> 1 cup butter or oleo
> 1 cup brown sugar

Then add

> 2 cups flour
> 1 6-ounce package of chocolate chips
> 1 cup nuts, chopped

Mix it, press it into a thirteen-by-nine-inch jelly-roll pan, and bake twenty-five minutes at 350°. While it's still warm, cut it in bars. If you forget to, just break it up when it's cool.

Also on this day, in 1975, Mumu Harbottle took her inadequacies to the doctor, and in the very nick of time.

She explained that though she had tried and tried, her spice shelf never resembled the impeccable sparkling spice shelves in the magazine pictures. Dr. Neitzelgrinder then explained that only model kitchens to be photographed have spice shelves like that, because in real life, whatever spice you suddenly need isn't available in your pattern at the only store that's open then. It only comes in some tin box that won the Prix de Ugly at the Cans Festival. It also gets gummy, as time goes on.

He suggested, however, that Mumu separate the exotic things, like Fenugreek and Tumeric, from the everyday standbys, and put them in a shoe box with a legible list of contents pasted to the outside. If Mumu would keep this on the top shelf of a darkish, cool closet, he said, it would unclutter the spice shelf while increasing the longevity of the spices. It would also do something for Mumu's mental health, he added, because she wouldn't be perpetually reminded of all the fancy stuff she wasn't cooking.

MAY 6   Sigmund Freud was born on this day, in 1856, so that Mental Health Month could be celebrated in May. (Many people find it easier to be mentally healthy outdoors than in.)

Dr. Freud would have had an interesting time with my husband's Aunt Abilene, who lives, if you can call it that, in Toledo, Ohio, and is too busy cleaning everything to read anything. So it's perfectly safe to write about her.

Aunt Abilene doesn't approve of self-polishing floor wax or packaged Parmesan cheese or sex (she speaks darkly of someone's having relations, and you know she doesn't mean for Thanksgiving dinner) or Democrats or split infinitives or dirt. Most especially she disapproves of dirt.

She doesn't realize that dirt is only misplaced matter—matter that was perfectly okay and had its own place in the scheme of things, back at its original port of embarkation. Dirt is only foreign bodies—tiny tourists, so to speak. And constant cleaning only ages the skin prematurely and creates more dirt, one way or another, the way a bath leaves a ring around the tub, and all that detergent makes the algae grow in the lakes so the fish can't breathe and they die and start to smell.

> ". . . Keeping a place clean isn't all that hard if you can afford the soap, and it doesn't take any great brain. I guess that's why women give it a lower priority now. My former wife had just about enough sense to find her mouth with her fork, but she still kept the cleanest house in fifty states."
> —Conger T. Hatt

Isabelline: A lovely soft pale gray, named for Isabella of Castile, who vowed she wouldn't change her underwear till Granada was retaken from the Moors, and it was a good long war.

MAY 7   "Still, you can't just bury your head in an
              ostrich. . . ."
              —Shirley Shimmelfenner (*Ibid.*)

> "For scrubbing ze floor or shooting ze marbles,
> safety-pin ze big sponges to ze pants-knees.
> *Trés confortable, n'est-ce pas? . . .*"
> —Brillo-Savarin*

---

* Brillo-Savarin was bucking for Chef at Le Tournedos in Marseilles till the day he burned the Béchamel. Since then he has been mainly in charge of cleaning things up.

MS. AESOP'S FABLES (No. 6)

Tiring of the nest, one bright spring day, a Mother Hen hired her teen-age Chick to housekeep it. "We're low on soap," she said, "so get some," and then she flew the coop for a job in another part of the barnyard.

That night, when she came home, the place looked the same except for a shelf full of aerosol Grass-Cleaner, Hay-Brightener, Straw-Softener, Egg-Polisher, Roost-Freshener, and Trough-Wax, plus a bill that wasn't chicken feed. But no soap.

So the Mother Hen told her Chick she could either pay for it herself or take it back and get some soap. Which the Chick did, and they all lived just as clean ever after.

Moral: An old broom knows how to sweep clean cheaper.

MAY 8   And so, as the busy honey bee buzzeth out-
               doors, heavy-laden with golden dust, the
houseperson raiseth a little dust too.

When it comes to housework—and somehow it always seems to—I'd like to know how to maintain a respectable level of accomplishment, day in and day out, instead of being an overachiever one day and an inert mass the next.

Perhaps it averages out, and the sum total of what's done during a week is the same. Still, the stop-and-start approach certainly uses more gas—probably causes more wear and tear too. Like light bulbs. Turning a bulb on and off wears it out about as fast as letting it burn. . . . Wouldn't a glowworm last longer if it just kept on glowing? . . .

"When you're hot, you're hot; when you're not, you're not."
                              —Shirley Shimmelfenner,
                                 and a lot of other people

"It is possible that Newton's law of action and inaction has something to do with the roller-coaster effect of many a housework pattern. And certainly the whirlwind-doldrum syndrome has its merits. Many a woman finds housework at least endurable if the place was so cluttered to begin with that she can see some results."
                              —Stella Trowbridge Hinky (*Ibid.*)

THE EASIEST NONTHINKING DINNER
THIS SIDE OF RAW

(For whirlwind days)

A good-sized eggplant, cup up any way, not peeled
A big can of tomatoes (or 3 or 4 fresh ones, unpeeled,
    just cut in chunks)
2 teaspoons rosemary, crushed between the palms or
    the oak trees; this doesn't matter

Put it all in an electric skillet and simmer it gently—lowest
possible simmering temperature—about an hour and a half.
Taste before adding any salt. (*Note:* No browning in oil—
in fact, no oil. Yet it has a rich meaty taste and will do, in
a pinch, as a main course.)

To Turn It into a Hearty Greek Stew: Add lamb, any
kind, cut up any way. Brown it first in a little oil, then add
the vegetables and cook the same way.

MAY 9   There Are Experts at Housekeeping . . .
            ". . . To assess her competence at cleaning, ex-
amine not the powder room, the sink, the living room. Regard, instead, the light-switch plate and the lamp shade;
the telephone and its very cord; the underside of the lid of
the step-on garbage can and the pedal that is daily stepped
on; the steps of the household stepladder, and the medicine
cabinet. . . . And, oh, examine most particularly the outsides
of wastebaskets and cleaning-cupboard doors, as well as the
shelf surfaces upon which the cleaning compounds and pol-
ishes have their being. All too often these are orphans. This
is because, when they are in use, the mind is beamed purpose-
fully elsewhere. One is emptying coffee grounds into the
step-on can, not inspecting the can. One is urgently seeking
the aspirin, not checking the sanitation level of the medicine
cabinet. . . ."—Stella Trowbridge Hinky

. . . and There Are Experts at Rationalizing, Another Handy
Skill

Let's assume that two jobs need doing: (a) shoveling out
The Child's room, which resembles a petrified storm, and (b)
writing a steering-committee report.

Which one you do depends on which one seems the less
repellent at the time. If the thought of the steering-committee

business makes even The Child's room look inviting, tell yourself: *Though community involvement is important, one must
know one's personal priorities; and with me, The Family
comes first.*

However, if the thought of The Child's room makes your
gorge rise and the report sound good, tell yourself: *The
Child must develop organizational and cleaning skills. To do
his work for him would be to deprive him of a Learning Experience.*

MAY 10   While intermittent probing sun
                Proveth indoor work undone,
                Intermittent gentle rain
                Bringeth crab grass back again.

An auspicious day for straightening up outdoors, which
is usually easier. When a tree or a bush drops something,
you can safely assume it doesn't want it any more.

A fast dinner for an outdoor day:

4-ITEM MEXICAN CASSEROLE

*(Taste the chili beans first, and if they lack authority,
add a teaspoon of chili powder, or ½ teaspoon each
of cumin and oregano. Also: If you forget to take
the corn soufflé out of the freezer a couple of hours
before dinner, it will thaw faster in a watertight bag
immersed in tepid water.)*

1 can chili beans with meat
1 cup taco-flavored corn chips, slightly crumbled;
      that should be enough to make an adequate layer
      on the bottom of a middle-size casserole dish
1 frozen corn soufflé, defrosted
1 cup shredded yellow cheese

Layer those things in that middle-size casserole dish—all the
corn chips, all the chili—then spread it with the corn soufflé
and sprinkle the cheese on. Bake it uncovered at 350° for
about thirty minutes, till the soufflé is slightly puffed and the
cheese melts.

MAY 11   On this day in 1976, the Hot Dog with
              Mustard on a Plain Soft Bun won the
nationwide Pupularity Poll with schoolchildren between the
ages of seven and eleven. From ages twelve through fifteen
they wanted chopped sweet pickle too.

Facts like this are one of our country's greatest natural
resources, and yet few people know where they come from.
Actually, their source is an enormous silo about fifty miles
north of Des Moines, Iowa, where they are kept to ferment
for a while, before the silage is shipped to newspapers in all
fifty states.

I happened to be walking past it once when the lid blew
off, and a bunch of crisp facts blew out, frisking about like
autumn leaves. Naturally, I grabbed a handful and ran.

> People with blue eyes and red hair are more apt to be
> nailbiters than people with brown eyes and brown hair.

> Only one out of thirty men over twenty-five can tell you
> (within 25 cents) how much change they have in their
> pockets; only one out of fifty women over thirty can
> tell you (within a dollar) how much change they have
> in their handbags.

> Families with three or more children eat pancakes three
> times a month.

> Twenty-two out of twenty-five people of Caucasian heri-
> tage put on their right shoe first.

MAY 12   For a Warm Day, a Cold Soup!

COLD WATERCRESS CREAM

Put together

> 2 cans condensed cream of potato soup; delump it in
>   the blender or a sieve
> 1 soup can light cream
> 1 cup chicken stock (made from chicken bouillon cubes
>   or powder)
> 1 bunch of watercress minus stems; should be about
>   a cupful

Simmer it five minutes and chill it for the rest of the day—

at least five hours. At serving time thin it with a little more light cream if it needs it.

MAY 13   Our Green-growing friends

"Screaming and bickering households are not, as a rule, ideal surroundings for growing plants. I must define screaming and bickering as opposed to the yelling and hollering of children. Plants prefer a stable pattern of noise, rather than constant surprises like 'Boo!' and jumping through a doorway. Vicious and vindictive quarreling will turn almost all plants into neurotic introverts. . . ."

—Jerry Baker

"Horse apples."

—One-Hoss

MAY 14   Stella Trowbridge Hinky's Handy Dandy

LEMON PUD

(To make into pie or to eat as is)

6 lemons	3 cups granulated sugar
½ cup butter	6 eggs

Get the juice out of the lemons, some way, and grind up three rinds. Mix it. Now melt the butter in the top of a double boiler, stir in the lemon mix and the sugar. When it is all dissolved, stir in the beaten eggs and and cook it all over simmering water—don't let the water boil. When it's as thick as thick molasses, cool it and pour it into jars to refrigerate.

This is handy to have on hand. You can eat it from little dishes, as pudding, or spoon it into any unbaked pie shell or crumb crust and bake it fifteen minutes at 375°. If you want to use up still more eggs, top it with a meringue and shove it for a minute or two under the broiler. If not, don't. Or use a squirt of whipped cream.

MAY 15   The St. Torquatus Olive Tree in Cádiz always blooms on this exact day every year, or is, at any rate, at least as accurate as the Capistrano swallows are.

And on this day in 1976, Winston Harbottle, age nine, of 52 Oak Trees, Illinois, concluded his fourth-grade science project on the Life Cycle of the Kidney Bean. He planted some in coffee cans, which he then set out on a tree stump, his experiment proving conclusively that raccoons certainly do like kidney beans.

MAY 16   Fulle sweete, the merrie month of May
                To lusty lads in raimente gay! . . .
But how sorry a thing it is (not only for the poet but for us all) to see honest old words so smogged over with new colorations that they can never again be scrubbed clean. When *gay* was liberated, the language was the loser.

And so it has always been, I suppose—the language changing daily, even hourly, being nibbled at, added to, and continually in the process of becoming, like the shore line of a continent. Not too long ago, a young woman could say, quite properly, "Yes, he made love to me but there was nothing improper about our intercourse." Not so very long before that, Spenser's "gentle Knight was pricking on the plaine." And now the innocent old query "How did you make out?" shows a rather unhealthy curiosity. . . .

Or consider the pimple. The not-very-attractive word *pimple* is well-calculated to produce an immediate image of the not-very-attractive thing itself. (There used to be a *pumple*, too—probably a larger or more mature pimple.) But after many generations of pimplehood, the eruption became—mysteriously—a *hickey*, which within present memory turned into a love bite, and now a pimple is a *zits*. No one seems to know where the zits come from, except from too many potato chips, chili burgers, and surging adolescent hormones.

"The Cucumber or Cowcumber . . . chopped as herbs to the pot and boiled in a small pipkin with a piece of mutton, being made into potage with Ote-meale, even as herb potage are made, whereof a messe to breakfast, as much to dinner, and the like to supper; taken in this manner for the space of three weekes together without intermission, doth perfectly cure all manner of sauce flegme and copper faces, red and shining fierie noses (as red as red Roses) with pimples, pumples, rubies, and such like precious faces."
                                    —John Gerard's *Herball* (circa 1575)

CHILLED DILLED CUCUMBERS

Slice a large cucumber thin enough to read through, but instead of doing that, beat together

   ⅓ cup salad oil
   3 tablespoons vinegar
   ½ teaspoon dried dill weed (or 1½ teaspoons fresh)
   ¼ teaspoon each sugar and salt

and pour it over the cucumbers. Chill till dinnertime.

"Eat your green salad, it's good for your eyes," said Mrs. Ace to her little boy Goodman. "Did you ever see a cow wearing glasses?"

MAY 17   And now beginneth THIN EATING to prepare
              for the bikini season.

"You've got to get the lead out to get the lard off."
              —Shirley Shimmelfenner,
              The Valley of the Dishes, vol. 3

A HEALTHY SKINNY BREAKFAST

(240 calories)

   ½ cup orange or tomato juice
   1½ cups high-protein nonsugar cereal
   1 teaspoon sugar
   ½ cup skim milk
   black coffee or tea

MAY 18   SKINNY FISH FOR ALL SEASONS

Dip fresh or thawed fish fillets—almost any kind—in well-salted milk. Roll them in fine crumbs mixed with paprika. Lay them out companionably side by side in a well-greased shallow baking pan. Drizzle just a little melted butter on top. Bake from eight to ten minutes in a 500° oven.

MAY 19   SKINNY MEAT LOAF

Mix together

2 pounds lean ground beef	1 cup skim milk
2 tablespoons melted whipped butter	2 tablespoons minced onion
	½ teaspoon white pepper
2 eggs, slightly beaten	2 teaspoons salt substitute

Pack this into a greased loaf pan and bake it about an hour at 350°. Or use a greased angel-food tin, which is more interesting, because you can fill the hole in the middle with some skinny stringbeans when you serve it.

MAY 20   bringeth something to hoot about!
                On this day, 1975, One-Hoss trapped the big old bird that had been eating his baby rabbits and really creamed him, to make the first owleomargarine.

MAY 21   And now beginneth the sign of versatile
                GEMINI (controlling the Nervous System),
which extendeth through June 20 and bodeth well for
    having the tonsils out
    setting hens
    consummating a business deal
    weeding the petunia patch.
But the restless mercurial Gemini decideth with difficulty which to tackle first and so doeth a bit of each: one tonsil, one hen, one phone call, one thistle. . . .

"Decisions were always terribly hard for me," said the Gemini lady. "I would take the longest while to make up my mind. Tomato juice or grapefruit juice? Green shirt or yellow shirt? Allan or Henry? And suddenly one day, I thought, if it's that hard to decide, there can't be a gram's worth of difference in how I feel about either one. So I married Allan, and I guess I had to do that to find out that it really should have been Henry, after all. . . ."

MAY 22   "Before scrubbing ze well-blackened pot bottom, place newspapers in ze seenk or you will be toot sweet scrubbing ze seenk too."
                                        —Brillo-Savarin

MAY 23   This day in 1967, in Liverpool, Humphrey
                the Dimwitted Computer who cost $125,000
was sold to a British junk-dealer for $150.

Humphrey's only problem was that he couldn't think very
well. It took him a week to solve mathematical problems a
college freshman could do in half an hour.

But even if he'd been brighter, he would probably have
created about as many problems as he solved. That is the
way computers do. And according to latest reports, they are
having trouble programming the computer that's supposed to
replace the cook. They can't seem to get the proper inflec-
tion into its "This isn't as good as it usually is" when it sits
down at the table.

"... That night they had a big supper. . . . Mary Jane she
set at the head of the table, with Susan alongside of her, and
said how bad the biscuits was, and how mean the preserves
was, and how ornery and tough the fried chickens was and all
that kind of rot, the way women always do for to force out
compliments; and the people all knowed everything was tip-
top, and said so—said 'How *do* you get biscuits to brown so
nice?' and 'Where, for the land's sake, *did* you get these
amaz'n pickles?' and all that kind of humbug talky-talk, just
the way people do at a supper, you know. . . ."
                                        —Huck Finn

MAY 24   Now the weather groweth better and busier;
                a good day to cook and freeze ahead some
Johnny Marzetti, a virtually indispensable freeze-ahead casserole.

Cheryl ("Cherry") Pitts, of Pittsburgh, reports that before
she started making Johnny Marzetti, she and her husband,
a dog-lover, were seldom invited out to dinner, because her
husband was such a bore about his Bedlingtons ("That dog
thinks he's *human*"). However, since she started making
Johnny Marzetti, to freeze ahead in individual portions,
they're still not invited anywhere, but she doesn't mind. They
probably wouldn't get fed anything they like as well, she
says, and she can always read while she eats.

JOHNNY MARZETTI
10 to 14 servings

1 large onion
2 pounds hamburger
1 pound elbow macaroni
1½ pounds sharp yellow cheese, plus any odds and
ends of Blue Cheese, et cetera, that you want
to use up. If the yellow cheese isn't sharp
enough, add a tablespoon of wet yellow mustard
1 can mushrooms—the more the better—plus the juice
1 large can (about 23 ounces) tomato sauce

Sauté the finely chopped onion till it's tender, add the hamburger, and cook till the meat stops blushing. Drain the grease. Boil the macaroni as long as the package says to, drain it, then add everything else. Pour this into casserole dishes to wrap and freeze. Or spoon it into tough pliofilm sacks, and freeze. (To cook these later, use the top of the double boiler; to heat the casserole dishes, use a 350° oven for about forty minutes.) Put a little more grated cheese on top during the reheating.

MAY 25   A Day to Think About Moving
This was known as "Flitting Day" in bonnie old Scotland, where the Scots, for some reason, hated to stay put for more than a year. Usually the heather looked purpler on the other side of the moor, and May 25 was the day they moved.

In early February, therefore, all landlords would ask their tenants, *Sit or flit?* Mostly they flat, and understandably, really. Sometimes moving is the only way to get a thoroughly fresh start, like with the floor under the refrigerator.

Big Moving Day!
". . . In maybe 50 years or longer, I think habitation of places beyond the Earth will become technologically feasible. There are no planets in the solar system that could sustain human beings in an unprotected environment, so the best approach is to make a space city—perhaps many of them—closer to home.

"One interesting suggestion was made by Gerald O'Neill, a physics professor at Princeton. His concept is to use raw materials from the moon, fling them to places called the lunar Lagrangian points—places in space which are easy to get to and where things tend to hang around. It would be about as far from the Earth as from the moon. You would use the raw materials from the moon to build a space city. . . . Each might be self-supporting and have a living area about the size of the island of Bermuda. There would be artificial gravity so everybody could have his feet planted firmly on the ground. . . ."

—Carl Sagan

MAY 26   ". . . All the men there are in this world, and I had to pick the one that flunked birdhouses. . . ."
        —Shirley Shimmelfenner,
        The 5 Little Shimmelfenners & How They Grew, vol. 7

How to Make Closet-and-Shelf Room When You Can't Find the Hammer:
1. Remember that box room and shelf room are easier to come by than closet room, and many clothes are happier lying down than hanging up.
2. Get a flat-topped trunk to serve as an end table too, or paint and paper a moving crate. For a lid, have a thin piece of plywood cut to size and hinge it on.
3. Get some flat heavy-cardboard blanket-storage boxes to go under the bed. Most department stores have them.
4. Rest a thin, skinny board on two tall cans (or on two stacks of unreadable books) on a pantry shelf, to make a separate one for small objects like tuna cans.
5. Get a shoebag to tack inside the pantry door or the undersink door for polish, cleansers, and so on. Get another for coat-closet door for gloves, flashlights, rain hats, et cetera.
6. Or fill a sturdy shopping bag with the cleaning stuff and hang it from an inconspicuous doorknob.
7. Use a bookcase as a room divider instead of against the wall. If it has a back, pry it off, and put books in from both directions.

MAY 27   Now! Two Good Things to Go with Leftover Beef or a Ham That Won't Quit.

JET-SET NOODLES

Cook eight ounces of egg noodles the way the package says to. Meanwhile, combine

- **1 cup cream-style cottage cheese**
- **1 cup commercial sour cream**
- **½ teaspoon salt**
- **⅛ teaspoon pepper**
- **⅓ cup snipped chives or chopped green onion stems**
- **1 tablespoon butter**

Put it all together, mix it, and pour it into a good-sized casserole. Dot it with butter and bake forty minutes at 325°. If you'd like the noodles a little browner-looking, put it under the hot broiler a minute or so before you serve it.

RICE SHIMMELFENNER

- **3 tablespoons butter**
- **2 medium onions**
- **1 cup raw rice**
- **1 can consommé, beef or chicken**
- **1 teaspoon each rosemary and marjoram**
- **½ teaspoon summer savory**

Melt the butter in a skillet, sauté the chopped onions for five minutes, add the rice, and stir till it's a lovely beige. Then add the consommé plus enough water to total about three cups of liquid. Add the spices and simmer forty minutes more.

MAY 28   A Foolish Consistency Is the Hobgoblin . . .
              or, It all depends on how you're feeling at
the time.

". . . I think I can understand that feeling about a house-wife's work being like that of Sisyphus (who was the stone-rolling gentleman). But it is surely in reality the most important work in the world. What do ships, railways, mines, cars, government etc. exist for except that people may be fed, warmed, and safe in their own homes? As Dr. Johnson said, 'To be happy at home is the end of all human endeavor'. (1st to be happy to prepare for being happy in our own real home hereafter; 2nd in the meantime to be happy in our houses.) We wage war in order to have peace, we work in order to have leisure, we produce food in order to eat it. So your job is the one for which all others exist. . . ."

—C. S. Lewis

". . . Domestic drudgery is excellent as an alternative to idleness or to hateful thoughts . . . [but] as an alternative to work one is longing to do and able to do (*at this time* and Heaven knows when again) it is maddening."

—C. S. Lewis

MAY 29   A favorable day for perusing *Aunt Penny's Daily Thoughts*, linen-bound and hand-painted with violets.

> Clean when you are angry
> Shop when you are full
> Cook when you are hungry

But she neglected to add, And when the wind is right, skip all that and do what you were doing before you so rudely interrupted yourself.

"I don't do housework," Annie Dillard said flatly. "Life is too short, and I'm too much of a Puritan. If you want to take a year to write a book, you have to *take* that year, or the year will take you by the hair and pull you toward the grave. *Let* the grass die. I let almost all of my indoor plants die from neglect while I was writing the book. There are all kinds of ways to live. You can take your choice. You can keep a tidy house, and when St. Peter asks you what you did with your life, you can say, I kept a tidy house, I made my own cheese balls."

MAY 30   ". . . You owe it to us all to get on with what you're good at."

—W. H. Auden

MAY 31   "When Gary asked if I'd marry him, I said, 'I don't know, what are your views on take-out food?' He said he liked it, I said yes, and now it's nine years, one child, and lots of Chicken Delights later."

—Karen Geld, screenwriter

June

bringeth divers delights & dilemmas, including Marriage & Metrics & a 28-lb. Cat; giveth also the easy Rule for

> *a glorious Fruit Tart*
> *a swift spicy Chicken*
> *a most co-operative Main Dish*
> *a pioneer pone*

and other Good Things to know about

~~~~~~~~~~~~~~~~~~~~~~~~~~~~~~~~~~~~

Butterflies taste with the soles of their feet!
  I read it myself in a butterfly book
And thought, what a pleasure, whenever they eat,
  For it's bound to be sole food, whatever they cook.

Just think, could we do it, how nice it would be!
  Imagine the difference such talent would make!
Shall we stroll through the meadow? Or hike to the sea?
  Ah no, let us go for a walk on the cake!

On desolate dawns when I sulk in the shower
  And my coffee is cold and my orange is sour,
I merely remember (and morning is sweet)
  Butterflies taste with the soles of their feet!

JUNE 1   NOW IT IS AMOROUS JUNE when the
                Turtledoves sit upon the lytle green Boughes
in the sweet Ayre, billing & cooing & billing yet again. And
the Cat hath new Kittens & the Nightingale tunes his Throate,
though it availeth nought against the Aire-conditioners keening the Night away in city Street & countrie Lane. Yet young
Lovers do make merrie, and middle-aged Lovers too, whyle
there be old Lovers who are not doing so badde either. And
it be in spite of everything a rare faire Month for Weddyngs!

> "God saw thee most fit for me."
> > —Popular inscription in old Irish
> > wedding rings

> "Wedlock, as old men note, hath likened been
> Unto a public crowd or common route;
> Where those that are without would fain get in,
> And those that are within, would fain get out."
> > —Poor Richard

Now, in the traditional wedding service today, the bride
and groom get out of their bed in the morning and change
the baby before they all proceed to some body of running
water—ocean, river, park fountain, or open drain—to stand
barefoot and read aloud to each other from *Portnoy's Complaint* and *Jonathan Livingston Seagull* as they pledge their
continuing co-operative efforts at ecology-oriented goal at-
tainment, with background music by The Funky Chicken.

But this is only one more variation of a ceremony that has
changed continually over the years, and not necessarily for
the worse.

Among the Anglo-Saxons in the Middle Ages, the bride
was taken "for fairer, for fouler, for better, for worse" and
promised to be "buxom and bonny" to her future husband,
after which he hit her over the head with a shoe. As a point
of honor, too, he was officially allowed the privilege of
moderate castigation . . . three blows with a broomstick being about right, according to old Welsh law, "on any part of
the person except the head." However, the law thoughtfully
provided that the stick be not longer than the husband's arm,
nor thicker than his middle finger.

Sir Thomas More would have approved of today's wedding
customs, with the possible exception of the music. In his

Utopia, it was mandatory that young people behold each other naked before they were married; and in the case of his own two daughters, Sir Thomas didn't quibble. John Aubrey writes of the morning when Sir William Roper came to see Sir Thomas with a proposal to marry one of his daughters:

". . . My lord's daughters were then both together abed in a truckle-bed in their father's chamber asleep. He carries Sir William into the chamber and takes the Sheete by the corner and suddenly whippes it off. They lay on their Backs, and their Smocks up as high as their arme-pits. This awakened them, and immediately they turned on their Bellies. Quoth Roper, I have seen both sides, and so gave a patt on her Buttock, he made choice of, sayeing, Thou are mine. Here was all the trouble of the wooing. . . ."

The observant reader will notice that the goose never got a gander at the old prospective bridgegroom, who kept his clothes on; and there is no mention of Sir Thomas More's suggesting that he take them off. He is to be gently blamed for this. But it is written that no sensible man with two daughters is going to push his luck too far.

JUNE 2   And now Gemini ruleth the soil with the Moon in the sign of the Crab, surely as good a time as any to consider the Metric System.

It was about two thousand years ago, when Mayan priests were living where Guatemala is now, that one of them conceived the mathematical notion of zero.

1st Mayan Priest: Maya ask what you invented today?
2nd Mayan Priest (scuffing a huarache in the dust): Zero.
1st M.P.: That's nothing.

And so no one bothered to get the word around to other civilizations, and the Hindus had to reinvent zero around A.D. 800. But the fact remains, if that Mayan priest hadn't invented nothing, they wouldn't have had nothing down there for so long. And, actually, the world has been in trouble ever since. If we didn't have a zero, we couldn't have a national debt, which consists mainly of zeros, and this is probably why nobody worries about it very much.

In fact, that Mayan priest has a great deal on his conscience. If it weren't for him, we wouldn't have to learn the grams and meters of the Metric System. But as our country moves ponderously to get in step with the rest of the world, the houseperson must move too. Otherwise the H.P. will end up getting gypped worse in the marketplace than she already is, and—in the kitchen—more confused. *31.103 grams of precaution is worth 0.4536 kilograms of cure.*

It is nice to have something to munch on while studying. Gold Nuggets are good with a book or a cold drink or both, and they freeze well.

GOLD NUGGETS

In a blender or mixer, combine

    1 pound Kraft Old English cheese cut in chunks
    1 cube butter

Add

    1 cup flour

Mix it, drop it in dollar-size bits on an ungreased cooky sheet, and stick a walnut half on each. Bake at 400° for six minutes.

JUNE 3   This is the birthday of Garrett Augustus Hobart, the twenty-fourth Vice President of the United States, who was born in 1844. Regretfully we bypass the celebration in order to continue with the Metric System.

It is hard to recapture, precisely, my mingled emotions on learning that our country is changing irrevocably over to the Metric System. Mainly, though, I was aflame with an intense desire not to learn anything about it, because it sounded like the dullest thing since tapioca.

However, when I really started to look into the subject, what was my surprise to find it even duller than I had expected, full of nitpicking ramifications you wouldn't believe. And yet, nevertheless, there are a few basic metric terms we must face up to, or be able to visualize. *There is the crux:* we must be able to visualize that metric quantity itself, without having to translate it into inches or quarts. This will be a small hedge against disaster, and it will also save an entire step in thinking.

JUNE 4   More Interesting Facts About the Metric System

Now, *milligrams*, or *mg.*, are only for pharmacists and doctors, and for the convenience of cigarette manufacturers, so they can count out the proper number of tar-and-nicotine bits to put into each cigarette. Otherwise, the *mg.* or *milligram* doesn't often concern the average houseperson.

Neither does the *tg.*, or *telegram*, which doesn't matter much any more, because the system has pretty much gone to hell and they hardly ever deliver them by hand the way they used to; they only telephone. Just remember that you still get only ten words, Day Rate, not counting your name; and it is important to choose them with care, as the sailor did, sending a telegram to his girl. "I love you, I love you, I love you [signed] Gunther," he wrote. When the clerk pointed out that he still had a word coming, he added, "Regards."

JUNE 5   And now the wild flowers wink in the feathery grasses as the sun scatters warm gold, but here we are, still deep in our books.

Now, the *gram* is a different story. The gram is important to know about, even though it is hard to picture because it is so small. Only $\frac{1}{28}$ of an ounce. (Actually, the gram is to the ounce as Connecticut is to California, if that makes it any clearer. You could put twenty-eight Connecticuts into one California.)

It was important to find something that weighed exactly one gram, and so I experimented with various objects on the postage scale. Aspirin tablets and kidney beans were too light, and anyway they kept rolling off. It was sheer good luck that led me to raisins, which were sticky enough to stay put, and seemed to be exactly the right weight too. . . . Twenty-eight middle-size raisins equal an ounce. Therefore,

a raisin = a gram

For practical purposes, I think of grams as being twenty-five to the ounce, because that's an easier figure to multiply or divide with. Those three grams aren't going to matter in any recipe I'll ever make, believe thee me, Bunky. And inasmuch as there are eight ounces to the cup, there are—roughly—two hundred grams, or raisins, in a cup. Knowing this may help you, someday, guess the correct number of beans in a jar and win a free trip to Las Vegas.

JUNE 6   This is the day of the International Sewage & Refuse Exhibition in Munich, Germany. Celebrate it long distance with a bowl of

METRIC MUSH

(A myghty picturesque old Receipt)

Put fifty grams of rice (noninstant) and seventy-five grams of sugar in a casserole that has a lid. Add a liter* of whole milk and stir it up.† Add a little vanilla and cinnamon or nutmeg and bake it covered for 4½ to 5 hours, till desired consistency is reached, as the old book said, and this can be a stumper. How do you know what consistency is desired, and by whom? Actually, what you're after is sort of a gentle pablum. This was a popular dish for invalids some years ago, and it probably got them out of bed fast, knowing there was more where it came from.

JUNE 7   On this special day, the annual Mermaid Reunion is held in Weeki Wachee,‡ Florida.
On this special day also, Socrates was born, sometime in the fifth century, B.C. He was the Athenian philosopher who, being charged as an "evil doer and a curious person, searching into things under the earth and above the heavens, and making the worse appear the better cause, and teaching all this to others," refused to pay a fine for it, was sentenced to death, and drank the hemlock.

Know thyself. For a good beginning, measure thyself:
  • wingspread, both arms stretched wide
  • distance from tip of the third finger to the floor, arm straight at the side
  • thumb-to-little-finger stretch
  • length of stride

---

* Comes later.—Ed.
† This would translate to about two quarts of milk, four tablespoons raw rice, and ¾ cup sugar.
‡ Where the gents get Weeki from too much Wachee. —Ed.

All these measurements are handy for furniture or rug-shopping when thou forgettest thy measuring tape.

And so back to Metrics, and the *kilogram*, which is 2.2 pounds and presents a special problem.

Examining it, one soon realizes that the *kilo* is basically an awkward conception—a product, perhaps, of the same keen minds that brought us the airplane seat and the morning horoscope, for it never quite fits. Nothing grows into a kilo as a rule, though the garden abounds in one-pound canta-loupes, and rutabagas and so on. Few manmade things turn out to weigh a kilo either.

A large cabbage is considerably more; a large cauliflower is invariably less. A No. 2 can of peaches comes close, but who can always remember offhand which size a No. 2 can is? And while five average bananas weigh almost exactly a kilo, it is no real help. Only a very few people are that familiar with the heft of five bananas.

Finally I settled for an extra-large coconut (without the husk), a real boomer, not the kind you commonly find in grocery stores or bopping tourists on the head in tropical places. This was the closest I could come except for a two-pound box of chocolates with an extra-heavy bow.

So the kilo is basically a personal thing. It is recommended that everyone find his own, to plant solidly in his own head.

JUNE 8   It was on this day in 1848 that Paul Gauguin was born. It wasn't till he was forty-three years old that he dropped out and went to Tahiti. But then he made up for lost time, painting some of his finest pictures and enjoying the beautiful native girls and fruits. It is too bad they didn't have blenders then, for they could have made some chilled melon soup. But probably there weren't many refrigerators on the island then either, and from all accounts —certainly the ones I've read—Gauguin was busy enough as it was.

CHILLED MELON SOUP

a big ripe cantaloupe or two big ripe papayas
½ cup sherry
¼ cup sugar
1 tablespoon (more or less) lime juice or lemon juice

Cut the fruit in half, get rid of the seeds, and scoop out the meat. Put it in the blender, add everything else, and blend. Taste to see if you want more of anything. If so, add it. Serve it quite cold.

Also a favorable day for winding up the Metric System.

And so to the matter of length:

A millimeter (*mm.*) is the crack between the piano keys, big enough to spill things in but too small to clean them out of.

A *centimeter* (*cm.*) is a black piano key. And both of these are the tiny offspring of the *meter,* which is the root word as well as the main thing the houseperson must know about length. The *meter* (*m*) is $1\frac{1}{10}$ yards, which can be easily pictured as a skirt-length with enough left over for a ruffle.*

Then, for multiples of the meter, it is best that everyone nail down, as with the kilo, his own personal image. Five meters, to me, are about the width of my kitchen, or half as far as I can throw *The Joy of Cooking* overhand. A *kilometer* (*km.*) I think of as being a generous half a mile, or about the distance from our driveway to Ichiki's Grocery Store.

JUNE 9   Other Tables, Rules, and Misc. Information
                 Important to the Houseperson.

Rule of thumb:	Keep it out of the way when chopping vegetables with a Chinese cleaver.
Slide rule:	Nine times out of ten a molded salad unmolded over the sink will slide down the drain.
Carpenter's rule:	Time-and-a-half on weekends, double time on holidays.
Long rule:	Victoria's, 1837–1901.
Fish scale:	Easiest to remove while the fish is wet. Then scrape from tail to head, never vice versa, with a sharp knife.
Bathroom scale:	Best avoided between Thanksgiving and New Year's.

* The same way a liter is $1\frac{1}{10}$ quarts, or a couple of beers, with a dividend for the hostess.

Old walnut table: 1¼ pounds unshelled = 2 cups chopped.

Metric rule: Just when you think you're getting the hang of it, they bring out the hectares and kelvins and joules.

JUNE 10 It was on this day, 1974 (as recorded in vol. 12, *I Couldn't Stand the Heat So I Stayed Out of the Kitchen*), that Shirley Shimmelfenner spent five hours reducing the sauce in the French manner to pour over the whole chicken she had spent two hours boning in the French manner, which her well-sloshed guests polished off with no manners at all and in eleven minutes flat.

"Well then, says I, what's the use you learning to do right when it's troublesome to do right and aint no trouble to do wrong and the wages is just the same?" —Huck Finn

JUNE 11 Now bloometh the wild poppy, in meadow and on the heath, and twinkleth too the bright strawberry, in market and strawberry barrel. Today, make a

STRAWBERRY FOOL

which is equal parts of crushed berries and whipped cream mixed together with a little honey. Or just as easy and good, make a

STRAWBERRY NINCOMPOOP

which is bowls of washed strawberries, their stems left on, with raw sugar (light brown will do) and sour cream to dunk them in.

JUNE 12 And still another remarkably effective way to treat a Strawberry!

A SHORTBREAD TART

The crust:
Mix 1 cup flour with 2 tablespoons confectioners' sugar, and with a pastry blender cut in ½ cup butter till it resembles

corn meal. Chill it half an hour, then press into a nine-inch pie pan or tart pan and bake ten minutes at 425°. Cool it.

The filling: Rinse and dry three cups ripe red strawberries, pinch off the stems, and arrange them points up in the pie-crust. Melt a ten-ounce jar of raspberry jelly over low heat and pour it carefully over, to glaze each berry. Chill it. Just before serving sprinkle a few nuts around—almonds, walnuts, pistachios.

JUNE 13   Now the daytime groweth longer and the wickets stickier.

" . . . And something else that curdles my disposition is those recipes that don't say whether to cook it covered or not. Mostly you have to use your head, and I thought that was the cookbook writers' job. The way I finally figured it was, if you want it wet, you cover it. You want it drier with thicker sauce, you cook it *un*covered. If you can't make up your mind, split the difference—covered for a while, then take the lid off. On Mondays, Wednesdays, and Fridays I think it's harder to dry something that's too wet. On Tuesdays, Thursdays, and Saturdays I think it's harder to wet something that's too dry, especially since you're now out of sauce. . . ."

—Shirley Shimmelfenner (*Ibid.*)

JUNE 14   "What kind of cake recipe's that?" Joan Rivers said. "Three eggs, and it doesn't even tell you whether to boil 'em or fry 'em."

" . . . And that's only the start of it. Let's say you're rolling along with your Cheese-and-Chokeberry Suprise, till you trip over 'Cover and refrigerate up to twenty-four hours.' Is that the surprise? *Why* do you cover and refrigerate up to twenty-four hours? How long does it take a piece of cheese to buddy up to a chokeberry, for Pete's sake. This was supposed to be for tonight. All right then, wouldn't four hours be better than nothing? And what if you get busy and don't have it till day after tomorrow? What does it do after twenty-four hours, blow up? They never tell you these things."

—Shirley Shimmelfenner,
Crack-up!, vol. 13

JUNE 15 ". . . Regrettably, good cooks—like good painters—can seldom tell you exactly how they did it. . . ."

—Albert Wooky

Take a piece of mutton and let boil a pretty while, goes an old recipe, which isn't too distant in spirit from "beat it till it *feels* right, then add a dollop of sour cream." It was with an eye to clarifying such culinary smog, as well as other kinds, that Prof. Arlo Crumpacker formulated his handy

TABLE OF EQUIVALENTS

Culinary Scale
Add a (whisper)
2 whispers = a suggestion
2 suggestions = a hint
3 hints = a pinch
2 pinches = a smidgen
2½ smidgens = a dab
3 dabs = a dollop
2 dollops = a glob

Extent-of-Ignorance Scale
Doesn't know (beans)
2 beans = from nothing
2 from nothings = straight up
2 straight ups = enough to
              roll over
3 rolls = his arse from his
              elbow

Ease-of-Accomplishment Scale
Easy as (pie)
2 pies = falling off a log
2 falls = shooting fish in a tub
3 shootings = one holler down
              a rain barrel

Worthlessness Scale
Not worth (a hoot)
2 hoots = a tinker's dam
2 dams = a plugged nickel
3 nickels = the gunpowder to
              blow it up
2 explosions = a fart in a
              windstorm

Certainty Scale
Sure as (shootin')
2 shootin's = the vine grows round the stump
3 vines = death & taxes
2 d & t = fate
2 fates = the Lord made little green apples

JUNE 16 On this day begins the week of National Old-time Fiddlers Contest & Festival in Weiser, Idaho.

And a good day almost everywhere for fiddling around. But sometimes the urge to do so happens on the way back from the grocery store with a sack containing some frozen things; and the mere thought of them glooming in their puddles can spoil your fun. Herewith, good news:

> ". . . After thawing, frozen foods are no more and probably not much less perishable than they would have been before they were frozen. . . . It is amazing how many women live under the dread illusion that they must rush home like mad from the market."

> —Poppy Cannon

"Contrary to popular belief, frozen foods that have thawed can be refrozen, according to the director of Rutgers University's food science department. Dr. Walter Maclinn states that thawed foods can be refrozen 'as long as they seem edible in appearance and odor.' He explains that manufacturers are against the practice not for health reasons but because they fear that products won't taste as good after refreezing—and sales may suffer as a result."
—*Moneysworth* Magazine, October 13, 1975

JUNE 17   A great many Chinese babies were born on this day in 1922, as well as on almost every day after that date and preceding it; clearly the Lord loves Chinese people as much as He loves poor people.

With all these mouths to feed Chinese home economists through the ages have understandably devoted considerable thought to quantity cookery.

> "She who double recipe without first writing down new proportions invite double trouble."
> —Hu Shih* (circa 550 B.C.)

JUNE 18   On this dark day for personkind in 1874, Susan B. Anthony was fined $100 for illegally voting in a national election. Commemorate it with a good bowl of

---

* Hu Shih is sometimes confused with Hao Shih Minh, an earlier Chinese home economist whose recipes were terribly confusing.

BAIL-BOND BEANS

Cook more French-cut green beans than you can eat tonight till they are just tender. In a little saucepan heat together

2 tablespoons lemon juice
2 tablespoons olive oil
½ cup sliced black olives
some garlic salt and oregano

Pour it over the hot green beans and serve them.

JUNE 19   Add last night's leftover Bail-Bond Beans to a green salad for tonight. Very good.

JUNE 20   An exceptionally busy day all over. Tennessee celebrates rhododendrons, Denmark celebrates Vikings, and West Virginia celebrates the day it became the thirty-fifth state. A good day for Dr. Neitzelgrinder's

5-MINUTE CHILI CHICKEN

(He admits that the five-minute preparation time depends on how fast you can cut up aluminum foil; and if someone stole the kitchen scissors again, it's more like seven.)

He lines up
8 to 10 chicken thighs or drumsticks
1 package of Chili Seasoning Mix
¼ cup cider vinegar
some aluminum foil

and then he salts, peppers, and MSG's the chicken. Next, he mixes the Chili Mix with the vinegar, paints each piece neatly with it, and wraps each one snugly in a square of aluminum foil, so he won't have to wash the baking dish later. Then he bakes them at 400° for forty minutes.

JUNE 21   Now beginneth the sign of CANCER (controlling the Breast and Stomach) that continueth through July 22, this time being auspicious for
    cooking & freezing good things
    buying new clothes

manicuring the lawn & the window box
painting murals in the powder room.

And so the gentle, domestic Moon Child doeth these things,
to have all in readinesse for summer Guests. For summer
beginneth now, unless they changed it to yesterday, as they
will sometimes do. The longest day of the year, and plenty
of time to make a bowl of cheese potatoes that are good
with cold meat.

SWISS POTATOES
4 to 6 servings

*(It's best to make more than you need because they're
good fried the next day.)*

1½ big baking potatoes, sliced thin as possible	2 beaten eggs
	1½ cups milk, scalded
1 teaspoon salt	¼ pound Swiss or Gruyère
1 teaspoon minced dried onion	cheese, grated

Mix it all together in a medium-sized baking dish, sprinkle
more cheese on top, and bake uncovered at 350° for an hour,
or 300° for an hour and fifteen minutes.

JUNE 22 . No Problem Too Small! (Some problems
too large.)

". . . One morning I found a raw scratch on the fine old
English desk my in-laws gave us for a wedding present. I
knew it was a fine old desk because it said Sheraton on the
back, and Waldo told me the trouble his dad had getting it
out of the hotel. Well, Grandma always said to rub scratches
with a cut walnut meat. So I got some walnuts and tried it.
It seemed to work pretty well, and that really surprised me,
because most of those corny old household hints aren't worth
shucks. . . ."

—Shirley Shimmelfenner,
*I'll Tell You Who Threw the
Overalls,* vol. 6

JUNE 23   On this day in 1868, Christopher Latham
Sholes received a patent for the first practical typewriter.

And then writers quit writing those long novels, which
seems illogical.

Consider Sir Walter Scott, who died thirty-six years before the typewriter was born. He started out writing naughty ballads like *The Lay of the Last Minstrel* but later mended his ways and started writing extremely long novels (which is why it is called "longhand") in pen-and-ink. Sir Walter would take six pages to say it was raining and another six to say how hard, and once he really got moving he could stretch one sentence from here to Glasgow with enough left over for a kilt.

However, many scholars believe there are sound reasons for the length (long-windedness) of novels before the invention of the typewriter, and for their comparative shortness thereafter. All handwriting being difficult to read, in quantity, authors were understandably reluctant to reread what they had written. Too, they were afraid they would find out how dull it was and feel they should rewrite it. So they would just take it to the publisher, who didn't want to read it either, and just handed it to the printer. Those were the days.

But after the typewriter appeared, writers could see how dull they were getting, and stop sooner.

Adhesive tape came along several years after the typewriter did, and it is a good thing it did, because it is such a help in cleaning striker keys. Press a piece on, then peel it off, and most of the impacted ink-and-lint will come with it. This improves even the fuzziest prose.

JUNE 24   A Foolish Paragraph!

". . . Pay attention to the cat of the house, for he can tell one not a little about the secrets of its larder. A good cook knows that her skill and the good name of the house are mirrored in the cat's coat and conduct, and that the absence of a cat is always interpreted in a sinister sense. A sleek cat, majestically slow in its movements, which languidly and voluptuously brushes your legs and occasionally, only very occasionally (for cats are naturally well-bred animals, if cynical individualists) stands up by your side to remind you with the velvety pressure of a paddy paw that grouse is grouse, as much for *felidae* as for human beings, is a sure sign that your hostess has acquired a minor *cordon bleu,* or is quite capable of shaping one. . . ."

—P. Morton Shand

This illustrates a trouble with writers—how a pretty conceit will occur to them, something deft or whimsical or in some other way so appealing that they can't resist embroidering it, a lazy-daisy here and a French knot there. Presently they are so enamored of it that they don't care whether it's so or not. But there it remains for all time, or at least through its dusty life on the final mark-down table—a delightful ornament, a button that doesn't fasten anything.

The fact is, cats and cooks have no real connection, no more than adverbs and aardvarks, or mandolins and peanut butter. Indeed, it is tempting to argue the other way around: the fatter the cat, the worse the cook. I have generally found, myself, that card-carrying cat-lovers feed their cats the best tuna and kidney and chicken and the creamiest cream, with never a thought to what they feed themselves. If an ailurophile invites you to dinner, don't go.

Yet, here again is a generality constructed on the flimsiest of foundations. I know only three devout cat-lovers well enough to know what they cook and eat. The scientific method would demand intimate knowledge of three hundred to three hundred thousand, before any such theory could be formulated, which is a lot of cats and cooks. I am sure Mr. Shand hasn't known that many, any more than I have.

JUNE 25   It was on this very day in 1961 that a sow owned by Aksel Egedee of Denmark threw a litter of thirty-four piglets, though the record doesn't say how far.

On this day too, the mailman cometh with a letter from Rosemary of Yakima, who not only has a twenty-eight-pound cat with athlete's foot and a sinus condition, but also a semi-invalid purple finch and five children. Rosemary stands five foot, one inch tall, when she feels like standing. She used to be five foot nine but her kids picked on her a lot. She also has a neat husband.

". . . Here I am, Mrs. Casual," she writes, "married to Mr. Clean. Come summer he's out there weeding the flower bed with my eyebrow tweezers. Winters, he bleaches our snow. In his spare time he waxes the driveway. What am I doing? Putting the dinner plates down on the floor for the cats to lick. . . .

"Anyway this is a good casserole for times when people straggle in at all hours. You can shut it off and reheat it again till the cows come home or the family does."

ROSEMARY'S GREEN-PEPPER BEEF

pound ground beef	1 large green pepper, cut in
teaspoon salt	rings
tablespoons mustard (plain or	1 clove garlic, minced
horseradish type)	1 can Mexican corn
medium onion, cut in rings	½ cup chili sauce

Mix the first three things. In a large skillet sauté the onion and green pepper rings, not much, just enough to break their spirit. Add the ground beef mixture, mess it about a bit, and cook till browned. Add garlic and corn and simmer covered for fifteen minutes. Add chili sauce and mix lightly, re-cover, and simmer another ten.

JUNE 26   A fine fresh morning to *bake* some BACON.

For this is the Law of the Kitchen,
As old and as true as the sky:
Where bacon's concerned, you should bake it
(Though she who would break it may fry).

And the way of doing it is this: put the bacon on a rack in a shallow pan. Then put the pan in a 400° over for ten to fifteen minutes.

PLUSES: It needn't be turned at all, or watched much. Also it will bake along with the biscuits and be a little less greasy.

MINUSES: Your oven uses 4,500 watts per hour and your small burner only 1,800, so your electric bill will be higher. When you come right down to it, it's a little like shooting rats with an elephant gun, and maybe frying is better, after all. Then you can skip the biscuits and make some

OLD-FASHIONED HARD-CORE PONE

1 cup white corn meal	boiling water
½ teaspoon salt	

Add the salt to the corn meal, then enough boiling water to make a soft dough but not a batter. Use bacon fat to grease a medium skillet, have it hot, and apply the mixture, flattening it into one big thin cake with a spatula. When it is brown on the bottom side, turn it over and keep cooking till it's brown and crisp on the other.

JUNE 27   Now Cherries Are Ripe!

"... A pleasantly sour wild red cherry tha[t] my grandfather called bird-cherry (*Prunus pensylvanica*) ripened in Missouri in June. I remember helping to pit them and Granddaddy saying that cherry pits contained a mil[d] poison. There is a temptation to ferment cherries whole fo[r] wine, but unless you wish to slowly poison your drinking cohorts, cherries should be pitted before use, he said. I hav[e] seen hogs devour cherries by the bucketfull and not show discomfort, but then, I can't tell a discomforted hog grunt from a comfortable grunt."

—Grace Firth (*Ibid.*)

JUNE 28   "... There lives the dearest freshness deepdown things. ..."

—Gerard Manley Hopkins

And appeareth now the frilled green lettuce.

"Whoever thought up the idea that salad bowls should not be washed should be tossed summarily into a pot of rancid oil."

—Craig Claiborne

JUNE SALAD DRESSING

Blend together

1 cup sour cream or Imo   2 teaspoons celery seed
½ teaspoon garlic powder   ½ teaspoon salt
2 tablespoons lemon juice   a dash of pepper
1 teaspoon dry mustard

See that it's smooth, then chill it to serve later with fresh lettuce.

"... Sometimes I'll pick nasturtium seeds or use the pretty blue flowers from chives for salads. Geranium leaves are excellent in blackberry jam."

—Emalee Chapman

JUNE 29   On this day in 1976, Edie Grumwalt secretly set over the buttons on all her husband's jackets so that they barely fastened, thus frightening him quite out of his burgeoning potbelly in time for their August vacation.

JUNE 30   ". . . What are you to do if your conscience is clear and your liver in order and the sun is shining?"

—"Elizabeth"

July

*bringeth hot Weather & Hang-ups; consid-
ereth the Wayward Self as well as divers
strange green-growing Objects; giveth also the
easy Rules for*

> *short rich Firecrackers*
> *the amazing Soccatumi Cake*
> *18 little-known Vegetables*
> *a most excellent Fruit Leather*

and still other memorable Delicacies!

~~~~~~~~~~~~~~~~~~~~~~~~~~~~~~~~~~~~

I moved to the country
And grew a big tomato,
O, willy waly, willy waly.
I moved to the country
And grew a big tomato,
O, willy waly, willy waly O.

I moved to the city
and met a big tomato,
O, willy waly, willy waly.
I moved to the city
And met a big tomato,
O, willy waly, willy waly O!

JULY 1   NOW COMETH FIERCE JULY to breathe
              red upon the Back of the Necke & green upon
the Vegetable Patch. Now sweateth the Judge in his Gowne as
the Laborer in his Levi's & the Secretary at her Bus Stoppe,
while the reluctant Cook steameth like unto the fresh lytle
garden Peas in her Pot.

Now the apartment Aspidistra drowneth through excess
Zeal & Water, as the high hot Sunne doth burn Grass & melt
Macadam, driving all to the Seashore for Picnicks & Fire-
works; and little Children's Eyes do widen at these Wonders
more wonderful than Telstar or Moonwalk. Yet even at the
Beach there be problems, as the harried Houseperson shovel-
eth away the Detritus of the Picnick before him.

                              And there be Bugges.

JULY 2   A Time to Cover the Deviled Eggs and the
              Ankles!

Now, it is written that in the early 1500's, insects so
troubled Pope Clement VII that he commissioned Benvenuto
Cellini to make him a papal cursing bell, marvelously crafted
of solid silver, exquisitely chased with flies, gnats, mosquitoes,
and other sworn enemies of the drowsy season.

> So when they zeroed in, that hungry horde
> Of uninvited bugs to share his board
> (The micoscopic fleas, the bees that sting,
> The tiny flies that bite like anything),
> Though hot and itchy grew the papal choler,
> Unseemly 'twas for popes to scratch and holler.
>
> And so he'd swing the trusty Cursing Bell
> To damn them each and all to bloody hell
> . . . A fairly futile gesture, probably,
> Though—grant it—godlier than DDT.

Certainly many bug preventatives have been tried, including heavy black eye make-up in Cleopatra's time. They hoped
it would scare the bugs away, but it didn't, much to the
surprise of the folk who tried it, and this is probably the
origin of the word "bug-eyed." Fringed hats have been hopefully worn too, but many bugs like to swing on the fringe.

What Is Known About Repelling Insects, Which Isn't Much:
1. Wear light colors. (Bugs prefer dark colors.)
2. Don't sweat, or else carry a fan to dry it off. (Bugs prefer moist surfaces to sit on.)
3. Don't use perfume. (Some bugs love it, and, in any case, it cancels the effect of any bug repellent you use.)
4. Ditto suntan lotions. (The chemical mix will probably add up to zero.)
5. If you use a chemical repellent, use it all over, not just in spots; any place uncovered will get bitten.
6. Be born a girl and stay that way. (Bugs find girl babies least inviting.)

"Don't water your lawn or flower beds for at least twenty-four hours before any outdoor party. An hour before the party starts, use a killer spray or light a bug-repellent smoke product in the area."
—Max Gunther

And there be Slugges. A pie tin full of beer will drown them, but it is a bad waste of good beer. And salt will melt them, but it is a sad thing to see. Better take a gallon of water, add a cup of sugar, mix in four 500-mg. vitamin-C tablets, pour it into pie tins, and leave it where the slugs were. They shortly become so healthy they can't stand it, and so they die, but presumably happily.

JULY 3   Now the sun pours tawny hot syrup on the sand, and a good thing, for otherwise everybody at the beach would catch cold.

"The ladies used to wear bathing suits down to the ankles and then they was wearing 'em down to the knees and now they ain't even wearing 'em down to the beach."
—One-Hoss

What to Do About Knock-Knees:
"A correspondent's advice and testimony are as follows: "I commenced the practice of placing a small book between my knees, and tying a handkerchief tight around my ankles. This I did two or three times a day, increasing the substance at

every fresh trial, until I could hold a brick with ease breadth ways. When I first commenced this practice I was as badly knock-kneed as possible; but now I am as straight as anyone. I likewise made it a practice of lying on my back in bed, with my legs crossed and my knees fixed tightly together. This, I believe, did me a great deal of good."

—From Mrs. Beeton's *All About Everything,* circa 1869

JULY 4   Today, also, the nation celebrates the birthday of Calvin Coolidge (in 1872), the thirtieth President of the United States. Commemorate it with a simple, shrewd, honest, and trouble-free picnic. Or, as they liked to put it then, Keep your cool with Coolidge.

CALVIN COOLIDGE PICNIC

Firecrackers
Baked Fried Chicken
Crumpacker's Cucumber Coleslaw   Whole Fruit
Potato Chips or French Bread
Soccatumi Cake
Beer or Iced Tea Punch

FIRECRACKERS

½ cup butter	several drops of Tabasco
¼ pound sharp Cheddar, grated	1 cup flour
¾ teaspoon salt	1¼ cups Rice Krispies
½ teaspoon red pepper	

Cream the butter with the cheese, add the seasonings, then the flour and cereal. Shape into marble-size balls on a lightly greased sheet, flatten with a fork, and bake at 350° about twelve minutes. These are crisp, short, and hot. To cool them off, omit the Tabasco.

BETTY'S GOOD
BAKED FRIED CHICKEN

Sprinkle some chicken parts with garlic salt. Coat them with mayonnaise, roll them in Ritz-cracker crumbs, and spread them out on a baking sheet. Bake them at 300° for as long as it takes the New Ashmolean Marching Society followed by the Tri-County All-Girl Brass Band to get from Twenty-second & Main Street down to the Town Square, or, say, an hour and a half, though another half hour won't do a bit of harm.

CRUMPACKER'S CUCUMBER COLESLAW

(Coleslaw is to the vegetable compartment as meat loaf is to the whole refrigerator, according to Crumpacker's Coleslaw Equation, or 18th Law. Any raw vegetable sliced fine can go into it—radishes, turnips, zucchini, carrot. . . . This is a good basic rule.)

Shred a head of cabbage fine, then mix in two cups of chopped cucumber and ¼ cup sliced green onions. Chill it while you mix the dressing:

2 eggs	1 tablespoon sugar
½ cup vinegar	2 teaspoons dry mustard
1 tablespoon salt	¼ teaspoon white pepper

Cook this till it's thick, and cool it. Then add 2 cups of SOUR CREAM, mix it, and keep it cold till you eventually put the coleslaw together. Add as much as you like to the shredded vegetables, then keep the rest handy for potato salad sometime later. Or for more coleslaw.

THE AMAZING SOCCATUMI CAKE

(Invariably rich, moist, and delicious. Actually, Soccatumi is the name of the Indian princess who often made it for the larger tribal functions. "Wow! Soccatumi!" the braves would yell as they waited for a piece, and a passing anthropologist thought it was the name of the cake.)

1 box yellow cake mix	4 eggs—add them one at a time,
½ cup sugar	unbeaten
¾ cup melted butter or Buttery-Flavored Wesson Oil	1 cup sour cream

Mix it all together with a big spoon, then beat it for five minutes with an electric beater. Pour it into a Bundt pan or angel-cake tube pan. Bake it for an hour at 350°. Doesn't need frosting. Good all alone. Or with somebody else. Or with ice cream.

ICED TEA PUNCH

1 rounded tablespoon Instant Lemon Tea
½ cup concentrated Hawaiian Punch
2 cups cold water
Plenty of ice

This serves 4 . . . multiply it as you like.

JULY 5   The Dog Days begin now, for dogs and every-
one,
As Sirius, the Dog Star, rises with the Sun.
Now stare in mild paralysis at all the chores
to do.
Plants wilt; ice melts; resolve does, too.

A Day to Ponder the Wayward Self.

"I am always saying to myself, *Look at you, and
after a lifetime of trying.*"
—Florida Scott-Maxwell, at age 82

I am forever finding myself hung up on certain jobs—a
particular letter that must be written, an especially miscellane-
ous cupboard to sort—all the things I know I ought to do
and know I'd feel better if I did do. But don't do. Because
I have a hang-up.

HANG-UP: a cumulatively negative reaction to a particular stimulus, resulting in minimum achieve-
ment with subsequent significant risk to ego
satisfaction and pattern maintenance domes-
ticity-wise.

That would be the psychologist's definition, though it is
only double talk for being caught on a barbed-wire fence by
the seat of your mental britches so you can't move.

But I have learned at least one thing about managing my
pigheaded Id when it gets hung up in this fashion. I have
learned not to nag it—that is, not to let my Ego nag it. For
then my Id will only dig in its heels. Apparently it hates to
be nagged, and I am worse off than before.

And so, for me, it is better to assume philosophically
that perhaps I am fated to live with the letter unwritten or

the closet mussed up; better to give the thing only an occasional flick of the mind. Then I sometimes find, to my surprise, that my Id up and does the job when I least expect it, like a child who will sometimes, unbidden, scour the sink to surprise his mother.

Now that women have been more or less freed by the three *c*'s—cars, can openers, and contraceptives—it seems too bad that the fourth one, Conscience, so often has to butt in.

A Report on Limbo:

Limbo is the suburb on Hell's outer fringes reserved for all those well-meaning but unfortunate souls either born too early or dead too soon to become Christians; people whose main error was timing.

Probably a corner of it is reserved for people whose flowers arrive at the hospital in time to greet the patient coming out, people whose soufflés rise high and ready before the salad greens are located and washed, people who are forever locking the stable door as the horse disappears down the road.

But apparently Limbo isn't a bad place; crowded, perhaps, but comfortable. According to C. S. Lewis, an authority on these matters, ". . . there are grand libraries in Limbo, endless discussions, and no colds. There will be a faint melancholy because you'll all know you missed the bus, but that will be a subject for poetry. The scenery is pleasant though tame. The climate endless autumn."

I think I'm going to like it there.

JULY 6   Thomas More is good and dead
                 And hardly a man alive
                 Remembers the day he lost his head
                 In 1535.

The Hangup (*continued*):

And then there is another kind of hang-up: the inaction that results from thinking something is harder than it actually is, despite all evidence to the contrary. There are small, stubborn cooking hang-ups.

Diced leftover chicken. Who has chicken left over? I don't, so I bypass recipes that call for it. Down where the truth lies, I know it isn't hard to simmer a couple of pieces of frozen chicken for half an hour with an onion and a celery stalk, then take the meat off the bones. But still . . .

Pastry tube. To me, that's like a GO BACK, YOU ARE GOING THE WRONG WAY sign on a freeway exit. When I come to a pastry tube in a recipe, I start over and make something else.

And just pastry. Some people bypass pastry on principle, even the prepared mixes. This is a good pie for them. It looks like a pie, tastes good, and uses only two apples.

NAKED APPLE PIE

Beat one egg in a middle-size bowl.
Then add

½ cup brown sugar
½ cup white sugar
1 teaspoon vanilla
pinch of salt
½ cup flour sifted with 1 teaspoon baking powder

½ cup chopped walnuts or pecans
2 medium-sized apples—peeled, then coarsely chopped or sliced

Spread it in a greased nine-inch pie plate and bake it half an hour at 350°.

And yet, when you come right down to it, what is so bad about a hang-up? Back in the comfortable old days, before quirks became problems that were supposed to be solved, a hang-up was a crotchet—just part of a person's engaging *is*-ness. I often think of Miss Jenkins, an elderly friend of the family when I was a little girl, whom we usually referred to as Miss Jenkins bless-her-heart.

Miss Jenkins bless-her-heart had a hang-up about keeping things covered. She felt that everything should be decently covered and stay that way. (She wouldn't have cared for Naked Apple Pie.) And, certainly, nearly everything in her house wore its own little sweater or jacket—her telephone, her teapot, her toaster, her terrier. . . .

You can imagine her dismay, then, when she developed a vitamin deficiency, and her doctor considered it advisable to administer the first of six vitamin shots, in the hip.

It was a traumatic moment for Miss Jenkin's b-h-h. Weeks went by before she could bring herself to return to the doctor's office. It was a hang-up.

But she managed to live with it, most ingeniously. When

she finally reappeared for the second shot, she had scissored a tiny slit in her underwear—approximately where the doctor had used the needle the last time—and neatly buttonhole-stitched it.

These were her going-to-the-doctor bloomers, and they worked just fine.

MISS JENKINS BLESS-HER-HEART'S PINK SALAD

She used to fix a three-ounce package of strawberry Jell-O the way the package said to, and chill it till it was half-thickened. Then she added a cup of unsweetened applesauce and let it chill till it set. She always brought this when she was invited to dinner, if the hostess mentioned turkey or chicken or pork or ham, and actually it was quite all right if you were ready for it.

JULY 7   On this brilliant blue-and-gold day in 1898, with the shiny palms waving like hula girls and the turquoise waves scalloping the shore, Hawaii was annexed to the United States.

Hawaii was first settled by Polynesians. Later, it was somewhat unsettled by Whalers and Sailors, as well as by a good many Missionaries. Many of them acquired pineapple fields and felt that Hawaiian pineapple should be pushed at all times. Indeed, this was the official missionary position.

Therefore, on Annexation Day, all U.S. restaurant owners swore a unanimous vow to call any dish containing pineapple Hawaiian-style, even if the pineapple came from Taiwan or Puerto Rico or Mexico, as it probably did. From that day to this, not one of them has broken his vow.

There are many ways to cook pineapple, but it is still best served fresh, as in a

FRESH PINEAPPLE SALAD (or dessert)
for 4

Quarter a pineapple but don't remove the leaves. With a sharp knife, remove the flesh and cube it—then put it back in the shell mixed with a few strawberries, banana slices, or whatever fruit you have. A squirt of lime juice never hurts, and it will keep the bananas, if any, from turning brown.

JULY 8   Quite probably muggy and unpleasant. A
                favorable day for a good book, a cool corner,
and a cold drink. *SANGRÍA,* anyone?

> First, find thyself a quart of ruby wine—
> Not kitchen Burgundy, nor yet *too* fine.
> A quart of sparkling soda cometh next,
> Plus juice of lemons (2), an' be thou vex't
> By tartness unrelieved, let sugar try
> Its gentle blandishments to mollify
> Thy sorely puckered palate—half a cup
> Is adequate. So add and stir it up.
>
> Next, oranges! Thou needest but a few—
> One half a dozen fat ones will suffice.
> Of juice itself, a gen'rous cup will do,
> Forgetting not the roundly lucent slice
> To charm the thirsty eye (for wise men know
> 'Tis eye that leads the trusting tongue). And so,
> Well armed 'gainst summer *angst,* thou shalt not brood
> But, beamish, lift thy ruby glass, *!Salud!*

JULY 9   Elias Howe was born on this very day back
                in 1819. He is the one who invented the
sewing machine, though he is often confused with Eli Whitney,
who invented the cotton gin, which mustn't be confused with
GIN-AND-GRAPEFRUIT JUICE, another good July drink. This
one has the additional merit of coming with prose directions:

Mix the gin and juice in whatever proportions taste best, and
dip the wetted rim of the glass in salt (before you fill it).
Now it is called a SALTY DOG and it seems to taste best
served in shorts or a bikini.

JULY 10   It was on this important day for the art
                 world, in 1834, that Whistler's Mother pro-
duced Whistler.
  If she could have foreseen that rocker bit coming, she
probably would have dropped him on his head. Just think
of the rich full life Mrs. Whistler must have enjoyed (for
however it was, and even if she didn't enjoy it much, it must

have been more interesting than simply sitting in a rocker in a bare room). Yet that is the only way posterity will ever know her. It is a real shame.

JULY 11   Still upset over Mrs. Whistler, let us name a good recipe for her:

MRS. WHISTLER'S ZUCCHINI BOATS

(The general principle here is the simple one of scooping out the innards to improve them, then piling it all back in to bake.)

1 cup chopped onion sautéed in
  butter till tender
6 medium zucchini
1 tablespoon additional butter
1 tablespoon flour
1 teaspoon instant chicken
  broth dissolved in ¼ cup
  hot water

¼ cup light cream
¼ cup bread crumbs
2 tablespoon grated Parmesan
  cheese
⅛ teaspoon pepper

While the chopped onion bubbles gently in the skillet, make boats out of zucchini: slice off the ends and cut a long vertical slice off each, a third of the way down. Simmer both tops and bottoms in salted water no more than ten minutes, scoop out the meat from both, and throw away the tops. Chop it, dry it a bit with a towel, and add it to the skillet.

Now make a white sauce: melt the one tablespoon butter in a small saucepan, stir in the flour, cook till bubbly, then add the chicken broth and cream. Stir till medium thick, then put in the skillet along with the bread crumbs, cheese, and pepper. Simmer five minutes, then pile it into the zucchini shells, put them in a greased pan, top with more Parmesan, and bake at 450° for fifteen minutes. Serve with a lemon wedge.

JULY 12   On this date, Dr. Emmett Neitzelgrinder throws his Annual Hand-wrestling & Pinochle Party, at which he invariably serves the doubled bean recipe of his that is on page 72.

          "Men, cooking, are generally extremists. Stingy or

lavish. Speedy or slow. Sloppy—you'd think the
hurricane hit the gravy plant—or *neat* (some will
even scrub the grout between the tiles just to shame
you). As for their cooking, it's either good or terrible, with few in-betweens. The terrible men-cooks
develop recipes like Fried Bologna & Rancid Mayonnaise on Charred English Muffin when their wives
are away. The good ones do things like Quenelles
and Filet en Croûte, but only when and if they feel
like it."

> —Stella Trowbridge Hinky (*Ibid.*)

> "If you can't fry it or toast it, forget it."
> —One-Hoss

JULY 13   Now Mars crosses the path of Saturn, and
               apologizes. The nights are hot. Perhaps it
would be well to freshen the bed, and it isn't hard to do,
just as it was done back in the 1700's.

Then, a lady mixed water, wax, and flour together, then
added powdered cloves and damask rose water. So do that,
and brush it on the mattress ticking with a brush made of
pig hair. You "fhall fmell your bed all over ye chamber,"
it being "both comfortable to ye head and ye ftomach and
inoffencive to a woman in child bed."

> —Book of Simples (mid-eighteenth century)

JULY 14   Avocados looking good now.

"... That was the summer I went to visit
Mother, and she threw me a (are you ready for this?) Tea
Party. So I was lunging around for things to talk about and
landed on Avocados, and you should of seen the fur fly.
These dolls agreed there was only one way to do Avocados,
but they all had a different one way, and I felt like the fellow
and his restaurant soup, wished I'd never stirred it up."

> Shirley Shimmelfenner (*Ibid.*)

Dr. Neitzelgrinder prefers his avocado pitted, halved, and
its middle filled with catsup. His wife likes a puddle of
vinegar-and-oil dressing in hers. Albert Wooky likes a squirt
of lime juice and a spatter of salt. One-Hoss fills his with rum,

and Edie Grumwalt sets hers on lettuce, fills it with soy sauce, and surrounds it with mandarin oranges while tooting on her Chinese flute. She makes quite a thing of this recipe—even sent it to the newspaper. She named it Avocados Grumwalt.

". . . It is a blurry line between creation and accident, between adaptation and plagiarism, in food as it is in literature. Should Dracula turn transvestite, has the writer created a new horror, or only fouled up an old one? Similarly, with the cook who adds pineapple to a tuna-cashew nut casserole . . ." —Albert Wooky

JULY 15 On this very day in 1869, margarine was patented by Hippolyte Mege-Mouries, of Paris. This first of the lower-priced spreads was compounded of suet, skim milk, pig's stomach, cow's udder, and bicarbonate of soda.

This is also St. Swithin's Day; and should it rain, it will rain for forty days more. That is because (legend saith) St. Swithin wanted to be buried outdoors, but his devoted followers brought him inside. At this, the spirit of the saint waxed wroth (became intensely annoyed) and made it rain till they moved him back out again.

It would seem to be a sort of reflex action on St. Swithin's part now. Whenever it sprinkles, he is reminded of that uncomfortable day when they were trucking him in and out like an old sofa, and he gets hot under the surplice all over again and makes it rain a lot.

However, I have noticed that on a couple of recent St. Swithin's Days there were showers, but it didn't keep on raining for forty days. It stopped almost immediately, as a matter of fact. Time heals most wounds, and apparently St. Swithin's spirit isn't so wroth any more.

JULY 16 "Now, you take a vegetable . . ." said Aunt Henry Macadangdang. "If he grew *above* the ground, that's what he's used to—uncovered, warm in the sun. That's the way he likes it and that's the way he wants to be cooked: uncovered." She examined, critically, the carrot she'd just peeled before she dropped it into the pot.

"However; on the other hand," she continued, "if he grew under the ground, he likes his privacy. So cook him covered. That's what *he's* used to."

"He's probably used to worms, too," I said. "Should I throw some in?"

"None of your sass," said Aunt Henry. She doesn't like sass.

"Yes, but what if he's a frozen green bean?" I said. "He grew in the sunshine, but the directions always say 'Cook covered.'"

"Certainly," said Aunt Henry. "He's been living in that dark little box longer than he's been growing, and now he's accustomed to it. So cook him covered."

You've got to get up early in the morning to get ahead of Aunt Henry.

JULY 17 From Stella Trowbridge Hinky's
         Handy Garden Guide to Little-known Vegetables

"Some people would rather they stayed that way. But as more and more amateurs start vegetable gardens, more and more innocent bystanders are the puzzled recipients of the overflow, from kale to Chinese mustard. However, cooking and eating these things saves money; and some of them taste better than you would expect. Even the worst of them taste good to the person who grew them, the way a baby mud toad looks cute to its mother, and so it's really better to take the offensive and grow some yourself."

ANISE-FENNEL. Sometimes called fennel, sometimes anise, but don't worry about it or cook it either if you don't like licorice. If you do, cook your fennel like celery. It also keeps fleas away from dogs. Plant fennel near kennel.

BEAN SPROUTS. Fresh, glisteny, crisp. Chill in ice water, dry thoroughly between paper towels, and add to salads.

BLACK RADISHES. Cook like turnips, if you ever do. Good in stews.

CACTUS LEAVES. In Mexico they're called *nopales* till they're chopped and then they're *nopalitos*. It's a mean job taking the thorns out. Then after they've cooked ten minutes and been BSPed* they still only taste like green beans.

CARDOONS. A shirttail cousin of the artichoke; looks like a big thistle. Pare the prickles, destring it, treat it like celery.

CELERIAC. A.K.A. Celery Root. Very good with Hollandaise or melted butter. Peel it, chop it small, simmer in chicken bouillon till tender. Drain and add the sauce or butter, or drain and add to salad.

CHAYOTE. A confusing little affair that's also called Mango Squash, Vegetable Pear, or Mirliton. You want them dark if you want them at all, and hard. Wash, cut in quarters, steam till just tender, and BSP.

CHINA PEAS. Pretty, shiny, flat green pods that look like a case of arrested development with those little tiny bumps, but they're not; they're a different sort of pea. Wash, cook in boiling salted water two or three minutes only, and BSP. Good with sautéed mushrooms.

CHINESE BROCCOLI. Don't bother with it unless you're quite hungry. If so, wash it, steam it briefly, and pretend it's spinach.

CHINSES LONG BEANS. Really long: fifteen to eighteen inches. Trim the tips, treat like green beans.

CHINESE MUSTARD. One of Nature's graver blunders. Crumbled cooked bacon helps some.

CHINESE OKRA. Resembles enormous okra; not bad Frenchfried. Scrape off the brown ridges, wash, slice, steam five minutes, then drain. Dip in beaten egg plus a tablespoon of water, then in cracker crumbs. Pan-fry in butter or oil.

DAIKON. An overgrown Japanese radish. Good raw or thinsliced in clear soup. Good in sandwiches: lightly salted sliced daikon and buttered homemade bread.

JERUSALEM ARTICHOKES. Scrub and simmer, unpeeled, in

* Buttered-salted-and-peppered

salted water about twenty minutes. Peel, cut in pieces, BSP. Or reheat in light cream. Also okay cubed in salads. Keep the peelings out of the garbage disposer or they'll tie it in knots.

LEEKS. Like an oversized green onion (shallot) but with its own taste. Wash, cut in edible-size pieces, simmer covered in a heavy skillet with a chunk of butter and some chicken bouillon. Good with cheese sauce.

SALSIFY. Shouldn't be creamed but often is. Good fried in butter if you like fried oysters. First, wash and simmer it fifteen minutes. Then put gloves on (it stains your fingers) and peel. Cut it in strips, put the fibrous inner cores in the garbage can. Dip strips in flour, pan-fry in butter, BSP.

WATER CHESTNUTS. Chestnutlike bulbs that stay crisp cooked. Wash, peel, slice (or not), and add to stews, salads, chow mein, whatever.

ZUCCHINI. Sauté a little chopped onion in butter. Add sliced zucchini, no water, simmer low for ten minutes. SP. Or alternate salted and peppered layers of it, coarsely grated, with layers of grated yellow cheese, ending with cheese, and bake uncovered, thirty minutes, at 350°. Or see Mrs. Whistler's Zuchinni Boats, page 163.

JULY 18   An auspicious day for canceling any scheduled outdoor camping trips in favor of a healthful vacation in Akron, East St. Louis, or the General Motors parking lot.

"Fritz W. Went, a botanist at the University of Nevada, said that the fragrant pine, the pungent sage, and other related trees emit 1,000 per cent more pollutants than all man's fires, factories, and vehicles. . . .

"The botanist said that these trees send molecular substances known as terpenes and esters into the air, stimulating a chemical reaction similar to that caused by manmade pollutants. The reaction is 'summer haze' or 'blue haze,' the professor said.

"The terpene, from which turpentine gets its name, comes from pines and other trees, and is 'incredibly toxic,' he added."   —New York *Times*

JULY 19   On this day in 1695, the first matrimonial advertisement appeared in an English newspaper.

A middle-aged Englishman declared that he would like to "match Himself to some young Gentlewoman that has a fortune of 3000 pound-sterling or thereabouts."

It started something. Thereafter, it wasn't unusual for men to advertise their availability. However, it was unheard of for a lady to do so, and in 1727 when a lively spinster got into the act, advertising for a husband, the outraged citizens of Manchester demanded that an example be made. Forthwith, the Lord Mayor had her committed to a lunatic asylum for four weeks.

In Memoriam

Commemorate we now a gallant lass
    Unloved, unwed, and up till now unsung,
Most foully sentenced by some pompous ass
    To live four weeks the lunatics among.

Yet clear the moral shines, howe'er despotic
    The Mayor was, and loud the civic strife:
To want a husband's purely idiotic,
    But clearly sensible to want a wife.

On this day, too, in 1848, Elizabeth Smith Miller introduced the first pair of bloomers to the First Women's Rights Convention. History doesn't record what she called them. But it wouldn't sound right to put on your Millers, or your Smiths, or even your Lizzies, though that's better. It took Amelia Jenks Bloomer, a bit later, to put the item on the map—additional proof, if any were needed, that much depends on names.

JULY 20   The moon comes up, for thoughtful consideration. It was on this day in 1969 that we landed on it.

A good night to sit outdoors and stare at it . . . wondering if they took the poetry out of the moon by landing there, or whether in the last long analysis they put some in.

JULY 21   The sun also rises, and Ernest Hemingway
                   was born on this day in 1898.

". . . Ernest was just as great an eater as he was a talker.
He made a sandwich that I have always liked. Take a good
piece of white bread, preferably French or Vienna. Butter
the bread on one side quite heavily. Don't use margarine—
the only good use for margarine is for children's suppositories.
Spread a generous amount of peanut butter over the butter.
I like the chunk style best myself. Then spread a heavy layer
of chopped raw onions over the peanut butter. This sandwich leaves just nothing to apologize for to anyone. When
you are saying your prayers say one for Ernest Hemingway."
                                  —George Leonard Herter

JULY 22   Aunt Henry Macadangdang says she doesn't
                   know what anybody else is doing about the
energy crisis, but she's taking lots of naps.

JULY 23   Now beginneth the sign of LEO (controll-
                   ing the Heart) that extendeth through
August 22 and bodeth well for
        restyling the hair
        picking blackberries
        finding new horizons
        getting married.
And strong prideful Leo doeth all these things, and well,
though he roareth myghtily if crossed, like unto the finest
Lion in the Jungle.

JULY 24   ". . . Fertilization of cucumber flowers by
                   insects is also said to be affected by the
moon. When the moon is a new sliver, the bugs rest at night
and are vigorous by day. As the nights grow brighter with
the waxing moon, fertilizing-type creatures romp all night
and are too pooped to pollinate the cucumbers by day. . . ."
                                  —Grace Firth (*Ibid.*)

When your CUCUMBERS get ahead of you, slice them thin,
salt, pepper, and flour them, and fry them in butter.

JULY 25   Tonight try to dream about carrots!

". . . These tasty roots in a dream prophesy an unexpected legacy or money windfall."

—*The Dreamer's Dictionary*

JULY 26   "FRUIT LEATHER MAY BE MADE AT HOME!" (headline)

And then again, it may not; it all depends on whether you have enough fruit and sunshine. People who live under a peach tree in a warm climate can do this:

Peel and slice about ten big ripe peaches, or enough to make ten cupfuls. (Or the same quantity of apricots or strawberries.) Put it in a big saucepan with one cup of sugar. Bring it to a boil, stirring till the sugar is dissolved. Then pour it, in several batches, into the blender and purée it.

Now cover baking sheets tautly with plastic wrap. On each, pour some purée and spread it to the depth of about ¼ inch. Dry it all day under the bright, hot sun. (Obviously you'll have to do something to keep the bugs off, but you can't simply lay a piece of cheesecloth on it, for it would stick. So stretch a piece of cheesecloth, or screening, tautly between two chunks of two-inch-by-four-inch boards placed far enough apart to straddle the cooky sheet.)

After its day in the great outdoors, bring it inside and finish the job in a 150° oven. It's done when the purée can be easily peeled off the plastic.

To store it, roll it up in the plastic, then wrap in more plastic and seal it tightly. At room temperature, it will keep for about a month; in the refrigerator, about 4 months; in the freezer, about a year.

JULY 27   Auspices good for making meat loaf.

". . . Meat loaf is one of the few purely creative endeavors left to the American cook. Not only is it creative, it is educational. As she serves it forth, she learns that (a) the family likes leftover poppy-seed noodles in their meat loaf, or (b) the family doesn't; while the family learns that (c) they'd better eat it anyway because (d) that's all they're going to get."

—Stella Trowbridge Hinky (*Ibid.*)

JULY 28   Social Notes from Mervyn Meadows, Calif.
"At the Friday Club's monthly Potluck, Mrs. Charles ('Edie') Grumwalt made a big 'hit' with her EASY-CHEESY MEAT LOAF, which 'Edie' confessed she just made up on the spur of the moment! What she did was make her regular meat loaf and then roll it into a rectangle, spread it plentifully with sharp cheese cubes, and roll it up like a jelly roll! Then she baked it in the regular meat-loaf pan at 350° for forty-five minutes. Your correspondent, who had a smidgen, agrees that it was a real 'breakthrough!'"

JULY 29   Dear Aloise,
I wonder if everybody knows about putting dry onion-soup mix in meat loaf. I use a package to about 2 pounds of ground meat. It gives a really great flavor and sure beats chopping up a bunch of onions!

I. K.

Dear I. K.,
You're a sweetheart! I tried it and you're right! It's people like you that make the world go 'round! I love you!

Aloise

JULY 30   From Our Science Correspondent:
"When you are wondering how hot it is, and only know it's too hot to go find out, listen for a cricket and count his chirps. If you add thirty-seven to the number of times he chirps in fifteen seconds, it will about equal the temperature. (The hotter it gets, the faster they chirp.)"

JULY 31   It was on this day in 1976, an extremely hot afternoon, that Mumu Herbottle managed to open a childproof container of aspirin tablets in the nick of time to stave off a severe headache. "I'd never in the world have been able to do it," she said later, "without the help of the children."

August

descendeth like a sigh, to keep July & September from sticking together; doth bring hammock Games & a Consideration of the personal Letter & Receipts for notable Edibles including

Gigi's fish
some remarkably good Toffee
a salad to remember
a swift & excellent ice cream

and still other good Things

~~~~~~~~~~~~~~~~~~~~~~~~~~~~~~~~~~

". . . Ideally, the body of a woman should feel like a hot water bottle filled with Devonshire cream. You feel like a paper bag crammed with curtain rods. Think of your muscles one by one. Let them go slack. Relax. Let the brain go blank. Relax . . ."
—Kurt Vonnegut, Jr.

AUGUST 1   NOW IT IS AUGUST, parched season
                    of the Puffball & the Milkweed & the
peeling Nose. And in the fayre Rivers (such as there be)
swimming is a sweet Exercise, for the Sunne abateth not.
Nor doth the Package Tourist slacken his Pace, all ardent to
digest 22 Countries in 21 Days, nor even the Turtle, who
striveth turtlefully in the International Turtle Creepstakes in
Chicago (which is in Illinois). Yet can this be an amiable
time for the reluctant Cook and the harassed Houseperson to
fall back & regroup & read Novels of beautiful Folk & sin-
ful Doings, or watch from some cool Shelter a Spyder go
about her Homespynning, and think long Thoughts.

"The true business of people should be to . . . think about
whatever it was they were thinking about before somebody
came along and told them they had to earn a living."
                                        —R. Buckminster Fuller

HAMMOCK comes from the Spanish *hamaca,* also from
Sears, Roebuck.

AUGUST 2   A Good Day for Hammock Games
                    Games of 4's, 5's, and 6's

Four roads to skepticism:
    "Best of all, on this one you never feel the slightest bit
    hungry."
    "I know you folks don't feel like sitting around all night
    listening to speeches, so I'll make this short."
    "The decrease in administrative confusion will more
    than offset the slight increase in taxes."
    "Take the Lone Pine exit off 101 past the second red
    light beyond the Oak Creek turn-off this side of the next
    overpass and you'll be there in ten minutes."

Five ways to turn me off:
    "Dear, I'm not trying to start something. But . . ."
    "You're making a value judgment."
    "But, Mother, you *said* . . ."
    "If you'd read the book, you'd know what's the matter
    with the movie. Now, in the book . . ."
    "May I be honest with you?"

Six ways to get my undivided attention:

"How nice you loo—Wait a minute. Turn around."

"Is that your red car parked across the street? Well . . ."

"Mom, I know you told me never to do it, but this afternoon . . ."

"Does your husband have a redheaded secretary, a real doll?"

"Now, I'm just going to tap that molar ve-e-ry gently with this little mallet, and you tell me if you feel anything."

"Due to changes in our billing procedure, some of our customers have been overcharged. We are pleased to advise . . ."

OR TAKE A MAGAZINE QUIZ TO DETERMINE THE EXTENT OF YOUR MALADJUSTMENT

Q. Do you think you smell as good as most people?

A. Yes.

Q. Are you now or have you ever been a member of an ethnic group?

A. Yes, want to make something of it?

Q. Do you often have feelings of inferiority?

A. Sure, if I compare myself to certain people, but if I compare myself to certain other people I feel pretty good. What a dumb question.

Q. Are you the same girl your husband married?

A. No, and I'll bet he's glad. My temper and my cooking have improved some, and I know how to take a vacuum cleaner apart and get it back together again.

Q. Do you daydream a lot?

A. Yes. Sometimes I daydream that dinner's all ready, and sometimes I daydream I'm floating in a cool mountain lake at a posh resort, and sometimes I daydream I won the Nobel Prize, and sometimes for a real treat I daydream the kids are back in school.

AUGUST 3   It was on this day in 1893 that the Peary Expedition arrived in Greenland.

This shows how far some people will go to escape the heat. It is too bad that the Admiral didn't get the idea just one year sooner, so that Lizzie Borden could have joined the expedition, for it was precisely on

AUGUST 4   1892 (Look-Out-Behind-You Day) that Borden took an ax and gave her mother forty whacks, and when she saw what she had done, gave her father forty-one. Clearly it was a case of one of those extremely sticky August days when the temper runs short.

This is something to beware of, when the mercury climbs high and stays there. When people get mad, they're apt to say nasty things they mean, as Penelope Gilliatt has pointed out; and sometimes it helps to leave the room and come back with a couple of revitalizing cold drinks.

A TEMPER-SWEETENING MILKSHAKE

Keep small cans of baby-type mashed fruit in the refrigerator. Blend the contents of one with a scoop of ice cream and a little skim milk. A spatter of nutmeg will dress it up.

AUGUST 5   From *A Consideration of Womanual Labor*, by Stella Trowbridge Hinky:

". . . Periodically, then, ask yourself: Do I dust all floors daily and polish them weekly? Do I check all 'busy traffic' areas daily, to sort and put away, and do I give them a thorough cleaning every week? Do I . . ."

It is irresponsible talk like this that gives housekeeping a bad name. These words appear in Stella Hinky's master's thesis, which she wrote before she had a house and a family. But she smartened up fast. Now she dusts when it's dusty enough to make a difference, and she expects people to sort and put away their own things. If they don't, she throws them all into a big barrel at the bottom of the cellar stairs.

AUGUST 6   Now the corn crop is looking good, tassels as high as an elephant's armpit, and Aunt Henry Macadangdang reminds us all that corn-on-the-cob is sweeter and tenderer if there is a little milk in the cooking water. She also admits there is nothing the matter with canned corn, especially in the following recipe, good to know when dinner is cold cuts again.

AUNT HENRY'S CORN-AND-CHEESE

Mix together

½ cup bread cubes	½ teaspoon salt
2 cups cream-style corn	2 beaten eggs
3 teaspoons minced onion	½ cup hot milk
¾ cup Cheddar cheese, grated	

Pour it into a greased soufflé dish or baking pan, and put it in a pan of hot water. Bake at 350° for forty-five minutes to an hour or till it's firm.

AUGUST 7   JOHANNA'S DRESSING

but she paused long enough to write down her favorite way to treat salad greens. On humid days, she explained, with energy at one knot per hour gusting to two, dinner is generally cold meat—some kind—and salad. This makes plenty; lasts for weeks.

In a blender, blend

1 cup olive oil	1 teaspoon each
4 tablespoons minced onion	Worcestershire sauce
2 tablespoons Parmesan cheese	dry mustard
3 teaspoons salt	basil
	oregano
	sugar
	pepper

Then add and blend for another thirty seconds

½ cup red wine vinegar
2 tablespoons lemon juice

Keep it cold and count on it.

According to University of Maryland researchers, the spurt speed of a snail is three inches per minute.

As for the previously mentioned cold cuts, they are apt to end up in a sandwich. Johanna finds it speeds up the sandwich-making (and improves the product) when she keeps a pot of her Better Butter ready in the refrigerator.

BETTER BUTTER FOR COLD MEAT SANDWICHES

One-half cup butter creamed with a teaspoon each of minced onion, prepared mustard, horseradish, and a dash of garlic powder. She keeps a pot of it cold.

AUGUST 8   On this warm August day in 1976, Charles ("Chuck") Grumwalt of Mervyn Meadows, California, cleaned from his swimming pool enough long brown hair to make a handsome doormat.

Hair is hard on swimming pools, which are equally hard on hair.

RECEIPT TO THICKEN THE HAIR AND MAKE IT GROW AGAIN ON A BALD PART

"Take Roots of a Maiden Vine, Roots of Hemp, and Cores of soft Cabbages, of each two handfuls; dry and burn them; afterwards make a lye with the ashes. Before you wash your head with this lye, the part should be rubbed well with Honey, and this method persisted in for three days together."
                    —*Toilet of Flora* (15th century)

AUGUST 9   On this historic day in 1841, the first U.S. train drawn by a steam locomotive chuffed and puffed its way from Albany to Schenectady.

And now returneth the Traveler from far exotic places, full of great food and conversation about it. Invite him to dinner before he has time to get his shapshots developed, and serve him a lovely French fish dish. This one serves four at 109 calories per serving, or possibly 110, depending on the amount of beurre.

GIGI'S FILLETS DE FISH

un lb. de fillets de fish blanc
demi-oignon dans les slices
un quartier lb. des mushrooms (aussi slicé)
un quartier coup de lait (skimmé)
la juice de demi-lemon
un demi tsp. de la sauce du Worcestershire

Maintenant! Puttez les fillets dans un pan greasé, et couvrez

les avec les oignons et les mushrooms. Mixer les autres
thingés tout ensemble et pourez les sur la fish. Appliez les dots
de beurre, aussi du salt et poivre. Bakez le decouvert 15-20
minuits a 400°. Servez votre guest et dites-lui, Fermez la
bouche.

AUGUST 10   Bad Smell Report
              ". . . The smell of a house is important
always, but it is especially so in warm weather. Take careful
note of any flowers in old putrid water, any vegetables
rotting in cupboard or refrigerator. Remember that fresh air
is a wonderful antidote for stale smells, ashes, smoke. . . ."
              —Stella Trowbridge Hinky (*Ibid.*)

    "She who wax ash trays do slick cleaning job quicker."
              —Wun Bum Lung
                (Chinese sage, 1930–1951)

AUGUST 11   Good Smell Report.
              ". . . The most popular fragrance is the
rose, closely followed by lilac and pine. Next in order are lily
of the valley and violet, coffee, balsam, and cedar. Sixty-
seven per cent of the group studied liked wintergreen, with
the young group bringing up the vote for chocolate. Then
in close succession come carnation, orange, and vanilla.
Among popular resinous scents are camphor, cedar, balsam,
pine, witch hazel, menthol, and turpentine."
              —Mary Davis Gillies

It is odd that no one mentioned clover, or bacon broiling,
or hot buttered popcorn. Or the smell of a new car or an
old book or a clean baby.

AUGUST 12   Now the end of the Dog Days brings a
              promise of coolness to come. A day to
catch up on correspondence and to consider some hurdles
in the way.

    . . . It is discourteous to be too long in replying, and dan-
gerous too. I have noticed, myself, that I begin to dislike the
poor innocent friend to whom I owe a letter (for how *not*

dislike a person who makes you so uncomfortable?). And the longer I postpone the writing, the heartier my resentment, to the point that it seems foolish to write a letter to anyone I dislike so much.

Writing a good letter means summoning up the person you are with that particular person. Sometimes this is impossible. Then your letter doesn't sound like you. (It actually does, of course, but it's a different aspect of your self from the one your friend may know.)

If you write someone twice a week, there is much to tell; twice a year and there is hardly a thing.

Any mimeo or carbon-copy letter of any kind from anyone at any time is a bore.

Finding the right complimentary close can be hard, if you ponder nuances. *Sincerely* or *Faithfully* shouldn't be necessary, though if they are, *Insincerely* and *Unfaithfully* should be correct sometimes too; and to few people can you honestly promise that you are theirs truly. *Love* is perhaps best, even for business letters. There are many kinds of love, including a generalized bewildered affection for one's fellow passengers on this wheeling planet. Moreover, the word might take some of the sting out of those letters from banks and other large corporate structures that don't know how to sound friendly even if they want to.

A letter-writer's address should invariably be on the writing paper itself as well as the envelope, because many people throw away the envelope before they answer the letter.

Weather is as lame-brained a topic in a letter as it is in a conversation and it is just as handy.

It is usually more interesting for the letter-reader to hear what the letter-writer thinks or feels (unless the writer is an unusually poor thinker or always sick), but usually it is easier for the letter-writer to write what he did.

People should never apologize for typing letters; only, sometimes, for handwriting them.

It is a waste of good ink to apologize for not having written sooner, unless you were adrift on an Arctic ice floe or locked in a Turkish jail. Most other excuses ring phony as a lead dime. (If this were a love letter, you know you'd have somehow found the opportunity to write it if you'd had to pen it in blood or carve it in soap.) The truth is that until this very minute you didn't want to write the letter quite enough to make time for it. This has nothing to do with affection or even devotion; it is simply the way life is.

One of the big pleasures of rereading old letters is that they don't need answering.

> "You can always tell what you really think of somebody, anybody, by considering the first impression you get at the first sight of a letter from said party."
> —Lou Boyd

AUGUST 13   It is especially important on this thirteenth day of the month to get out of bed on the right side instead of the left, no matter how many people you have to crawl over. However, either side of the bed is the right side, depending on whether you're lying in it or looking at it, so don't worry about this.

AUGUST 14   *From Our Women's Page:*
Dear Aloise,
You may not believe this, but just for an experiment I planted an unpeeled garlic clove in a pot, and it grew just like chives. Handy!

M. S.

Dear M. S.,
In my book you're the tops! I tried it and it works! If everybody was like you the world would be a better place! I love you!   Aloise

AUGUST 15   On this historic day, the Social Security law was enacted, back in 1935.
And for quite a while now, Bessie Tyler Damm of Wichita

Falls has been living on it. The following recipe for toffee is in honor of them both, because Mrs. Damm put herself through Writers' Correspondence School making and selling it. Not once did she ever get a rejection slip for her toffee, and so what with one thing and another, she decided to skip the short stories and stick to candy. She has kindly given permission to include her recipe here.

BESS DAMM TOFFEE

Butter a nine-inch square pan. Pour in, and spread evenly, a cup of chopped nuts—anything but peanuts. (Walnuts are Bessie's personal choice.) Now boil for seven minutes

> **1 cup firmly packed brown sugar**
> **¾ cup butter**

This should bring it to the hard-ball stage—from 250° to 266° on the candy thermometer. Anyway, that's what you're aiming for. So try it: drop a bit in cold water and see if it forms a hard ball that is still yielding. If so, pour the mixture over the nuts. Now sprinkle some semisweet chocolate bits—as many as you like—on top, and a few more chopped nuts on top of that. Press it all down firmly with a piece of aluminum foil, chill it, and break it in chunks.

AUGUST 16   ". . . My own house runs like clock-
                 work. Sometimes it goes slow, sometimes
it goes fast, often it stops altogether—just like clockwork."
                                      —Katharine Whitehorn

AUGUST 17   A Sad Moment!
                 Waiting for take-off on the air strip, in-
side the big DC-10, the agile planes dipping and soaring in
the distance, the three-year-old next to me was crying. He
wanted to go on an airplane. He didn't know he was on one.

AUGUST 18   A FAST, EASY STROGANOFF TO
                 MAKE WITH CUBE STEAKS!

Start with 1½ pounds of cube steak, cut in one-inch strips.
Then you'll need

1 medium onion, shredded
4 tablespoons butter
¼ pound sliced, cleaned mushrooms
1 cup beef broth
2 tablespoons lemon juice
1 cup sour cream

Sauté the onion a little while in 1 tablespoon of butter, till it's golden. Take it out, add another tablespoon and cook the mushrooms in it about five minutes. Flour the steak strips lightly and brown them in the rest of the butter. Put everything else back in the skillet, plus the broth and lemon juice. Simmer fifteen minutes, add the sour cream, heat it through *gently*. Serves six.

AUGUST 19   Now the provident harvest mouse waits in readiness for the first plump wheat grains; and the provident Houseperson, in the cool of the early morning, rolls scoops of vanilla ice cream in coconut and puts them back in the freezer to serve later with fudge sauce.

AUGUST 20   A Historic and Marital First!
Mr. and Mrs. A. D. Brandon ("Brandy" & "Ellie") of Los Altos, California, got lost on this day, in 1975, driving to a friend's new home for dinner, the reason being that Mr. Brandon had failed to get explicit directions. Promptly acknowledging his error, however, Mr. Brandon stopped at a public booth to telephone his friend for a verbal map, then later stopped again at a gas station to ascertain the correctness of his approach. The Brandons arrived approximately on time and in the best of spirits.

AUGUST 21   Things to Do Today:
Buy a roll of reflector tape to keep in the glove compartment, possibly to paste (some dark night) on the headlight glass. You can't predict when a headlight will burn out, these summer nights, on the long road back from the beach.

AUGUST 22　　　It was on this very day in 1974 that Mrs. Edward Ainsworth of Orinda (Calif.) cooked a salmon in her dishwasher. It was a seven-pounder. She placed it on a cupped sheet of heavy aluminum foil, poured on enough dry white wine to make it feel cherished, added an onion slice and an herb or two, wrapped it *snugly*, then put it through the dishwasher for two cycles. No detergent. She said it was beautifully poached, tender, and delicious . . . a good thing for anyone to know, she added, especially anyone who is faced simultaneously with a small salmon and a busted oven.

AUGUST 23　　　Now beginneth the sign of VIRGO (controlling the Bowels) and a good thing too, as it extendeth through September 22, a fine fayre time for

> pulling teeth
> buying new overalls
> taking risks
> mowing lawns.

And the conscientious Virgoan doeth all these things, and nicely, though Perfectionism may hone itself to Nit-pickery as the Mercury climbeth.

A good time for fishing, and a good time to poach

SOME HANDSOME SALMON STEAKS

Combine in a large skillet

1 cup each water	2 teaspoons salt
white wine vinegar	1 teaspoon peppercorns
orange juice	¼ teaspoon ground allspice
lemon juice	1 teaspoon dried dill weed

Bring it to a boil and simmer ten minutes. In it, put

4 salmon steaks (about ¾ inch thick)

and simmer ten more minutes or till the salmon flakes when tested with a fork. Don't overcook it. Take it off the heat and chill several hours (and it's all right to chill it for twenty-four). Finally, to serve it, take it out of the broth and garnish it with something pretty.

AUGUST 24　　　Another Cold Supper Day
It is commonly said that hot foods are

cooling on a hot day. But this truth is inoperative, so far as the cook is concerned. The idea is to stay out of the kitchen entirely, if that is possible. If it isn't, then it is next best to have everything possible done in the early cool of the day. This Mexican-oriented salad is a hearty summer lunch or supper, with a loaf of good bread and a bottle of beer. It is also fast to fix.

SOUTH-OF-THE-BORDER SALAD
for 6

In the morning, mix and chill

½ cup mayonnaise	1 teaspoon Beau Monde
½ cup chili sauce	several drops Tabasco
1 teaspoon chili powder	1 teaspoon vinegar

Just before supper, put these things in a bowl:

    a medium head of iceberg lettuce, in edible-size pieces
    ½ cup sliced pitted black olives
    1 cup grated Cheddar cheese
    1 small purple onion, sliced thin
    seasoned salt and pepper
    a large chunked avocado
    2 cups crumbled corn chips

Add the dressing, toss, and serve.

AUGUST 25   On this day in 1975, Mumu Harbottle
              went to see Dr. Neitzelgrinder.

"I want to quit smoking, Doctor," she said, lighting up.

"Then why don't you?" inquired the doctor, with interest.

"Well . . . because everything depends on something else," Mumu said uncomfortably. "I don't want to quit smoking till I've lost fifteen pounds. And I don't want to start dieting till after my vacation, because it would be silly to diet on my vacation. And I can't take my vacation till my Department Manager takes hers. And she can't take hers till her in-laws go back to Tennessee. And her in-laws can't go back to Tennessee till the plumbers finish replumbing their kitchen. And—"

"I see," said Dr. Neitzelgrinder. "You can't quit smoking on account of some Tennessee plumbers you never even met."

"That's right," said Mumu. "I know it sounds silly to you but—"

"No, I understand how it is," said the doctor. "I want to start jogging again, to get rid of this potbelly, but I left my warm-up suit at my son's house in Colorado Springs. Only he's always away troubleshooting now, at the St. Louis plant, because the Chief Engineer is taking some cure in a Swiss clinic and maybe he'll stay another month if his eighteen-year-old daughter decides she wants to get some skiing in. So—"

"So you can't lose your—er—bay window on account of an eighteen-year-old ski buff you never met either," Mumu finished for him.

Dr. Neitzelgrinder nodded: "No man is an island," he said.

"No woman is either," said Mumu.

"All right, I'll tell you what, Mumu," the doctor said. "Why don't we start running our own ball game? I'll go buy another warm-up suit if you'll quit smoking."

"Just like that?" said Mumu.

"Just like that," said the doctor.

And so they did.

Beardsley Ruml had two maxims that he said were sufficient to live by. One was IT TAKES NO LONGER TO DO IT TODAY. The other was IN GOD'S GOOD TIME. These, he said, took care of most situations.

AUGUST 26   An Interesting Old Custom!
              "Since Saxon days the people of Cheopham Bivney have brought in the snedge on August 26. Today at dawn the snedgebringers will assemble in the old tithe-barn. Then, led by the Master-Snedger, they will walk on stilts to the Gold Cross in the Market Place, singing the eighth-century huck-song, and wearing their gilt cardboard hats.

"The oldest woman in Cheopham Bivney, Mrs. Brass (104) will then read out the scrin-list, after which four young men will haul the snedge from Cow Down to the crossroads. It is a picturesque ceremony, and Professor Towell states in his East Mercian Folk Ceremonies that it probably goes back to the days of Eggfrith the Bald.

"PRODNOSE: But what is the snedge?
  "MYSELF: That has never been disclosed."
                              —J. B. Morton

AUGUST 27   Confucius was born on this day in 551
B.C. And it wasn't long thereafter that
Confucius say, *Hostess at pancake breakfast have most ups
and downs*. Therefore, hostess who serve Very Slim Buttermilk Pancakes reduce two ways.

VERY SLIM BUTTERMILK PANCAKES

In 1 cup buttermilk, put

> **1 teaspoon each of baking powder**
> **baking soda**
> **salt**

Beat 2 egg yolks and to them add

> **1 tablespoon sugar**
> **½ cup flour**
> **the buttermilk mix you just mixed**

Beat the egg whites till stiff, fold them in, and fry the pancakes on a lightly greased skillet.

AUGUST 28   A Little More about Confucius.
Confucius said a great many sound
things in his time, and I've always felt that the reason he
has lasted so well is that his advice was never exactly advice,
but, rather, comments and observations from his undoubtedly
vast store of experience. He stated what he considered to
be a fact, and you drew your own conclusions. —None of
those "If I were *you*" solutions that friends and other amateur sages are always so happy to contribute. (The sticker
here is that I am not You, and You are not Me. Neither
of us actually knows what weapons, if any, the other has in
his arsenal.)

For instance. Recently, with only a few hours' warning, I
was afflicted with two surprise guests for dinner, bed, and
breakfast—a knowledgeable pair who had eaten widely and
well in most of the world's gourmet meccas. Naturally concerned about what to stuff them with further, I was ponder-
ing the situation aloud with my neighbor, a skilled cook.

"If I were you," she said promptly, "I'd do a butterflied
breast of lamb on the barbecue, and then I'd have that mar-
velous bulgar pilaf with the lemons and pecans—you remember, I gave you the recipe. . . ."

But my neighbor is not me. This is the sort of thing she

does naturally. What *I* do, naturally and swiftly in a situation like this, is go to the telephone and make reservations for dinner at a local beanery. There we sit at ease, making snide remarks about the food, in which I join, Allah forgive me, for it is nearly always better than I would have been able to produce on short notice myself.

MS. AESOP'S FABLES (No. 7)

A certain Cat who had been roaming the countryside suddenly remembered an important Catfight he had been anticipating eagerly, back home. He turned around, and—traveling fast—soon came to a broad stream that must be crossed before he could continue his journey.

On the bank sat a friendly Dog, and so the Cat enquired, "When is the next ferry?" The Dog said, "There isn't one till tomorrow. If I were you, I'd jump in. You can paddle across in no time."

The Cat jumped in, before he remembered he couldn't swim. "Oh, you dirty Dog," thought the Cat as he went down for the third time.

AUGUST 29   Ice Cream Facts
On this very day in 1974, Winston Harbottle, age nine, completed his third tour of all 31 Flavors and said Chocolate-Chip-Peppermint was still the hands-down winner.

Observers report that while the average grownup gets 170 licks from an ice cream cone, the average child gets 300. And yet the average child is right there, bright-eyed, sticky-chinned, and ready for another one while the grownup is still fumbling to pay the man.

EXCELLENT EASY BANANA ICE CREAM

2 cups mashed bananas	1 cup sugar
1½ cups buttermilk	1½ teaspoons vanilla
1 9-ounce container of frozen whipped topping	

Blend it thoroughly in the blender, pack it in cartons, and freeze it.

"As for tasting other people's ice cream cones,

never do it. If it tastes good, you'll wish you had
ordered it; if it tastes bad, you'll have had a taste
of something that tastes bad."

—L. Rust Hills

AUGUST 30   The best breakfast on a hot August
morning is ¼ cup All-Bran sprinkled
over a good scoop of vanilla ice cream.

AUGUST 31   August Andante

Regretfully the sun leaves, and dark comes late.
The soft shadows deepen now, along about eight;
And through an open window with the scent of
   warm clover
Comes the sound of Jane's piano, just a green yard
   over.

Listen . . . that's a scale now; she crosses hands
   here,
And now a little tune starts, halting, shy, clear. . . .
Rondo? Memories of Love? Elegy? Romance?
Or possibly a chorus of *The Primrose Dance?*

Summer isn't locusts, and shrill bright heat,
And the hot sun strumming with a harsh gold beat.
It's little cool piano notes, as falteringly sweet
As gentle petals falling
               through a dusky summer twilight
                   down a quiet summer street.

September

toucheth lightly upon Time & the Saving thereof & the start of new Endeavors; landeth harder on some lightning Receipts including

> *Souper Chicken*
> *I Hate To Cookies*
> *4-way Meat Loaf*
> *the fastest fudge sauce*
> *the fastest lemon pie*

and other Swifties there isn't time to mention

~~~~~~

"... For the days grow short
when you reach September. ..."

SEPTEMBER 1   NOW IT IS SEPTEMBER, Summer's
                     farewell, the brisk time, the gold
time. Now travelers do return to Offices throughout the Lande
to tell great Lyes of their Adventuryings & now the windes
begin to knock the Apples' heades together on the trees &
the fallings are gathered for Pyes. And Mothers do wave
Children off to School, these little ones now being a lump
in the Throate that were so recently a pain in the Necke.
And yet this be the lively time, the yeasty time, the Year
in Geare, when all seemeth possible & is, to the reluctant
Cook & the harried Houseperson, given another Two Hours
in the Daye. And so to ferret these out be our worthy Endeavor.

SEPTEMBER 2   People so often talk about killing
                     time but never about killing money.
Perhaps we are more reverent about money.

The big difference between Time and Money is this: you
can save pennies in an old pickle bottle and watch them pile
up. But Time can't be saved that way; the snippets disappear.
The capful of detergent in the tub saves a ten-second swish
later on. But where do the ten seconds go? Out like a candle
flame, melting into the time-space continuum.

Another example: the instant TV. No thirty seconds to
warm up. But what can you do with thirty seconds besides
make instant mashed potatoes? And this isn't the time for
that, it's time to watch the news.

Why must we do everything fast? I'll bet it won't be long
(I thought) till they break the four-minute book the way
they did the old, slow, four-minute mile. Then we'll have
the 3:58 book to aim at, then the 3:56 book. . . .

The idea bothered me, and so I decided to pay a call on
our state councilman in charge of Speedup.

"Dr. Sonikboom," I said, for it was none other, "I'm
sorry to bother such a busy man on a busy Monday. But I'm
confused about all this speed."

"Perfectly all right," he said, swallowing a cigar. ((He
swallows them instead of smoking them because it makes him
feel just as bad, and it's faster.) "Nothing scheduled today

anyhow, just a little project to provide free skate boards at the Art Museum. Do you realize that people have spent as much as a week in there and still haven't seen everything? On a skate board they can wrap it up in precisely—" he paused impressively—"one hour and forty-eight minutes, allowing a full five-second stop in front of the El Greco."

"Mercy me–" I said.

"Nothing to it," he said modestly. "Just a matter of taking the pleasure out and putting the speed in."

"But what about outdoor walking?" I said. "Some people still like to ramble around and look at the—"

"Clouds, trees, hills, all that stuff," he finished for me, nodding impatiently. "But we're fixing that. Stationary walkers. In the basement."

"Like mechanical bicycles?" I said.

"Right!" He beamed. "Strap yourself in, stand there, move your feet up and down and count the cobwebs! No fun at all! One hour is nine miles!"

"Heavens to Elizabeth!" I said. "But Dr. Sonikboom, people still spend a great deal of time listening to rock bands and opera and symphonies, don't they?"

He frowned. "It's a problem," he said. "The thing is, we still haven't figured out how you can listen faster than somebody plays. But we're programming it," he added confidently. "And we'll get there."

Still, there are two good reasons for doing something fast: because life is crowding in hard, and if the thing isn't done fast it won't be done at all, or because doing it isn't half so rewarding as doing something else.

Therefore: iron fast, or not at all, so you can paint slow. Shop fast, so you can sew slow. Cook fast, so you can study slow or read slow or write slow or take your time organizing an office or decorating a room. Or so you can spend some time with a child before it disappears into an adult.

SEPTEMBER 3   "You take some recipes, be my guest, they've got 14 ingredients before you come to the stuffing. This one has three, so you can remember it at the grocery store at quarter to five, and it tastes darn good."

       —Shirley Shimmelfenner,
      Breaking the 4-Minute Chicken, vol. 14

SOUPER CHICKEN

Mix

>   1 can undiluted mushroom soup
>   1 can undiluted onion soup
>   1 cup dry white wine

Pour it over two to three pounds of chicken parts, cover and bake at 300° for 2½ hours. Serve it. If you want gravy instead of sauce, thicken the juice with two tablespoons cornstarch or flour mixed in ⅓ cup cold water. And if you want stew, add some little onions and carrot chunks about thirty minutes before it's done. And if you just can't stop, put some refrigerator biscuits on top, about twenty minutes before it's done, and leave the lid off, for a nice Pot Pie.

Or make some

COCACHICKEN

Salt and pepper a flock of chicken parts—two or three pounds—or a whole chicken, cut up. In a skillet, warm ¾ cup catsup, add the chicken, and pour one cup of Coca-Cola over the whole thing. Cover it; cook half an hour. Then uncover it, cook another half hour, and it's done. And don't knock it till you've tried it. Then you can. But fair's fair.

Don't knock bottled barbecue sauce either. There are some good brands around—some smokier, some spicier. Get one you like, to keep handy for

BARBACHICKEN*

Simmer the chicken pieces in a little water for ten minutes, then drain them. Lay them out in a shallow pan, pour some sauce on top, and bake at 350° about forty minutes.

SEPTEMBER 4 An Auspicious Day for making sandwiches to freeze.

What not to put in them: mayonnaise, salad dressing, jam, jelly, hard-cooked egg whites, lettuce, tomatoes, and carrots.
But to solve the mayonnaise problem you can make a

---

* That same barbecue sauce is good on any leftover roast meat if you've eaten it plain too long. Cut the meat in small chunks and heat them in it.

freezable cooked dressing. Then the sandwiches will be ready to eat when they thaw.

FREEZABLE DRESSING

Over simmering water, mix well

 2 tablespoons sugar
 1 teaspoon salt
 1 teaspoon prepared mustard
 1½ tablespoons flour

Then beat an egg in ¾ cup of milk and blend it in. Now stir in ¼ cup of vinegar and keep right on stirring, over the hot water, till it's thick—about twelve minutes. Blend in one tablespoon butter, then cool it and refrigerate in a covered jar.

SEPTEMBER 5 Labor Day is a legal holiday on the first Monday in September, a day of rest and recreation, a day to bask in. . . .

Wash. Clean house. Cook. Locate everybody's back-to-school gear. Explain to eight-year-old that the back-to-school dress from Grandma isn't barfy. Explain that all her friends will be wearing barfy dresses too. Explain that okay, she's going to wear it even if it is barfy. Then explain that if she doesn't stop yowling you'll give her something to yowl about. Then fish eight-year-old's patched cut-offs out of wastebasket, barf, wash cut-offs, add additional vital patch, and figure out something to tell Grandma.

SEPTEMBER 6 Look, Jane! Look, Jane, look!
Look at the school bus! The school bus is coming!
The school bus is coming to pick up the children.
See?
See, Jane? Did you see the school bus?
The school bus came and picked up the children!
Jump, Jane! Holler, Jane!
Jump high and holler!

SEPTEMBER 7   A good day to make

I HATE TO COOKIES*

(Not a great cooky but a good cooky; a cheap cooky, a fast cooky, an easy cooky. No creaming, sifting, rolling out, cutting out, or pan-greasing.)

Melt

> ½ cup butter (not margarine)

In it, stir

> 1 cup brown sugar
> 2 cups quick-cooking rolled oats
> ½ teaspoon baking powder
> 1 teaspoon vanilla

Mix it, press it into a nine-by-fifteen-inch pan with a rim (a little bigger wouldn't hurt) and bake at 400° for ten to twelve minutes. It will still be bubbling when you take it out. When it's barely cool, cut in squares.

SEPTEMBER 8   The 4-way Meat Loaf, or

YOUR BASIC MEAT MIX

(from Hinky's book of the same name)

"Face it. The fastest food is raw food. Next comes the quick chop, steak, cutlet. Next, the Meat Mix, frozen in small balls to thaw fast and use half a dozen ways. In fact, the family can eat meat loaf most of the time and never know it." Buy

> 1 pound bulk sausage
> 3 pounds hamburger

preferably on sale, but if it isn't, buy it anyway. (People who hate to cook hate to shop, so bargains are a matter of luck.) Now add

½ cup milk
4 eggs
4 slices bread, crumbled
4 tablespoons parsley
2 tablespoons Worcestershire sauce

1 cup minced onion
Salt, pepper, and garlic salt; or dry mustard, celery salt, marjoram, thyme, or a bit of each

* Registered.

That's the MIX. Put ¼ of it in a meat-loaf pan and bake at 350° about fifty minutes. Make the rest into one-inch meat-balls and divide them into three separate packages, about equal size, to freeze.

Second week: STUFFED PEPPERS. Remove tops and seeds from four green peppers, simmer them five minutes, then stuff them with the frozen meatballs right out of the freezer. Pour something wet over them—cheese sauce, tomato sauce, whathaveyou—and bake at 350° forty-five minutes.

Third week: JUST PLAIN MEATBALLS. Take out another package, flour the meatballs frozen, and brown them in a skillet. Put them in a casserole dish. Make gravy out of the pan drippings (or if you prefer a gravy mix, use that). Either way, add to it a half-cup of sour cream, pour it over the meatballs, and bake them covered at 350° for an hour.

Fourth week: STUFFED CABBAGE. Buy a small can of cream sauce or make a cupful, using 1½ tablespoons flour, 1½ tablespoons butter, and one cup milk. Now chop a small head of cabbage coarsely, cook it in boiling water five minutes, and drain it. Grease a big casserole dish. On the bottom put a chopped raw tomato. Next, half the drained cabbage. Next, a package of frozen meatballs. Now add the rest of the cab-bage, dot with butter, cover and bake for an hour at 350°. *Before serving,* heat the cream sauce, add a pinch of nutmeg, and pour it over.

. . . Now, actually you needn't hold this down to four pounds of mix. If you have enough muscle and a big-enough bowl, make more. Those meatballs could show up with pastry wrapped around them, for a variation of Cornish Pasties. Or layered with pasta, mozzarella, and tomato sauce for free-style lasagna. . . .

SEPTEMBER 9   A day that augurs well for starting a project.

The civil war within: When I know beyond a doubt that I want to do a specific thing—will be happier, healthier, nicer, or richer for doing it—why then don't I do it? What absurd mental isometrics keep me immobilized? It is one-half the

brain pitted against the other: the will and the won't. . . . A
person divided against herself cannot stand, she sits.

SEPTEMBER 10   A Common Complaint!
          My brain is not a satisfactory one.
If I had a car like my brain, I would take it back and tell
them they gave me a lemon. It is hard to budge out of neutral
and it screams like an eagle when I shift gears into second,
and the windows are usually stuck, only halfway open.

SEPTEMBER 11   A Comforting Reflection!
          And yet, I suppose everyone knows
more than he thinks he does. There are so many kinds of
knowledge.

Think of all the things you know but don't believe!: A
table is only a mass of nervous electrons. Greenland is icy
and Iceland is green. You are not as bright as you feel, after
the second Martini.

And the things you believe but don't know. One kind of
toothpaste is better than another kind. Cold showers are good
for you. A male calico cat is worth a thousand dollars.

And the things you know but forget when possible. You
probably look your age. If you try to get all your suntan in
one weekend, you'll be as sorry as you were the last time.

And the things you take on consignment till they begin to
look too foolish. The fattest people are the jolliest people.
Everybody loves a good listener. You can trust anyone who
looks you straight in the eye. The best things in life are
free. . . .

SEPTEMBER 12   A Wise Observation!
          ". . . Every act of conscious learning
requires the willingness to suffer an injury to one's self-esteem.
That is why young children, before they are aware of their
own self-importance, learn so easily; and why older persons,
especially if vain or important, cannot learn at all."
                                        —Thomas Szasz

SEPTEMBER 13   A Valuable Word!
          The *clochandichter,* in northeast
Scotland, is the last rock that can be put on a heap of rocks

before the whole lot collapses.—Not the rock that makes it collapse, mind you. (That would be the straw that broke the camel's back.) The clochandichter is the one just before it.

On a crisp September morning exactly a year ago, in Cleveland, Ohio, a certain Mrs. Andreyev (Frisia) Taloff woke to find the house unusually chilly. After investigating, Andreyev reported that they were out of oil. Frisia said she would telephone the fuel company as soon as their Customer Department opened.

Next, she washed a few dishes for the family's breakfast (the dishwasher was full of dirty ones because last night the dishwasher-detergent box had proved to be empty), then got Andreyev off to work and the children aimed for school, seven-year-old Boris having spilled his cocoa only once, to the considerable amusement of thirteen-year-old Natasha as she watched her mother clean it up.

From 9 to 9:30 at the telephone, Frisia got a busy signal from the fuel company. So she decided to stop and place the order, since their office was on the way to her own at the City Vocational Guidance Center, where she worked from 10 to 4.

Dressing, she discovered that Natasha had worn her mother's only pair of runless pantyhose to school, and so Frisia wore the pantsuit she had intended to drop at the dry cleaner's.

En route to the office, she had a flat tire that she replaced, herself, at the corner of Third and Taft, with her spare, which the garage told her, when she eventually limped in, was worse than the flat. So, $38.88 later, she arrived at the office, just in time to miss the department-head meeting during which she had been appointed Building Collector for the Heart Fund.

All afternoon it rained. At 4:30, returning to her car, she found she had left its windows open. At 5:15, arriving home after a stop at the supermarket, she found that Boris had a runny nose and that Natasha had thoughtfully run the dishwasher but used ordinary detergent, so the suds were now up to the kitchen sill.

By the time Frisia had wiped and dried the floor, the counters, and the dishes, Andreyev was home. She opened a can of corned beef hash.

Natasha wanted to know why they never got anything but corned beef hash around here. Frisia responded that sometimes they did, but not tonight.

Boris wanted to know if he had to eat a yucky poached egg on his. Frisia said, "Yes."

Then Andreyev said, over his shoulder as he twiddled the TV dial, "Say, it's still cold in here. Did you get the fuel company?"

Frisia said, "No."

Andreyev opened his mouth to say something else. But he happened to be looking at Frisia at the time. He closed his mouth again, promptly. He didn't say anything else. Fortunately, Andreyev recognized a clochandichter when he encountered one.

SEPTEMBER 14   "Woman's place is in the home, and that's where she should go just as soon as she gets done at the office." —Anonymous

SEPTEMBER 15   On this day, 1847, the first ten-hour workday law became effective in New Hampshire.

On this day, 1975, Artemus Thorncrotch, Economist, calculated that at his salary of $25,000 per year, one hour of his time was worth precisely $12.81.

Calculating in similar fashion for his wife, Alicia, who also holds a degree in Economics and pounds a typewriter down the hall for $10,000 per year, he informed her that one hour of hers was worth $5.12.

"Therefore," he said pleasantly, "when we spend an hour together, you should pay me the difference, precisely $7.69, or I'm wasting my time."

"You're wasting your time right now," she said, with equal cordiality. "Any decent call girl is $25 an hour—shall we say $3,600 a year? And the lousiest cook, which I am not, gets $600 per month—that's $7,200—plus minimum housework plus laundry, say $300 a month or another $3,600, plus weekend baby-sitter and chauffeur, that's another $6,000. So pay me my $20,400 annual back wages for fourteen years and maybe we can do business."

A smart girl, that Alicia. You can't say her degree in Economics went for nothing. Almost nothing, though.

SEPTEMBER 16   On this day in 1620, the *Mayflower* set sail from Southampton for Provincetown; and only twenty-eight years later the Pilgrims hanged their first witch, an occasion to commemorate with a magic fast

RICH WITCH CAKE

(The magic is in the way the fruit cocktail disappears. No one would ever guess.)

In a bowl, mix

1 cup white sugar
1 cup all-purpose flour
1 teaspoon soda
½ teaspoon salt

1 egg
1 small can (15-ounce) fruit cocktail

Pour it into a greased pan, about nine by eleven inches or thereabouts. Sprinkle the top with one cup brown sugar and ½ cup chopped nuts, mixed together, and bake at 350° for an hour. If you like, serve with ice cream or whipped cream. But think twice.

> "To gild refined gold, to paint the lily,
> To throw a perfume on the violet . . .
> Is wasteful and ridiculous excess."
> —Shakespeare

SEPTEMBER 17   A rare picturesque Phrase!
        In the olden days, girls and boys, dolls were different. They didn't walk or talk or have bust measurements and ski outfits. What they had was wax heads and necks firmly attached to thoroughly stuffed stockinette bodies. And in Boston, some decades ago, certain well-reared children were taught to fold their little mitts over their breastbones, when offered another helping they didn't want, and say, "No, thank you. Dolly's wax!"
To dolly's wax a football team, make a

HEARTY BEEF GOULASH

to serve on noodles

(If it's the entire team plus the coach, add more beef, any handy vegetables, and cook more noodles. Or double or triple the whole thing.)

In a deep skillet with a lid, brown two pounds stewing beef in four tablespoons of oil. Remove the meat, and in the same oil sauté for about three minutes—

    1 cup each onion, thinly sliced
                celery, thinly sliced
                green pepper strips
    ½ teaspoon garlic powder

Now stir in

3 teaspoons paprika	1 can bouillon (undiluted)
1½ teaspoons salt	1 cup thinly sliced carrots
½ teaspoon pepper	a crumbled bay leaf
2 tablespoons tomato paste	

Bring the whole works to a boil, then simmer it, covered, about two hours, till the meat is quite tender. Do it hours ahead or the day before. Just before serving time, heat it through, keeping the heat low, and stir in

                    ½ cup sour cream

Serve it on buttered noodles.

SEPTEMBER 18   Now beginneth a nation-wide week
                      of mad revelry yclept *Pickle-Tickle Time,* sponsored by Peter Piper and his pixilated pickle-packing peers.

    Beginneth also a

September Harvest of Extra-Simple Fast Recipes, each assembled before you can say *"precipitevolissimevolmente!"* and each one personally selected by Stella Trowbridge Hinky.

VEGETABLES & SALADS

SIMPLE SPINACH: Cook and drain a package of frozen chopped *spinach.* Press out the water. Add a one-ounce package of *cream cheese,* a dash of *garlic salt,* and stir over low heat till hot clear through.

CHEESE CABBAGE: Simmer quartered *cabbage* in a little water till tender. Heat and pour over it a can of undiluted *Campbell's Cheese Soup.*

SIMPLEST CORN CHOWDER: Pour a can of *cream-style corn* into a saucepan, add the same amount of *milk,* and heat, stirring occasionally. Pour into bowls, dot with *butter*, and serve.

CINNAMON YAMS: Open a No. 2½-size can of *yams*. Pour juice into the blender, add chunked yams, one *egg*, one teaspoon *cinnamon*. Blend, pour into a casserole dish, bake uncovered at 350° for forty minutes.

ONION RICE: In a saucepan put two cups of *water*, a tablespoon *oil*, a package of *Lipton Onion Soup Mix*. Bring to a boil, add one cup regular white *rice*. Turn to low, simmer twenty minutes, and don't peek while it cooks.

GOOD SALAD DRESSING: Equal parts *yoghurt* and *mayonnaise*.

GOOD SALAD DRESSING NO. 2: Thin *mayonnaise* with *catsup*.

SIMPLE FROZEN SALAD: Combine one can *whole-berry cranberry sauce* with one cup *sour cream* and one small can *crushed pineapple*. Freeze in oiled refrigerator tray, then cut in squares.

SEPTEMBER 19   Continueth the Hinky Collection, with two-and-three-ingredient recipes for

DESSERTS

FRESH FRUIT M*A*S*H: Leave one quart *vanilla ice cream* in refrigerator till slightly soft. Wash, cull, and/or peel one pint *fresh fruit*. Mash. Blend slightly with a big spoon. Chill in freezer before serving.

SWIFT FUDGE SAUCE: In the top of the double boiler, heat one can *Eagle Brand Condensed Milk*, three tablespoons *water*, three one-ounce squares *bitter chocolate*.

FASTEST LEMON-PIE FILLING: Mix a regular-size can of thawed *lemonade* with one can *Eagle Brand Condensed Milk* and one nine-ounce container of *whipped topping*. (Now it's ready to pour into a crust and chill.)

VANILLA SOUR-CREAM TOPPING: Prepare a small package of

Instant Vanilla Pudding according to directions, add a cup of *sour cream*, mix, and refrigerate ten minutes. A good dip for fresh fruit.

SHORTBREAD: Mix ½ pound softened *butter* with ½ cup *sugar* and three cups of *flour*. Mix thoroughly, press into pan of proper size, so the mixture is ¼ inch thick and extends to the edges. Bake at 350° for fifteen minutes, 300° for thirty more.

> " . . . It was the Count de Laplace who discovered a very elegant way of eating strawberries, namely, of squeezing over them the juice of a sweet orange, or apple of the Hesperides."
>
> —Brillat-Savarin

AND ODDS-AND-ENDS

GOOD HEARTY SIDE DISH: Mix cooked *macaroni* with *cottage cheese, poppy seeds,* and *salt* and *pepper* to taste.

ICE CREAM MUFFINS: Mix two cups self-rising *flour* and one pint softened *vanilla ice cream*. Spoon it into greased muffin cups, bake at 425° for twenty to twenty-five minutes. (Add a tablespoon of sugar for a good shortcake base.)

CHEESE SAUCE: Add three ounces grated *sharp yellow cheese* and ½ teaspoon *dry mustard* to a small can of *evaporated milk*. Stir, heat.

TO GO WITH HAM OR TURKEY: Mix a good tablespoon of *Orange Tang* with a can of *applesauce*. Stir well and chill.

SEPTEMBER 20   On this day in 1974, Billie Jean King licked the petticoats off Bobby Riggs in the Houston Astrodome. Celebrate with a

TRIFLE

" . . . Lay mackroons over the bottom of your dish, and pour upon them a glafs of fack; then have a ready a cuftard, made pretty ftiff, which lay over them. Make a froth of cream,

fugar, wine, and juice of lemon, cover your cuftard over
with it, and ftick citron in it."

—From *"The Complete Englifh Cook, or, The
Prudent Housewife,"* published 1746

SEPTEMBER 21   But if you can't decide where to
                          ftick the citron, make a

1976 TRIFLE

It takes

- 1 strawberry jelly roll—about a pound
- 2 small packages strawberry Jell-O
- 1 cup sherry
- 1 package cook-type vanilla pudding (not the kind
     you merely mix)
- whipped cream
- some maraschino cherries

and preferably a transparent bowl to put it in. Line the bottom with the jelly roll, cut in one-inch slices. Make the Jell-O
according to directions EXCEPT use only half the water it calls
for and make up the difference with sherry. (*Not* cooking
sherry, which is salty.) Pour it on the jelly-roll slices and
mush it together gently, then put it in the refrigerator to set
while you cook the pudding. Pour it on top of the Jell-O
and let it set. Before serving, decorate it with the whipped
cream and the cherries.

SEPTEMBER 22   Have down-to-earth talk with potted
                          house plants that have been vaca-
tioning outside. Explain that life isn't all beer and skittles,
and vacation is about over, and the first frost is coming. Then
move them closer to the house so you'll remember to bring
them inside. Or get it over with and do it now.

SEPTEMBER 23   So beginneth the sign of magnetic
                          LIBRA (controlling the Loins) that
extendeth through October 22 and augureth well for
    painting a picture

writing a novel
composing a sonata
traveling to far places
buying rare fine new clothes.
And the born Libran charmeth all with his talents and warmth,
yet keepeth his plans and projects ever to himself.

SEPTEMBER 24   Yet be not too careful at thy toilet.

"It is lucky to put on any article of
dress, particularly stockings, inside out: but if you wish the
omen to hold good, you must continue to wear the reversed
portion of your attire in that condition, till the regular time
comes for putting it off—that is, either bedtime or 'cleaning
yourself.' If you set it right, you will change your luck."
     —R. Chambers

SEPTEMBER 25   And mark with precision the day of
     the week before cutting thy nails!
Cutting Fingernails:
"Cut 'em on Monday, you cut 'em for health;
Cut 'em on Tuesday, you cut 'em for wealth;
Cut 'em on Wednesday, you cut 'em for news;
Cut 'em on Thursday, a new pair of shoes;
Cut 'em on Friday, you cut 'em for sorrow;
Cut 'em on Saturday, you'll see your true love tomorrow;
Cut 'em on Sunday, and you'll have the devil with you all
     the week."
     —Forby's *Vocabulary of East Anglia*

SEPTEMBER 26   On this day, try Wun Long Chin's

CHOP SUEY

for People Who Don't Like Chinese Food

*(Wun Long Chin, former chef at the Pewter Pavil-
ion, was fired recently because his cooking was too
Americanized. This isn't surprising, inasmuch as he's
never been out of Peoria. However, his Chop Suey
has a number of things going for it: kids like it, it*

freezes well, and it's handy for baby-sitter meals. Also you can make it with leftover turkey. Add some chopped ginger, some Chinese pea pods, some water chestnuts, and more soy sauce, to give it more thrust.)

Brown two cups finely diced fresh pork in three tablespoons salad oil. Add, and cook ten minutes

> 3 cups chopped celery
> 2 cups chopped onion
> 2 tablespoons soy sauce

Now dissolve two bouillon cubes in a cup of boiling water. Add it to the pork. Mix another tablespoon of soy sauce with three tablespoons cornstarch, one tablespoon molasses, and ½ cup water, and add this to the pork too. Finally, stir in a one-pound can of bean sprouts and a can of mushrooms, and stir till it's thick. Cook it another five minutes if it's to be served at once. If it's to be frozen, freeze it.

SEPTEMBER 27

Thirty days hath September,
Month of paler, cooler suns
(And if it didn't, who'd remember
The totals for the other ones?)

SEPTEMBER 28

"The old earth . . . is nearly half a degree cooler than she was 30 years

ago."

—*The Old Farmer's Almanac,* 1970

Helpful Healthful Facts!

COFFEE & TEA

". . . Coffee may be used with benefit by laboring men; but black tea is the best drink for sedentary persons. . . ."

SMOKING

"In consumption, catarrh, and nervous exaltation of the system, moderate smoking is always beneficial."
—*Frank Leslie's Illustrated
Family Almanac, 1872*

SEPTEMBER 29   This is the anniversary of the day Louise Riehl married Leo Todd, in Paducah, Kentucky, and it was a lovely wedding.

However, Louise, always active in the Women's Movement, wasn't about to give up her own name. Now Riehl-Todd, with four children, two in diapers, she hasn't yet found a way to lib herself from getting dinner. But she has found the following recipe to be of considerable help, because it is so easy, and the whole family likes it.

"This isn't the greatest-looking casserole in the world, why should I lie to you?" she writes. "But it *tastes* good—good and rich, for some reason. So cover the top with crumbs or cheese. It's really a dependable stand-by, sort of a foundation I can build on when I'm trying to figure out the week's meals."

LOUISE'S ALL-IN-ONE FOUNDATION

Brown 1½ pounds ground beef in a skillet with a little oil. Then mix into it

    1 can Veg-All, drained
    1 can chicken-with-rice soup, undiluted

Cover and bake at 325° for forty-five minutes, and if you decide to add the crumbs or cheese, bake it an additional ten minutes with the lid off. Serve it on Chinese noodles.

SEPTEMBER 30   Adam and Eve were banished from the Garden on this day, a long time ago.

And St. Jerome died on this day in A.D. 420. He was the one who removed a thorn from a lion's paw and wrote the Latin version of the Bible.

This is also Botswana Day, a national holiday for people who live in Botswana.

> Thirty days hath September,
> Thirty shining golden beads.
> Thirty days hath September.
> Actually, that's all it needs.

October

toucheth mainly upon Appearances; offereth ways to combat Obligations & presenteth divers Daynties to cook for Companie, including

> *Spinach and Love Apples*
> *a most delicious Carrot Cake*
> *the invariably successful Florentine*
>   *Casserole*
> *a worldly Hot Fruit Dish*

and many more Delicacies too

'Tis meet that we should dream the dream
And wish upon a gentle star
—Should do our earnest best to seem
A trifle couther than we are.

And so we sort the tousled house
Ere Guest descend, and rare the wife
Who hath not said to errant spouse,
Goddammit, use the butter knife.

OCTOBER 1   NOW IT IS RED-GOLD OCTOBER
                but the Winde soon shaketh the Trees &
wild Hogs grow fat on harvest Nuts as doth the armchair
Footballer. Now sparkleth the new Season with theatre Open-
yngs & brave new Clothes all in the winey Ayre; and kind
Hearts & true Lovers lie close but do ponder, on arising, their
Sociall Obligations. For it is known to both reluctant Cook &
harried Houseperson that they who Entertain little will be
but little Entertained; and the Holidays draw nigh, which do
take unaccustomed Forethought & Cooking & ardent Attention to Appearances.

> ". . . Everything that was of use, Mrs. Dancey hid
> away. Anything that was of no use to anybody, she
> proudly displayed. That was another reason Linnea
> knew she was a lady."
>
> —Ardyth Kennelly

> ". . . At long last they had finished the painstak-
> ing, arduous, and expensive job of re-doing their
> house. All it lacked now was a discerning guest to
> appreciate how much more charmingly, luckily, and
> richly situated they were than he was."
>
> —John Crispin

. . . The real reason for not dropping in at the dinner hour
is not (except in the wilderness) that people would feel con-
strained to invite you to eat with them. It is because dinner
is so personal a thing, personal as undershirts, hair-curlers,
and other comfortable slovenries, and only distantly related
to the way people eat when you come as an invited guest.
Many people hunker over the TV set while eating, for nearly
as many people watch TV and don't admit it as eat TV dinners and don't admit it. And people read while they eat, and
eat in strange positions and make strange noises, and what
they eat is often strange, too.

OCTOBER 2   On this day in 1975, Mumu Harbottle
                forgot to buy her customary sour cream
for the baked potatoes and served them plain with butter
and salt. A guest telephoned the following day to say, among
other things, that she had forgotten how delicious a com-

paratively unadorned baked potato can be, and she thanked
Mumu for bringing the fact to her attention.

Style is sometimes a happy accident, while planned effects
are not always effective. At one time, to hide a bad haircut,
I was featuring a white turban—severe, yet not without a
certain dash, or so I thought, until a doorman asked with
real curiosity, "What happened to your haid?" Then, once I
couldn't find any cuff links to wear with a French-cuffed shirt
and wore the shirt anyway, open at the wrists. A friend told
me later that she thought, *How chic!* and decided to wear
her French-cuffed shirts that way too.

With me, other people's houses always get the benefit of the
doubt. I see the odd off-color wall and think, *How carefully
thought out, how interesting!* I look at my own and think,
Missed again. . . .

". . . But a golden glow does seem to hang over the houses I
visit; bald envy leaves me with a considerable re-entry problem into my own, and a depressing conviction that there's
almost no place like home, dammit."

                                        —Katharine Whitehorn

OCTOBER 3   A certain Mr. John S. Thurman did
                     patent the motor-driven vacuum cleaner
on this very day in 1899, a day that boded only good for
universal personhood, that freed us (when we cleaned a
room) from dusty bondage to the broom, from aches and
pains and blistered mitts and periodic sneezing fits—that gave,
from all of this, surcease, that we might henceforth sweep
in peace. All hail!

From Aunt Henry Macadangdang's *Practical Entertaining
Manual* that she has been making notes on for forty years:

Sometimes I sit at the dining table where guests will sit and
look up (as they may do) at the undersides of things. I find
considerable dust this way. Not that I necessarily do anything about it. But I find it.

Candle-lit rooms need less dusting than electric-lit rooms.

Flowers in the powder room get you more points than flowers on the table.

Raw vegetables are easier than hot canapés, and cheaper, because some are usually left over, for salad tomorrow.

When meat is expensive, serve salad as a first course, with plenty of breadsticks.

Always give people a chance to refuse dessert.

Always explain that it would be a crime to camouflage the vegetable's delicate spring taste, when you don't want the bother of making a sauce.

Don't ever admit the recipe came off the box. Say it is from a funny old cookbook that's been in the family forever.

It's really better to invite all the dull people one night and all the bright ones the next. The dull won't know it's dull, because it's always that way.

October is also Eat More Spinach Month. If the taste is sufficiently covered up, it isn't too bad, as is the case with Aunt Henry's two sound approaches to the problem:

1. MACADANGDANG SPINACH MEDLEY
(which provides a starch too)

2 tablespoons butter	4 eggs, slightly beaten
½ cup chopped onion	½ cup milk
1 pound spinach (fresh or frozen and thawed)	2 teaspoons salt
1 teaspoon garlic powder	¼ teaspoon pepper
3 cups cooked rice (1 cup raw)	1 cup shredded mozzarella cheese (about 4 ounces)
½ cup grated Parmesan cheese	

Melt the butter, add the chopped onion, and cook till it's tender. Add the spinach, garlic, rice, and Parmesan, and mix it well. Now combine the eggs, milk, and seasonings and stir this into the rice mixture. Turn it into a shallow rectangular baking dish, top it with the mozzarella, and bake at 350° for half an hour.

2. SPINACH AND LOVE APPLES

Get three or four big *tomatoes* and slice them into eight thick chunks. Lay them out in a flat buttered baking dish. Sprinkle with garlic salt. Now cook two packages of frozen spinach and drain it. With it, mix

¼ cup bread or cracker crumbs	⅓ cup grated Parmesan
⅓ cup chopped green onions	½ teaspoon garlic powder
4 tablespoons melted butter	½ teaspoon thyme
¼ teaspoon salt	2 beaten eggs

Spoon this on top of the tomato slices, shape into neat little humps, sprinkle more crumbs and Parmesan on top, and bake at 350° for fifteen minutes.

OCTOBER 4   A good day to celebrate Rutherford
                  Birchard Hayes's birthday, because this
is it. A good honest man, and a day for a good honest cake.

HONEST SHEEPWAGON CARROT CAKE

(Remember to start it the day before you want it.)

In a middle-size saucepan put

1⅓ cups sugar	2 large carrots, finely grated
1⅓ cups water	1 tablespoon each cinnamon
1 cup raisins (or chopped can-	cloves
died fruit if you like)	nutmeg
1 tablespoon butter	

Simmer it all together for five minutes, then cover and rest it for twelve hours. Why it gets so tired is one of those little mysteries. But do it. Then add

1 cup chopped walnuts	½ teaspoon salt
2½ cups sifted flour	1 teaspoon baking soda
2 teaspoons baking powder	

and mix it all up. Bake it in two oiled loaf pans or one tube pan at 275° for two hours. Cool, then wrap it in foil. A good-tasting, rich-looking, moist, sturdy pioneer cake this is, and good for every meal including breakfast.

OCTOBER 5   This is Opening Day of Unicorn-hunting
                  Season. Should you find one, treat him

with utmost gentleness, for the unicorn is shy . . . a magic animal that only a maiden can catch. But you will recognize him instantly by his tail like a lion's and his hind legs like an antelope's. If you are persuasive (and only if he is looking for a place to sit down), he might consent to serve briefly as a center-*cum*-conversation piece, and a stunning one he would be, with his black-and-white-and-red horn growing out of his forehead—perfect for pretzels or doughnuts.

OCTOBER 6   An Unlucky Day. Sufficient unto it are the problems thereof.

". . . Cooking is a fickle and faltering art. Didn't Rembrandt ever ruin a picture? Then why shouldn't I have the right to ruin a dish? . . ."

—Raymond Oliver

". . . knights errant used not to complain of any wound, although their guts did issue out thereof."

—Don Quixote

. . . That night my salad was awfully good, but the sauerbraten tasted like fly spray. Thinking a simple admission of error was in order, I said philosophically, "Well, cooking is full of ups and downs," and my ten-year-old said, "It comes up right after it goes down." I didn't know whether to slit my wrists or hers, so I compromised and brought the dessert. *It* was good. . . .

Thinking about it later, I came to the conclusion that it was vanity, simple vanity, that troubled me. I didn't want my guests to think that this was my idea of something good to eat.

Vanity. Why don't I clean a room as thoroughly for myself as I do for a guest—any guest? You'd think I expected Queen Elizabeth, closely followed by Mrs. America and the Board of Health. Vanity again, vanity and hypocrisy overcoming my natural sloth. . . . And it is the same when I make something myself, say a pillow or a dress. I am torn between a desire to brag about the fact that I made it, and a desire to pass it off as the work of a professional. If I give in to the first urge, as I generally do, then I invariably point to a flaw: "But the zipper puckers a little—see? Right here." Not modesty, but vanity. I am only trying to forestall their saying, "Who in the world laid that one on you?" Or thinking but not saying, *Doesn't she know a sloppy zipper when she sees one?*

"You are ungraceful [and you say] 'Excuse me, pray.' Without that excuse I would not have known there was anything amiss. . . . The only thing bad is the excuse."
                                                                    —Pascal

OCTOBER 7   Now doth the Noise of the Green Bay Bellywhoppers and the Back Bay Mastodons in valiant Battle joyned for fleeting Possession of the Pigskin make loud the Daytimes and yea the Eventides in darkened Livyngrooms throughout the Land.

A DOZEN THINGS A MAN CAN DO WHILE WATCHING FOOTBALL:

1. Isometrics: he can suck in his stomach hard and count to seven while trying strenuously, feet planted on the floor, to push them together without moving them.
2. Shell nuts.
3. String popcorn to freeze for the Christmas tree.
4. Give himself a manicure.
5. Give himself a pedicure.
6. Give you a pedicure.
7. Sort out your sewing box, getting the thread ends in the proper spool slots.
8. Roll newspapers into fireplace logs and fasten them with wire twists.
9. Polish silver.
10. Run in place.
11. Address Christmas cards.
12. Press flowers, just sitting there.

OCTOBER 8   A Heavy Trip!
                   On this day in 1906, the first permanent-wave machine was patented. It involved a dozen brass curlers weighing 1¾ pounds apiece, it took six hours, and it cost $1,000.
    On that day, also, Great-Aunt Emily was probably thinking about her next party.

GREAT-AUNT EMILY'S FRIDAYS

My Great-Aunt Emily lived in a little Kansas town with red brick sidewalks where sage-green moss grew quietly between the bricks. This was a good while ago. I never saw her. But my mother has told me how she kept her social life in good repair.

On the first Friday of every month, dependable as the new moon, Aunt Emily had what she called her At Home, to which she asked perhaps a dozen people. Her habit was to prepare a large pot of beef stew, or Brunswick stew, or beans, or chicken-and-dumplings—with brown bread or biscuits, as the situation demanded, with raw carrot strips and celery her usual vegetables. She would bring out what pickles she had, and fruitcake, from her inexhaustible homemade supply, and that was it.

The big thing wasn't the menu. The big thing was that she always had something ahead to invite people to, a regular monthly occasion, which she could count on for keeping in touch with her old friends and repaying her social debts. The only entertaining she ever did, it was apparently enough. Great-Aunt Emily got around a good deal.

The theory is sound. Systematic entertaining is like a drawer to put things in—everything neat and in its place.

OCTOBER 9   A Reasonable Menu for a Punctual Friday Party

Parmesan-Wine Meatballs
on Noodles or Spaghetti
A Green Salad   Shivering Elizabeth
Breadsticks or Crisp Rolls
Rain-or-Shine Moose (p. 19)

PARMESAN-WINE MEATBALLS
for 10

Mix together

2 pounds ground beef	4 tablespoons dried minced
1 cup soft bread crumbs	onion
1 cup milk	1½ teaspoons salt
2 eggs, slightly beaten	1½ teaspoons pepper
1 cup grated Parmesan cheese	

Shape it into balls, pan-fry them briefly till brown, then take them out of the skillet and make the sauce: Add a little butter to the hot skillet, mix it with ⅓ cup flour, then gradually add

2 cups consommé (chicken or beef)
1 cup cream, sweet or sour
juice from 8-ounce can mushrooms
½ cup dry white wine

Stir till it thickens but don't let it get too hot. Then put the meatballs back in, add salt and pepper to taste, and the mushrooms. Cover and simmer about twenty minutes.

SHIVERING ELIZABETH

1 package orange gelatin
2 small cans mandarin oranges
   (drain but save the juice)
2 tablespoons lemon juice, plus enough of the mandarin juice
   to make a cupful
1 pint orange sherbet

Heat the juice, then pour it over the gelatin and stir till the gelatin is dissolved. Take it off the heat, cool it, and watch it —or better yet, set the timer; it firms fast. Maybe ten minutes. When it starts to, add the sherbet and orange sections, stir it, pour it into a well-oiled six-to-eight-cup mold, and put it away in the refrigerator. (A good dressing: mix 1 cup sour cream with ½ cup chopped chutney and juice of half a lemon.)

OCTOBER 10   On this day in 1925, Art Buchwald first saw the light of this bewildering planet. A shrewd analyst and observer of the contemporary scene, founder and defender of the Ban the Peace Movement, he was first to point out that we could build ten hydrogen bombs with what it takes to build ten African universities. Send him a birthday cake. If you're too busy, a card will do nicely.

Also on this day, in 1639, the first U.S. apples were plucked from trees planted in Boston, Massachusetts. The record mentions "ten fair pippins."

OCTOBER 11   ". . . It was about this time I learned that when it comes to your own cooking, you can't be a shrieking violet, you've got to *pass* things again.

"My hang-up was, I was bored with whatever I'd cooked by the time I got it on the table, and anyway it's a pain when people push things (they say, *Otherwise I'll just have to throw it out*, and you want to say, *Go ahead*). But sometimes people are actually hungry. Eating out one night, I never got a second chance at anything and came home and made a sandwich and thought, *Even if you're not the greatest cook in the world, there's no point getting a reputation for being stingy too*.

"So you never know. But, probably, if you cooked it, you can't judge it, so give it a chance. . . ."

—Shirley Shimmelfenner, *If I'd Known You Were Coming I'd of Bought Some Cupcakes* (*Shimmelfenner's Complete Works,* vol. 19)

FLORENTINE CASSEROLE
for 8 to 9

(An exceptionally good recipe that your scribe hath copied out for divers folk more times than she hath hairs on her head and she be in no way bald.)

6 ounces noodle bows or elbows—doesn't matter so long as they're noodles—cooked till barely tender, according to directions

2 to 3 cups spaghetti sauce made from a mix in one of those foil packets, using the tomato sauce it calls for

1 pound of ground beef, browned in a little fat, and crumbled into the sauce (get the habit of freezing ground beef in thin patties instead of a big chunk and it thaws fast)

1 package (10 ounces) frozen chopped spinach, thawed and well drained

1 cup sour cream

½ cup grated Parmesan cheese

After adding the beef to the sauce, mix it with the noodles. Cool it, then layer it with the spinach, sour cream, and cheese (noodles, spinach, sour cream, cheese; noodles, spinach, sour cream, cheese). Bake thirty minutes at 375°. Freezes fine.

OCTOBER 12   Year older, wind colder, geese drumming, guests coming

". . . Finger bowls are dismal, but hot steamy scented guest towels are a great help after the entree as well as a great nuisance. *For those who care to bother:* have them steaming in the vegetable steamer over water to which you've added a drop of some man's after-shave lotion. Put on your oven mitts, roll the towels neatly, pass them on a tray. *For those who don't:* get some individual wash-and-dry towels, remove them midafternoon from their ugly commercial jackets, and repackage them in plain foil or any foil gift-wrap that suits the decor."

—Stella Trowbridge Hinky (*Ibid.*)

". . . Mrs. Guinea answered my letter and invited me to lunch at her home. That was when I saw my first fingerbowl. The water had a few cherry blossoms floating in it, and I thought it must be some clear sort of Japanese after-dinner soup and ate every bit of it, including the crisp little blossoms. Mrs. Guinea never said anything, and it was only much later, when I told a debutante I knew at college about the dinner, that I learned what I had done."

—Sylvia Plath

One wonders why Mrs. Guinea didn't give her a cue. What was she doing meanwhile with her own finger bowl? Had she dabbled her fingers in it, Sylvia would—presumably—have followed suit. Therefore, we can assume that Mrs. Guinea didn't. Why not? But apparently she didn't drink it either; and one would expect her restraint to have been a hint for Sylvia. After all, if your hostess simply sat and did nothing with *her* bowl of blossom-strewn water, wouldn't you suspect something? And quit drinking yours? Anecdotes like this leave quite a large number of tantalizing questions unanswered.

Once I, too, had a finger-bowl problem, at a dinner in a New York editor's apartment. The maid brought in the finger-bowls, a fact that didn't escape me. But I was talking so busily that when I finally dabbled my fingers, it was in the strawberry parfait, because she had already removed the finger bowls and had brought in the dessert.

OCTOBER 13   Simple Often Means Reassuring

"... Unfortunately for Phyllis, she was too good a cook and a perfectionist as well. Her dinners were exquisite, talked about, marveled over, but never emulated. —Nor even, for that matter, was she invited back. Uneasy feelings pervaded the women of Fall River, followed by feelings of embarrassment and guilt. Presently they crossed the street when they saw her approaching, and she wondered what she had done wrong."   —John Crispin

"I think food should be uncomplicated and undisguised. A ham is beautiful to behold, but it has no business being decorated to look like a violin."   —Helen Corbitt

"My social instincts are primitive, centering around a fireplace and a pot of chili and beans."
     —Adela Rogers St. John

OCTOBER 14   Of course there are ways to avoid cooking entirely.

"... For a while there, living in town, I had it made. I'd just call up some people and say, 'I'm dying for Chinese food—if you'd come over I'd have a swell excuse to send out for some.'"
     —Shirley Shimmelfenner (*Ibid.*)

OCTOBER 15   And there are uncomplicated entrees that frighten no one, including the cook.

YANKEE CASSOULET

(Beans with a French accent; good with caviar, fruit salad, Irish brown bread, and champagne)

2 cups small dried navy beans	2 (8-ounce) cans tomato sauce
2 cups water	1 cup dry white wine
1 teaspoon salt	1 pound bulk sausage
1 onion, chopped	2 cups cubed meat (chicken,
1 teaspoon garlic powder	beef, whatever you have)
½ teaspoon thyme	1 tomato, chopped
2 cups chicken broth	1 cup buttered bread crumbs

Bring the beans, water, and salt to a boil in an electric skillet or a Dutch oven and let them cook fifteen minutes, then stand for an hour. Add the onion, garlic, thyme, and the chicken broth. Cover, simmer for an hour, then add the tomato sauce and the wine. Recover it and simmer another hour.

Now brown the sausage and pour off the fat. Add it with the cubed meat and the chopped tomato to the beans. Pour it all into a bean pot or a casserole dish, sprinkle with crumbs and bake, uncovered, at 325° for an hour. If the top looks anemic, brown it under the broiler a minute or three before you bring it to the table.

OCTOBER 16   Ting Ling was born on this day, A.D. 450. A beautiful Chinese belle, she eventually married the Emperor and had to give large parties. It is an honor to present

TING LING'S CHINESE STEW
for 10 or more, and easy to double

(When her kitchen staff asked her what to top it with, she told them to use their noodles.)

Put two tablespoons of oil in a big skillet. In it, sauté for five minutes

> 1 cup chopped onions
> 1 cup sliced celery
> and add
> 2 pounds crumbled ground beef

When it is brown, add

2 cans undiluted mushroom soup	1 flat can water chestnuts, drained and sliced
1 cup uncooked rice	4 tablespoons soy sauce
1 can bean sprouts with juice	salt and pepper

If you're making this in the morning, stop there and finish it later. If not, pour it into a big casserole dish and bake it covered for thirty minutes at 350°. Then add a package of frozen pea pods, thawed enough to separate, and stir them in. Then top it all with a can of chow mein noodles and bake for another thirty minutes, uncovered, same temperature. A green salad with some mandarin orange slices and cashew nuts added is good with this. Use a plain vinegar-and-oil dressing, three parts oil, one part vinegar. For dessert, sherbet and cookies.

OCTOBER 17   There has always been a long, long
                        Cocktail Hour.

Or reasonably always. Many years ago, when Antony and Cleopatra were living it up in Alexandria with a group of similarly blithe spirits known as "the Inimitable Livers," Cleopatra's cook invited a friend of Plutarch's grandpa to visit him, some night, and see the goings-on in the kitchen. When the friend did, he was goggle-eyed to see eight wild boars roasting whole.

" 'Surely,' he said, 'you have a great number of guests.' The cook laughed at his simplicity, and told him there were not above twelve to sup, but that every dish was to be served up just roasted to a turn, and if anything was but one minute ill-timed, it was spoiled.

" 'And,' said he, 'maybe Antony will sup just now, maybe not this hour, maybe he will call for wine, or begin to talk, and will put it off. So that it is not one but many suppers must be had in readiness, as it is impossible to guess at his hour.' "
                                        —Plutarch's *Lives*

And thus it was that the long, long cocktail hour was allowed for. It was only a matter of time, then, till the cocktail was invented to go with it, and finally—an invention of lesser import to the gaiety of nations—the canapé, hors d' oeuvre, or appetizer, to go with the cocktail.

". . . Don't rush into complicated *hors d'oeuvre*. You have not the right, nor the time. In any case, they only attenuate the voluptuousness of your hunger for the principal dish, so use them with parsimony." —Edouard de Pomiane

". . . Eventually one must take a stand. Pro-world, anti-nation. Pro-cat, anti-bird. Pro-people, anti-cockroach. Pro-dinner, anti-cocktail dip."   —Albert Wooky

OCTOBER 18   ". . . Well, the way it worked out, I
                        was always one thing behind. First it
was fondue, a big gummy lake of it, fondue from here to Whiddy Island. But the minute I got in step, it was quiche,

everybody into quiche, and once I got a quiche pan, here
came the crêpes. . . ."
—Shirley Shimmelfenner (*Ibid.*)

". . . Certainly there are fashions in food as in hem lines
and wallpapers. Wise is the reluctant cook who disregards
these seasonal breezes and makes only those dependable items
that have earned her confidence. . . . However, she would be
dim-witted indeed to disregard the obvious merits of the
fondue served with cocktails when no dinner is to follow.
Serving the ready-made fondue, either frozen or plain-
packaged, is so easy it's worth the price of a fondue pot. Long
fondue forks, chunked French bread, and that's it."
—Stella Trowbridge Hinky

A Good Canapé to Know About:

THE MINIQUICHE

Make a rich pastry of

> 1 cup butter
> 2 3-ounce packages cream cheese
> 2 cups sifted all-purpose flour

(Beat the butter with the cheese and gradually add the flour.)
Chill it. Then form it into big-marble-size balls and press
them into very small muffin tins or a tartlet pan. Put a teaspoon of deviled ham in each. Or crumbled bacon.

Mince a middle-sized onion and sauté it in two teaspoons
of butter. Add ¼ cup grated cheese (American, Swiss, or
Gruyère), mix it up, and spoon a bit of it on top of the ham
in those little pastry cups.

Then make an uncooked custard; combine

> 1 large egg (or 2 medium)
> ⅓ cup milk
> ¼ cup more grated cheese
> a touch of nutmeg
> a dash of pepper

and spoon it evenly into the cups. Don't put in as much as
you think you should; it will bubble up and run over. Now
bake them at 450° for 10 minutes, then reduce the temperature and bake another fifteen minutes, till the custard sets
and the quiches are golden brown.

Not so classy but easier: THE 4-WAY PIZZA

Get a frozen plain pizza. Score it lightly into four quarters. Put drained chopped clams on one, chopped ripe olives on the next, crumbled sausage on the next, anchovies or sautéed mushrooms on the last. Bake according to directions and serve in squares or slivers.

OCTOBER 19   On this day in 1975, Aunt Henry Macadangdang found some more notes in the bottom of her embroidery basket.

Parkinson's Law applies to giving a dinner: it always takes as much time as you've got. So set some limits.

When you invite people, find out who doesn't like what. Say, "I want to do this great curried-oyster thing." If they say, "Do you?" think of something else.

Don't take any recipe on faith. There are some hostile recipes in this world.

If there's no time to do both an interesting vegetable and a special dessert, opt for the vegetable.

Big casseroles can fool you on reheating time. The deeper the dish, the longer it takes, so double-check the deep center.

Things go farther if you do the serving.

If you need help clearing the table, ask a man. He'll plunk the plates on the first clear surface and leave. Women hang around being helpful and hiding things.

"... Few things are so annoying as unwanted help in the kitchen. When fools rush in, I tell them —as the great Samuel Johnson remarked on other provocation—'I do not say you should be hanged or drowned for this; but it is very uncivil.'"
                                        —Albert Wooky

OCTOBER 20   Max Beerbohm Day
                An English critic, essayist, and cari-

caturist, Max Beerbohm was given to frequent and rueful rumination about The Host and The Guest. It was he who discovered that people are born basically one or the other, the natural-born guest being—in general—an inferior host, and vice versa.

Mr. B. himself tended toward guesthood, but he was often hard to catch:

". . . If anyone hereafter shall form a collection of the notes written by me in reply to invitations, I am afraid he will gradually suppose me to have been more in request than ever I really was, and to have been also a great invalid and a great traveler."

In spite of everything, it is still Host and Hostess. Why was it never Guest and Guestess? That would be convenient too.

OCTOBER 21 God bless the cook who doesn't ask me how I want my sandwich. (With or without mustard? Lemon-pepper? Mayonnaise?) She may simply bring it out. Unless she is thinking of something really bizarre like cherry marmalade on the sardines, I'll take my chances. One of the great pleasures in being a guest is not making decisions.

OCTOBER 22 ". . . And so we gather together to eat and to make what someone called those mutually reassuring noises known as polite conversation. . . . Strange that we customarily give so much more forethought to the first activity than to the second."

—Albert Wooky

OCTOBER 23 Now beginneth the sign of mysterious SCORPIO (controlling the Secret Parts) that extendeth through November 21, a time bòding well for

    betting the horses
    mating the poodle
    catching a mouse
    heaping straw on strawberries.

And solitary Scorpio performeth these Duties but not to the Hurt of other Enjoyments, for he hath lusty Humors.

And on this day every year the Swallows leave Capistrano, but there is never much publicity about it.

OCTOBER 24   "Breakfast, an essentially unsociable meal, is an appropriate time to choose for disinheriting one's natural heirs."
                                        —P. Morton Shand

Once upon a time, two friendly couples who lived three hundred miles apart decided to visit each other. And so they both drove 150 miles the first day, to meet at a luxurious Motel Establishment where they had made advance reservations.

There, they talked, played tennis, swam, and talked some more, with no one responsible for host-and-hostessing except the motel management, which provided them with comfortable lodgings and an excellent dinner. (The ladies ordered the sweetbreads, which they never cooked at home because their husbands couldn't stand them, while the gentlemen enjoyed the prime rib.)

The following day, both couples swapped house keys and proceeded to each other's establishments, where they fed the rubber plant and watered the goldfish and enjoyed total privacy, new views, different places to go, as well as the glorious freedom from having to make small talk at unlikely hours.

At the beginning of the third day, they set forth once more, to meet again for lunch and the exchange of house keys, and then they drove back home.

Both couples agreed that it was the most satisfactory visit they had ever had. Each lady averred, as well, that there is nothing like knowing that your friend is going to have the run of your refrigerator for getting the damn thing really cleaned out and shiny.

OCTOBER 25   ". . . It was a chicken breast thing with anchovies and apricots that taught me complicated doesn't necessarily mean good. In fact, the more ingredients something's got, the bigger the chance it's going to be a lemon."
                                        —Shirley Shimmelfenner,
                                        Eat It Anyhow, vol. XI

"If there is one thing less appealing than another thing—and for the sake of discussion let us assume that there is—I cast my vote for the Steak-Lobster Combination Plate as featured in some of our drearier bistros. As Mencken remarked about vaudeville, some like it and some can stand it while they are drunk. With steak and lobster, I belong to neither category.

"But that is the way of it today. Silver screen, TV or bookshelf, pantry or restaurant, there is something for every warped taste." —Albert Wooky

Let no man bring together what God hath set asunder.

A GOOD SIMPLE FISH DISH

2 tablespoons butter, melted
1 to 2 pounds sole fillets
salt, pepper
4 green onions, thin-sliced, including some of the green
3 tablespoons minced herbs—parsley, tarragon, chervil
1 cup fresh bread crumbs
⅓ cup dry vermouth

Melt the butter in a baking pan big enough to hold all the fish in a single layer. Then salt and pepper both sides of the fish. Dip them in the butter, both sides. Put the green onions and herbs in the pan, lay the fish out on it, and cover it neatly with the crumbs. Pour the vermouth over it all, dot with some more butter—three tablespoons should do it—and bake uncovered at 375° till the crumbs are brown and the fish cooked—about thirty minutes.

OCTOBER 26 ". . . Certainly it is no trick now to put a special meal together if there is a food market nearby and money in your wallet. Steaks, roasts, and lovely frozen arrangements that might as well be emeralds. . . . But doing it out of the pantry is something else. The reluctant cook (who may well have spent the grocery money on something more interesting) will do well to keep handy the ingredients for a couple of easy out-of-the-pantry main dishes that still taste a little special. . . ."
—Stella Trowbridge Hinky

Mumu Harbottle is of the Minced Clam persuasion, *i.e.*, some grocer persuaded her to buy a case of canned clams on sale once (she'll never do *that* again), and she has been paddling her way out of a chowder sea ever since. But when she learned that clams can be nicely combined with pastry, she began to see lights on shore. Though her husband, Jimbo, is a real meat-and-potatoes man, he isn't so apt to ask, "Where's the rest of the dinner?" when he has finished a good wedge of Clam Pie.

JIMBO'S CLAM PIE

pastry for a 2-crust pie
2 eggs
2 7-ounce cans minced clams
¼ teaspoon pepper

½ cup coarse soda-cracker crumbs
¾ teaspoon salt
¾ cup milk

She lines the pie pan with half the pastry. Then she beats two eggs and (if she remembers) sets aside a tablespoonful to brush the top crust with later. Next, she adds ¾ cup of the clam juice (throws the rest of it out) to the eggs. Then she adds everything else.

She pours it all into the pastry shell, dots it with butter, covers the pie with the rest of the pastry, gashes it, and brushes it with the tablespoonful of egg she saved, if she can find it now. It bakes for forty-five minutes altogether—fifteen minutes at 450° and another half-hour at 350°.

Another good thing to know about is

TUNA PIE
for 6

Roll out enough pastry for a one-crust pie and put it in a nine-inch pie pan. Next, pour two tablespoons oil into a big skillet, and in it put

   1½ cups sliced carrots
   a large onion, chopped
   ½ teaspoon garlic powder
   ½ teaspoon anchovy paste

Cook it over medium heat about six minutes, and add

   ½ cup tomato-based chili sauce
      (not the Mexican pepper type, that is)
   1 teaspoon oregano
   ¼ teaspoon pepper

Then drain a can of tomato slices, keep the juice, and into

it stir two tablespoons flour. (If no canned tomato slices are around, small sliced fresh tomatoes are fine, but you'll need a half-cup of tomato juice from somewhere.) Anyway. Add the juice-flour mix to the onion-carrot business, cook, and stir till it's thick. Take it off the heat and add two 7-ounce cans of tuna, plus ⅓ cup sliced pimiento-stuffed olives (black will do if that's all you have) and ½ cup Parmesan cheese.

Pour it all into the pie shell, sprinkle with a lot more Parmesan, and bake at 375° about thirty-five minutes. Everything but the baking can be done several hours ahead.

OCTOBER 27   And sometimes the guest stayeth and
                 stayeth and goeth not home.

". . . Whenever he [Steffansson] has visitors, he receives them seated behind a desk on a low platform in his small study. A visitor is placed facing him in an aged, overstuffed chair so saggy that the seat touches the floor. 'The arrangement gives me a feeling of great superiority,' he says. . . ."
                                   —Robert Lewis Taylor

It was Ephraim Tutt who kept a special and subtly uncomfortable chair in his office for nonpaying clients (who always tended to stay too long). The front legs of the chair were an inch shorter than the back legs.

New At-Home Gown for Holiday Hostesses!

Send $10.98 plus $10.98 handling for a plain brown wrapper that fits all sizes, great for entertaining, stamped for embroidery, your choice of messages.

(1309A)	EAT IT & BEAT IT
(1310A)	CHEER UP OR PIPE DOWN
(1311A)	YES I'VE HEARD THAT ONE
(1312A)	GO HOME
(1313)	BED, ANYONE?

Shimmelfenner Products
33 Slippery Elm
Bugtussle, Oklahoma

OCTOBER 28   From the Mervyn Meadows *Sentinel:*
                 In an exclusive interview with the *Sen-*

tinel's "Chatterbox" editor, Mrs. Charles ("Edie") Grumwalt said that she doesn't think it's right to pay back a dinner with a brunch because after all, as she put it, fair's fair, though she admitted she'd certainly done it.

"If you don't run out of booze, you can get by with murder at a brunch," she said. "That's why they're so great—I mean, to give, not to go to."

AN EASY BRUNCH PUNCH

Equal parts champagne and orange juice and plenty of ice.

OCTOBER 29   On this day in 1929, the stock market collapsed. On this day in 1740, James Boswell was born and thereafter grew up to report, with unflagging enthusiasm and no electric typewriter to help him, every audible word spoken by the late, great, and vocal Dr. Samuel Johnson, who did on one occasion declare himself as follows:

"Sir, when a man is invited to dinner, he is disappointed if he does not get something good. I advised Mrs. Thrale, who has no card parties at her house, to give sweetmeats, and such good things, in an evening, as are not commonly given, and she would find company enough come to her; for everybody loves to have things which please the palate put in their way, without trouble or preparation."

A most palate-pleasing dessert:

HOT WINTER FRUIT

1 orange and 1 lemon	8-ounce can sliced peaches
2 to 3 tablespoons brown sugar	8-ounce can pitted Bing cherries (or plums)
8-ounce can apricots	1 cup sour cream
8-ounce can pineapple slices	

Grate the orange and lemon rinds into the brown sugar. Cut the orange and lemon pulps into thin slices, removing as much of the white inner skin as you can, and the seeds. Mix these slices with the rest of the fruit and put a layer of it in a baking dish. Sprinkle it with part of the rind-and-sugar business and a spatter of nutmeg. Repeat the layers, then heat it in a 300° oven about half an hour. Top it with the cold sour cream.

OCTOBER 30
A smoky bitter-sweet time,
A ghost and trick-or-treat time,
And night falls soon
With a round orange moon.

". . . I myself am a pretty good operator with the forked twig. . . . Once I had a dowsing twig cut under a waxing moon from an apple-tree growing beside a graveyard. It was super-sensitive! Ignoring the nearby Charles River, it located a pint of bourbon in a friend's hip pocket."
—Harlow Shapley

Now drive thy broomstick in for a lube job and make some candied popcorn for tomorrow's gneighborhood gnomes.

BALDERDASH

(A descendant of old-fashioned crackajack and much improved. Also known as crackatooth if some shells get in by mistake.)

Pop ⅔ cup raw popcorn (or enough to make 2½ quarts). Mix with a cup of nuts—more if you like, any kind. Spread it out in a shallow pan with a rim and put it in a preheated 250° oven to bake slowly while you make the syrup:

    ½ cup butter
    1 cup brown sugar
    ¼ cup light corn syrup
    ½ teaspoon salt

Combine those over medium heat and stir till the sugar dissolves. Then boil it without stirring till it reaches 248°—the firm-ball stage—on the candy thermometer. That will take about five minutes. Take it off the heat and stir in ½ teaspoon baking soda. Now pour it over the popcorn, stirring gently to coat everything, return it to the oven to bake for forty-five minutes. Stir it every fifteen. After it's cool, store in air-tight cans.

OCTOBER 31
A Capital Rejoinder!
Old graveyards would be restful places if only the permanent residents would keep quiet. But, no, they must point their skeletal fingers, forever admonishing.

"Reader, stop and self behold,
Thou'rt made of ye same mould,
And shortly must dissolv'd be,
Make sure of blest eternity."

It was Charles Lamb who commented, "Every dead man must take it upon himself to be lecturing me with his odious truism, that 'Such as he now is I must shortly be.' Not so shortly, friend, perhaps as thou imaginest. In the meantime, I am alive. I move about. I am worth twenty of thee. Know thy betters."

"It is no problem to find someone who can make a good cobalt bomb but it is getting pretty hard to find someone who knows how to make a good jack-o-lantern."
—George and Berthe Herter (*Ibid.*)

November

freezeth the marrow & December's dinner; pondereth a Houseperson's Miscellanie, including the winter Colde & the unwieldy Leftover, & presenteth Receipts for

> *some highly practical Chicken & Turkey things*
> *jellied Moose Nose*
> *Salome's Molasses Crisps*
> *a painless ham casserole*

and numerous other Daynties!

~~~~~~

> Although the choice is lavish now
> (They freeze whatever's salable)
> I never thaw a Purple Cow;
> I don't think they're available.

NOVEMBER 1   NOW IT IS NOVEMBER with the
Seas full roughe as the wild Goose
leadeth a tattered Banner of Birdes through the chill Ayre,
& the very Countrie doth rattle in a high Winde, for this be
the Tyme of the political Oration. And in the Cities do Door-
men & Apt. Supers show extra Courtesie from now till December 26, & in rural Places doth the long-tailed Fieldmouse
curl up for his Nappe in the Weed patch behind the Shopping
Centre. Now it is the nervous Tyme of late Meetings & Dinners postponed, of Bake Sales & Church Bazaars & all such
divers Curves thrown the reluctant Cooke & the harried
Houseperson, who do field them as best they can with what
Weaponry lieth to hand.

And be it not forgot: that the peanut-butter-on-whole-
wheat sandwich with an Orange & a Glass of Milke be an
almost nutritionally perfect Meale.

NOVEMBER 2   This is the birthday of Marie (Let-
'em-eat-cake) Antoinette, but she
never really said that.

This is also Daniel Boone's birthday.

And on this day in 1976, Shirley Shimmelfenner came down
off the mountain and delivered her Ten Freezer Command-
ments, en route to the airport and Kankakee, first stop on her
preholiday lecture tour.

"Sure, it's easier to get up in the morning when your dinner's in the freezer, but you better be sure it's something you
like and the family likes," said Ms. Shimmelfenner, looking
great in her mackinaw and high-heeled Keds. "Otherwise,
there you stand at quarter to six, freezer door open and your
shins getting purple, wondering if you've got the nerve to
unload that squid-and-gooseberry casserole on the family
again. Remember, you thought you were so smart to double
the recipe the first time you made it, so you'd have a frozen
one in reserve? Ha."

**SHIMMELFENNER'S TEN FREEZER COMMAND-
MENTS for People Who Hate to Cook**

1. Freeze a little of something new before you freeze a
big dish of it. Don't trust anybody, even me.
2. Even if it tastes great, hot the first time, maybe it will
freeze funny. Like, some flavors get stronger—cloves, garlic,

black pepper, green pepper, pimento, celery. And some poop out—onion, salt, chili powder. And potatoes freeze mushy, and so do some beans. And if vegetables were cooked enough in the dish you ate hot, they'll be overcooked in the one you froze, by the time it's reheated.

3. So better you cook two dishes to freeze, instead of one to eat now and one later. Do it some morning when you're eating out that night. That means three nights off. Better than money in the bank.

4. Don't give an all-frozen dinner party. You read these jolly articles, Be a Guest at Your Party!—Freeze it all ahead, lie around all day in your harem pants, then a couple of pirouettes and Presto, dinner's ready! Beautiful. But I'm here to say if it wasn't choreographed to a fare-thee-well, there'll be something limp and something over-garlicked and something stone-cold in the middle. Two prefrozen jobs is plenty.

5. You'd think frozen bacon and ham would stay good forever since they're smoked or pickled to start with, and would you ever be wrong. Two months for smoked ham in a 0° freezer, one month for bacon.

6. They make freezing sound so complicated it scares you. Special paper, tape, pencils, wraps, whatever. Nuts. Just so it's wrapped airtight and all the air squeezed out, you're okay—foil, solid paper, plastic wrap, nylon parachutes. Then borrow a freezer thermometer and make sure the freezer's at 0°.

7. Better arrange the food shelves in three sections: THIS WEEK OR ELSE . . . THIS MONTH . . . NO SWEAT. (That's for bread and ready-frozen things.)

8. Chances are good, whatever you're in the habit of making will freeze okay if it isn't full of mayonnaise and potatoes—check the freezer manual. Give your stand-bys a try.

9. If something looks dry when you take it out of the freezer—rice, noodles, and so on—add liquid, say ⅓ cup milk, broth, tomato juice, whatever's logical, before you reheat it.

10. Don't get suckered into too big a freezer. If you inherited one, use half for something else—wool sweaters, bathing suits, maybe popcorn chains for the Christmas tree. They freeze fine.

When there's a lot of it around, you never want it very much.
—Crumpacker's 22nd Law

NOVEMBER 3   ". . . I remember, after acquiring my
first freezer, stopping short before an
unexpected psychological hurdle. With a novice's enthusiasm
I had prepared and frozen some nice items: a Coq au Vin, a
Cassoulet, some lovely brioches. . . . Trying to choose from
the attractive array one afternoon, I couldn't help thinking of
old Franz Josef of Austria. One day he was reviewing his
troops, splendid in their scarlet tunics and gold braid and
shiny boots. And he simply stood there when it was over, the
tears running down his face at the thought of sending such
a beautiful little army off to war. That's the way I felt, looking at all those neat packages. That night I ate at a restaurant."   —Albert Wooky

NOVEMBER 4   A Day to Vote for Somebody

LIBERAL POTTAGE

(divers elements all stewing together)

Put a pound of lentils in a big kettle with three quarts of
water. Bring it to a boil, turn off the heat, and let it stand
two hours. Now fry

   6 big chopped onions
   2 garlic cloves
   1 pound lamb meat (shoulder, neck, whathaveyou)

for fifteen minutes and put it in a big bean pot or deep casserole. Drain the lentils (but save the water) and add them,
along with

   a green pepper, seeded and chopped
   a 15-ounce can stewed tomatoes
   several stalks celery, chopped
   4 chopped carrots

Stir it up and add some lentil liquor, just enough to cover
everything. Salt and pepper to taste, then cover and bake in
a slow, slow oven, about 250°, for two hours. Longer won't
hurt; just check once in a while for dryness and add more
juice if it needs it.

NOVEMBER 5   The Carnegie Library was dedicated
in Pittsburgh on this day in 1895.

". . . Never have I lost my early faith that wisdom is to be found somewhere in a book—to be picked up as easily as a shell from the sand."
                    —Robert Lynd

"To make tough beef tender, soak it in vinegar and water (½ cup vinegar to 1 quart of water) for about twelve hours."
—Mrs. Crowen, *The American System of Cookery,* 1870

"We derive a certain satisfaction from being sinned against. It is not only that a grievance adds content to our lives, but also that it makes less monstrous the flame of malice which like a vigil light flickers in the dimness of our souls."
                    —Eric Hoffer

"Take what you want," said God. "Take it, and pay for it."   —Spanish proverb

NOVEMBER 6   On this day in 1975, a certain Amaryllis Redd (of the Cincinnati Redds) calculated the cost of each individual almond and chicken chunk in the Frozen Chicken-Almond Casseroles she had been buying for the past year, and ever since then she has been inaccessible to her friends. Just sits in her bedroom staring straight ahead and keening softly.

". . . People who hate to cook and acquire a freezer generally start out by filling it with ready-frozen entrees, desserts, and fancy vegetable mixtures until they wake up broke, which generally doesn't take too long. Then if they have minimal sense, they settle for a few plain frozen vegetables by the sackful, plus a few simple guest-type entrees and vegetable casseroles they learn to make themselves. . . ."
—Stella Trowbridge Hinky

NOVEMBER 7   A DEPENDABLE BEEF BURGUNDY TO FREEZE

Cut two pounds of boneless beef chuck into two-inch chunks,

brown it in a little oil, then pour on a cup of red wine. Stir it around. Then add

1½ teaspoons salt	1 teaspoon marjoram
¼ teaspoon pepper	2 medium onions, sliced
1 teaspoon paprika	½ pound fresh mushrooms, or
2 seeded and chopped green peppers, cut in rings	the same amount canned

Cover and simmer it in the electric skillet (or in the Slow Cooker at medium or in the oven at 250°) for five hours. Then take the meat and vegetables out of the broth and keep them warm somewhere. Skim as much fat as possible off the broth. Better still, if you've time, semifreeze the broth so the solidified fat is easy to remove. Then boil it down to thicken it a bit, and if you want it thicker still, stir in a tablespoon of cornstarch or flour mixed to a smooth paste in cold water. Pour the whole works into a big casserole dish, or seven or eight little ones, wrap, and freeze. To serve it, eventually, reheat it in a 400° oven about forty minutes for the large, twenty-five for the small.

"Things that cooled fast in a bowl of ice water before they were frozen eventually taste better than things that didn't." —Shakespeare
(Erwin Shakespeare, *sous-chef* at Le Trianon, Kansas City)

"If a casserole calls for a crumb or cheese topping, do it before you reheat it, not before you freeze it. Otherwise it gets kind of a boardinghouse look." —Napoleon Bonaparte
(Napoleon Bonaparte Mazzuti, head cook at the Elba Room, NYC. His great-uncle learned a lot about freezing, that winter in Russia)

Two Dependable Chicken Things to Freeze:

1. McCORMACK'S CHOICE

(The idea here is four items, layered and baked: broccoli, chicken-in-gravy, cottage cheese, and noodles.)

1 package frozen chopped   ½ cup flour
  broccoli   ½ teaspoon salt
a 4-pound chicken, cut up   ½ teaspoon dried basil
a celery stalk   8 ounces egg noodles
an onion slice   1 egg
½ cup butter   16 ounces cottage cheese

Take the broccoli out of the freezer to thaw while you simmer the chicken in water to cover, with the celery and onion.
Then get the meat off the bones and dice. Next, make some
gravy: melt the butter, stir in the flour gradually, and add
salt, basil, and three cups of the water you cooked the
chicken in.

Cook the egg noodles eight minutes and drain them. Then
beat the egg a little and mix it with the cottage cheese. Finally: layer these things like this, in a big casserole dish:
chicken mix, noodles, cottage cheese, broccoli. Do it again,
ending with chicken mix. Bake forty-five minutes at 350°,
wrap it, and freeze. When you eventually reheat it, sprinkle
Parmesan cheese on top and reheat it, frozen, for two hours
at 350°.

2. McCLINTOCK'S BEST

*(A good Mexican-type chicken arrangement that feeds
8 to 10 people and freezes well. Transfer it from
freezer to refrigerator the night before you aim to
serve it. On dinner day, heat it a good two hours at
300°.)*

4 whole chicken breasts   1 can chili without the beans
  (or an equal amount of any   1 small onion, chopped
  chicken)   ½ cup milk
12 corn tortillas   1 cup green chili salsa
1 can cream of mushroom soup,   (or taco sauce)
  condensed   ½ pound jack cheese, grated
1 can cream of chicken soup,   ½ pound sharp cheddar, grated
  condensed

First, bake the chicken, wrapped in foil, for an hour at 350°.
Then take the meat off its bones. Tear the tortillas into one-
inch pieces. Now mix everything else except the cheese.
That's your sauce. Layer chicken, tortillas, sauce, and cheese
in a three-quart casserole, ending with the cheese, and bake
at 350° for forty-five minutes.

And a Dependable Vegetable Dish to Freeze:

SPICY BAKED EGGPLANT

Get a good-sized eggplant and don't peel it, just cube it. Sauté it in ¾ cup olive oil for about 5 minutes. Then add

a 15-ounce can of tomatoes	1 teaspoon garlic powder
small jar of pimentos drained and coarsely chopped	2 tablespoons chopped parsley
2 medium sliced onions	1 teaspoon capers

Cook all this about fifteen minutes more, then pile it into a casserole dish, wrap it, and freeze it. Before you eventually reheat it to serve, put crumbs on top, heat half an hour at 350°, and double-check to be sure it's hot clear through.

NOVEMBER 8   This is National Dunce Day, named for Duns Scotus, a champion thirteenth-century nitpicker. Known as Dr. Subtilis, he was famous for his attention to tiny details that bored the whey out of everybody. To keep his memory green, do three dumb things, your choice, or

1. make gay matching plastic bloomers for all hanging house plants
2. wash and iron your floor rags
3. dust under the light-switch plates.

NOVEMBER 9   This day in 1974 was a very big day for Mumu Harbottle.

That year—it was the year she was an Avon lady and away from home so much—Mumu had a traumatic time of it, thawing a frozen roast for tomorrow. She found that if she transferred it from freezer to refrigerator the night before, it wouldn't be thawed enough. On the other hand, thawed at room temperature, it would eventually be ankle-high in its own red juice, which meant considerably less juice left in the meat.

Then, on this particular November 9 at 7:43 P.M., as she was debating which dubious course to follow for tomorrow night's meat, she noticed on the pantry shelf a small styrofoam cooler that had cooled many a six-pack the previous summer. It occurred to her that if she'd put the meat in it, its own chilly exhalations would cool the small cubic area of the box enough so that it would be cooler than room temperature but certainly warmer than the refrigerator. And so she did and it was.

Greatly excited, then, Mumu wrote home to Mother about it, and to her old college roommate, and she also placed a long-distance call to Stella Trowbridge Hinky, a lady whose work she greatly admired.

NOVEMBER 10   On this day in 1974, Stella Trowbridge Hinky returned Mumu Harbottle's telephone call, Collect, and when Mumu delivered her big news, Ms. Hinky said that was very interesting, but why did she bother to thaw it at all? Why didn't she cook it frozen?

"I didn't know you could," Mumu said, crestfallen. (Her crest falls easy.)

"Certainly," said Ms. Hinky. "Just figure twice the ordinary roasting time for a roast that's frozen solid. Say, sixty-five minutes per pound in a 325° oven, for medium to medium-rare. To make sure, you can insert the meat thermometer after the meat has warmed a little."

Mumu said, "Oh."

"*And*," continued Hinky, "perhaps you'd be interested in knowing that the same thing is true for all kinds of steaks and chops. Cook them frozen—broiled or pan-fried at the same temperature you'd ordinarily use, but roughly twice the time. Actually, Ms. Harbottle, this preserves the juice and the flavor. Taste tests at Columbia University—"

"I'm sorry, I have to go," Mumu said, "my phone's ringing." After all, this was a long dime. That's the way with experts, she thought. Turn them on and you can't turn them off.

But that night in bed she had a sudden thought. When she was out all day and came home to a frozen three-pound roast, it would be three hours till dinner, Hinky's way, instead of an hour and a half the styrofoam-cooler way. Even if she put the frozen roast in the oven before she left in the morning, and set it on automatic, the meat would have thawed somewhat by the time the oven turned on. And she wouldn't be there to stick the meat thermometer in, and it would probably be well-done by the time she got home, and Jimbo would absolutely throttle her.

Why do things have to be so *fuzzy*, she thought, tossing

fretfully, and presently she thought, The heck with it, and went to sleep.

NOVEMBER 11   On this day, observe a moment of respectful silence for Kurt Vonnegut, Jr.'s birthday.

NOVEMBER 12   Sky snoweth
kine loweth
cold groweth
nose bloweth

For the Common Winter (or Rotten Uncomfortable) Cold:
". . . Take half a pound of reafons of the Sun Stoned and 1 ounce of liquorifh and 1 ounce of Elicompane made into fine powder beat your reafons then pour in them till they come to a conferve adding thereto 2 or 3 fpoonfulls of Red rofe water if a thick ruehm leffen your quantity of Elicompane & take of this morning noon and night. Probatum."*

—A Book of Simples, circa 1700

NOVEMBER 13   A Dissertation on Leftover Ham

From Shirley Shimmelfenner's *Hit It Again, Shirl!*, chapt. 27
". . . You read some great fiction in the food magazines. I mean, 'How Susie Thimblefinger Feeds Her Family of Four on $2.69 a Week,' all starting with this big ham she cooked on Sunday. Then it goes, MONDAY: Hot Clam Broth, Ham Timbales, Spinach and Mushrooms in Sour Cream, Herbed Carrots, Apple Crisp. TUESDAY: Ham-Asparagus Rolls with Macaroni, Broiled Green Tomatoes, Fresh Spinach Salad, Angel Fluff Pudding. And so on.—Out of sight! But anybody knows that in real life, Monday is Cold Sliced Ham with the rest of the scalloped potatoes, and maybe Tuesday is ham and eggs, and Wednesday is Cold Sliced Ham.
"After all, that's what you cooked it for, because it tastes

* It is proven.

all right cold, right? And why recook all the rest of the vitamin B out? I mean, quit messing with it till it gets right down to the tail end. It makes more sense to put your mind on something good to go with it. . . ."

NOVEMBER 14   Two good hearty dishes to go with a slice of Ham or any other cold meat:

1. JETTY SPAGHETTI

Into the blender put

2 cups parsley, stripped from the stems	½ teaspoon pepper
	½ teaspoon garlic powder
1 teaspoon each basil	½ cup olive oil
oregano	
marjoram	
salt	

Blend it at high speed; occasionally you'll have to push it down the sides with a spatula. Ten minutes before dinnertime, cook and drain a pound of spaghetti (this will serve eight to ten, so cut it in half for four or five; no need to make less sauce, though, because it keeps) and mix it well with two tablespoons of butter. To it add ¼ cupful of chopped pecans or walnuts, and ½ cupful grated Parmesan cheese. Add the parsley sauce, see that it's all hot through, and serve.

2. WINE SPOON BREAD

3¼ cups milk	2 tablespoons butter
1 cup yellow corn meal	4 eggs
1½ teaspoons salt	¾ cup dry white wine

Scald the milk and stir in the corn meal and salt. Put an oven mitt on your hand, because the stuff sputters, while you stir it for three or four minutes. When it's a good thick mush, take it off the heat and add the butter. Beat the eggs, and to them add the wine. Stir the mixture slowly into the hot mush, then pour it into a well-buttered casserole dish. Put the oven rack just a notch below the center of the oven and bake the spoon bread at 375° about an hour. When its top is a pretty puffy light brown, it's done. Serve.

NOVEMBER 15   ". . . But comes a time [Shirley Shimmelfenner continued] when the chips are down. Your ham looks like an ha'penny's worth of soap after a hard week's wash, and you'd love to give it to the dog. But with just two cups of chopped meat you can make a darned good

END-OF-THE-LINE HAM CASSEROLE

1 can cream of celery soup	3 medium potatoes, peeled and
½ cup milk	sliced
pepper	1 medium onion, ditto
	2 cupfuls chopped ham

Mix the soup and milk, add a good grind of pepper, then layer things like this, in a casserole dish: potatoes, meat, onion, celery-soup sauce. Cover and bake for an hour at 375°. Then take the lid off, which makes it easier to sprinkle some grated cheese on top, and bake it uncovered another twenty minutes.

Finally, if you can scrounge one more half-cupful of ham, you can make

AUNTIE SCROOGE'S BEAN SOUP

1 pound navy beans	½ teaspoon each celery salt
3 quarts water	and cardamom seeds
the chopped ham (and bone if	2 teaspoons salt
there was one)	2 drops Tabasco

Soak the beans in the water overnight. Next day, simmer them an hour, then add all the other things. Simmer for two more hours and it's done.

NOVEMBER 16   Tidy Tips for Thanksgiving Week

From Brillo-Savarin (as translated by S. T. Hinky)

1. Clean around doorknobs and damp-wipe the telephone before cleaning floors if there isn't time for both. Doorknob and telephone dirt is grime; floor dirt is just dirt.

2. With a rubber band, fasten an old sock to the end of a yardstick to reach high cobwebs and dusty places.

3. After you polish your shoes with shoe polish, spit on the toes and buff them again. Nothing works like spit.

4. Everybody hates embroidered guest towels except the person who embroidered them.

NOVEMBER 17   A Story of Virtue Rewarded!

Once upon a time, a young bride invited her husband's boss and his wife to dinner. The employer, a kindly man, was also a gentleman chicken farmer; and on the snowy morning of the night they were to come, he sent over one of his nicest Wyandottes as a hostess gift.

The hen arrived crated, fully feathered, and clucking. Chicken and dumplings on the hoof. The bride telephoned her husband.

"Oh wow," he said. "We'll have to butcher it and pluck it," and he promised he'd be home early.

His bride didn't know anything about killing chickens and wouldn't have had the heart for it anyway. But she thought it would speed things up to start the plucking, which she did, twitching off a feather or two at a time.

By sundown, when her husband phoned to say the guests weren't coming after all because of the bad weather, the hen was looking pretty chilly. And when he finally got home, he found that his wife had made it a cozy kimono from an old flannel nightgown, and found some corn meal for its supper, and fixed it a cozy bed from shredded newspapers. The next morning, the little red hen laid a nice egg for their breakfast, and they all lived happily ever after.

A bird on the nest is worth two in the pot.

NOVEMBER 18   Now doth the Mighty Hunter don his red cap and fill his flask and his gun in the dark and go forth into the predawn cold to prove his Manhood in valiant tourney with the Wicked Moose!

". . . The king [James I], pleased, yet flushed and pale with excitement, his hunting-garb soiled with mire and bog-water from spur to bonnet-plume, reins up just in time to witness the finish, when the royal pack has fastened upon the quarry's throat. And when the deer has been broken up, and whilst the foresters, all unbonneted, wind the customary *mort* upon their bugles, our royal woodsman is plunging his unbooted limbs in the beast's warm, reeking entrails: an extraordinary panacea, recommended by the court physician, Sir Theodore Mayerne, as the 'sovereign'st thing on earth' for those gouty and rheumatic twinges, which too emphatically reminded the Stuart in the autumn of his days, how 'every inordinate cup is unblest and the ingredient thereof a devil,' though the warning produced no practical result. . . ."

> —From a courtier's letter,
> circa 1611

"HOW TO COOK A MOOSE NOSE: Moose nose is cooked by cutting off the upper jawbone just below the eyes. Drop this jawbone in a kettle of water and boil it for about 30 minutes. Remove, and cool, and skin it, taking the hairs and bristles and dark skin off. Now wash it well and place the skinned nose into a fresh kettle of water. . . . Cut the white and dark meat into thick slices and pack them into jars. Cover with the juice from the boiling. This will jell when chilled, and it can be sliced and eaten like sandwich meat. . . ."

—*How to Hunt a Moose,* by James E. Churchill

"After you've bagged your hunter, don't drape him over your automobile or mount him when you get home. Merely the cap or jacket will suffice."

> —Cleveland Amory, founder
> of the Hunt the Hunters Club

NOVEMBER 19   What Was So Great About Grandma?

". . . And so I finally learned that just because they call a recipe 'Grandma's Whatzis' doesn't necessarily mean it's any good. Plenty of grandmas can't cook worth shucks. In fact, a lot of girls today cook rings around their grandmothers, because their grandmothers grew up eating Grandma's Old-fashioned Store-bought Cookies by the boxful. It's their granddaughters and great-granddaughters that are cooking up a storm, cooking French, Korean, Italian, Basque, you name it. Pickling, preserving, baking . . . The only thing my grandma could really make was frozen Daiquiris.

"I got the following recipe from a belly-dancer named Salome, christened Mary Elizabeth, in a commune down the road. She makes them for her old man all the time. It's about the best, crispest, easiest cooky you'll ever make. Trust me on this."

—Shirley Shimmelfenner (*Ibid.*)

SALOME'S MOLASSES CRISPS

Cream ½ cup butter with ¾ cup sugar and beat in an egg. Then sift together

> 1½ cups flour
> ¾ teaspoon baking soda
> pinch of salt

and add it to the butter-sugar business alternately with

> ⅓ cup molasses

Finally, add ¾ cup of chopped nuts, more or less—whatever you have. Drop them by the teaspoonful on a greased cooky sheet and bake at 350° for twelve to fifteen minutes.

"If they ain't molasses, they ain't cookies."

—One-Hoss

NOVEMBER 20   Beware of Suppers!

SOME RULES FOR PRESERVING OF HEALTH BY DIET:

"Two meals a day is sufficient for all persons after fifty years of age, and all weak people; for the omitting of suppers does always conduce much to the health of the weak and aged; since if no suppers be eaten, the stomach will soon free itself from all rough, slimy humors, wherewith it is slabbered over on the inside, and thereby the appetite will be renewed and digestion made more strong and vigorous. Moreover, all that are troubled with sweating in the night or any ill taste in their mouths, belching, and troublesome dreams, must avoid suppers. . . ."

—R. Saunders, 1770

NOVEMBER 21   Now on this day, or approximately,
                do all SANTA CLAUSES every-
where shake the mothballs and the moths out of their red plush pants.

And now is the wind sharp and the frost keen, and if one flower still standeth in the garden, it is with bowed head as though in mourning for its dead companions. And in such wise doth the reluctant Cook stand too, weighted down with sorry awareness of Thanksgiving dinner looming ever closer. And sometimes the Turkey doth even trouble her sleep.

"TURKEY: This bird has various meanings depending on the action in your dream. If you saw one strutting and/or heard it gobbling, it portends a period of confusion due to instability of your friends or associates. . . . However, if you ate it, you are likely to make a serious error of judgment, so be very careful regarding any important matters which may be pending."

—The Dreamer's Dictionary

NOVEMBER 22   Now beginneth the sign of SAGIT-
TARIUS (controlling the Thighs) that extendeth through December 21, all this time being mightily auspicious for
    picking chives
    exterminating the apartment
    getting a haircut
    going to Paris
    falling in love
    having teeth pulled.
And the born Saggitarian—restless, impetuous, impatient— doth survey with unease the year's numerous unfinished projects all so bravely begun, and even so (gallant optimist that he is) doth start some more.

NOVEMBER 23   On this day, when Stephanie ("Fats")
Stumflug found that she had gained another seven pounds, she paid a call on her friendly neighborhood physician, Emmett Neitzelgrinder, M.D.
"Well, now, I'll tell you, Fa—Stephanie," said the good doctor. "Of course you eat too much. And one reason is that you eat too *fast*. Now, I want you to observe something." He passed her a doughnut from his file drawer labeled *D*.
"Take a bite," he said. "Taste it. Okay? Now try to taste it while you're inhaling." Stephanie drew a deep breath as she chewed, and her eyes went round with astonishment.

"You see?" said the doctor. "You can't do it. You can taste only while you're exhaling or not breathing—*never* while you're breathing in. So just think of all the food you waste, taste-wise! If you will take smaller portions and smaller bites and consciously *taste each bite* when your lungs are comparatively empty, you'll get twice the taste enjoyment for half the calories. Come see me after Christmas."

"Goodness gracious and Gloriosky!" Stephanie said to herself in the elevator on her way down to the main-floor lobby; and when she came to the newsstand she bought a chocolate bar so she could practice her new technique on the way home.

> "To acquire or maintain the perfect mean between fat and thin is the life-study of every woman in the world."   —Brillat-Savarin

NOVEMBER 24   From *I'll Tell You Where to Stuff the Turkey* (Shirley Shimmelfenner, vol. 8, chap. 1)

". . . In the sink, because those bread crumbs really fly around, and otherwise you'll have the floor to sweep too. Somebody else's sink is best of all, because somebody else will probably be doing it then, not you.

"In fact, if you're any kind of a noncook, don't do Thanksgiving unless you potluck it. Doing the whole thing, you're out of your league—up against the pie purists, spud champs, and gravy artists, and every man there remembering the Thanksgiving dinner Mom used to put out. A wizard with a gizzard, Mom was, the way they tell it, even if she didn't know a giblet from her left foot. . . . And when you potluck it at someone else's place, put in for the relish and the dessert, and bring something Mom never heard of. You may not get Mom's reputation, but you'll get one for sure."

NOVEMBER 25   Make some

CRANBERRY CHUTNEY

In a big saucepan, combine

1 pound cranberries	1 tablespoon ground cinnamon
1 cup seedless raisins	1½ tablespoons ground ginger
1⅔ cups sugar	1 cup water

Simmer all this for about fifteen minutes, till the cranberries pop out of their skins and the mixture thickens. Then add

> ½ cup chopped onion
> 2 apples, pared and chopped
> ½ cup celery, sliced fine

Simmer it another fifteen minutes, then cool it and keep it cold.

NOVEMBER 26   On this day in 1789, the first nation-
                     wide Thanksgiving was celebrated.
George Washington chose the date as a day of national Thanksgiving, specifically for the adoption of the Constitution. But the purpose got lost in the general shuffle, and now we are mainly grateful for the long weekend and the chance to overeat and then to sleep it off.

A Good Thanksgiving Dessert:

KAHLUA CREAM
for 6

1 cup heavy cream   cupcake papers
1 pint vanilla ice cream   ⅓ cup finely chopped and
¼ cup Kahlua   toasted almonds

Beat the cream to the stiff-peak stage. Then put the ice cream in a bowl and beat it (with the same beaters) to soften it a bit. Then mix in the whipped cream and the Kahlua. Put the cupcake papers in muffin tins and fill them with the mixture. Sprinkle the almonds on top and freeze till firm.

NOVEMBER 27   A Reasonable Thing to Do with
                     Leftover Turkey

". . . Nothing is easier than Sour Cream Turkey Curry, but since the family probably won't settle for nothing (that's my little joke!) a Turkey Curry is a good second choice, providing, as it does, a distinct change from the turkey taste."
                              —Stella Trowbridge Hinky

SOUR CREAM TURKEY CURRY

3 tablespoons butter
2 teaspoons curry powder
⅓ cup chopped onion
3 tablespoons flour

1 can chicken broth
3 cups cooked turkey meat, chopped
1 cup sour cream

Melt the butter over low heat, and add the curry powder and chopped onion. Cook about five minutes. Then stir in the flour and the chicken broth, stirring till it's a smooth sauce. Then add the turkey and the sour cream. Keep it hot in the double boiler (have the water barely simmering so the sour cream won't curdle) while you cook some rice to serve it on. Actually one should have done this first, but one doesn't always think to.

NOVEMBER 28   A good Italian treatment for Leftover Turkey.

ATSA MY TURKEY!

First, cook and drain half a pound of fettucini or plain egg noodles. Then simmer over low heat for five minutes

3 cups chopped cooked turkey
½ cup condensed chicken broth
½ cup dry white wine

Add the noodles to the turkey now, along with

¼ cup milk
6 tablespoons diced mozzarella or Monterey Jack cheese
6 tablespoons Parmesan cheese

2 tablespoons butter
1 teaspoon salt
¼ teaspoon pepper

Cook it over very low heat, stirring frequently, for ten minutes. (Or use the double boiler.) A fruit salad is good with it.

NOVEMBER 29   On this day in 1783, the American Revolutionary troops decided they'd won that war, and so they all demobilized.

Also on this day, in 1975, the Second Methodist Church of Piscataway, New Jersey, reported 100-percent co-operation from the female members of the congregation in making something for the Annual Home-Baked Goods Bazaar. Every one of them brought something.

"Actually, it was easy," explained Mrs. Patterson Wibblee, chairman and organizer. "We just had the minister announce that only the younger women were expected to contribute."

NOVEMBER 30   Mark Twain was born on this day in 1835, a very good day for the country.

> Low'ring sky,
> blizzard ny.
> Flick'ring sun,
> blizzard dun.

Augurs well for the end of the old month and the start of the festive new. Rest quietly now.

December

bringeth a consideration of sundry good
things: the Gift & the Phlugerhaggen, the
Card & the Comfit & the Sweetmeat; includeth

> a gentle jubilation of Cookies
> a remarkable Fried Fruit
> the world-famous Scripture Cake
> an almond-cranberry Delight

and other Delicacies befitting the Joyful
  Season!

~~~~~~~~~~~~~~~~~~~~~~~~~~~~~~~~~~~~

Mary, Mary, quite contrary,
How does your Christmas garden grow?

Pine, poinsettias, holly berry . . .
The crocus sleeps now, under the snow.

DECEMBER 1   NOW IT IS DECEMBER and Frost lieth cold silver upon the Ground as the aging Yeare creaketh to the Finish-line. Now the Apartment-dweller raileth at the Super & the Homeowner complaineth to the Power Companie. And in 24 days shall the reluctant Cooke grapple with the reluctant Turkie (or the sullen immortal Ham). And now doth the harried Houseperson shut her Minde to the Cupboard that needeth sorting & the Room that needeth repainting, wisely postponing these Thyngs. For surely December bringeth problems enow & yet bringeth Joys too, with good Thyngs to make & eat & think.

DECEMBER 2   What Do You Wear on Christmas Day? ". . . The trick about dressing for Christmas is to get the dress *now*. Do it before the last of the money goes on presents for forgotten relatives. . . . You probably need something tough enough to cope with the kitchen, the children, serving the turkey, getting drunk in, and general slouching about, yet pretty enough to preside over your own family party or go out to someone else's. It should be loose enough to let you over-eat in comfort without reminding you of the ruinous effect your gluttony is having on your figure. . . ."

           —*The Observer* (London)

"Don't eat too many almonds; they add weight to the breasts."

           —Gigi (in *Gigi*, by Colette)

DECEMBER 3   Now lytle birds do search for seeds in the hard fields, and it is a time to replenish the Birdfeeder and quarantine the Cat.

DECEMBER 4   Cooky Notes from Our Columnists From "The Chatterbox," Mervyn Meadows *Sentinel:*
"Mrs. Charles ('Edie') Grumwalt's 'gang' is at it again! Last Thursday, 'Edie's' charming kitchen was the scene of a pick-up lunch and the Big Cooky Swap she instigated a month ago . . . each of eight 'girls' going home with four-

teen dozen cookies, seven kinds! Only specification was that they had to freeze well. They all looked just yummy. But would you believe they wouldn't give Your Correspondent a single bite? 'No bringee, no eatee!' laughed 'Edie' as she whipped up the Margaritas. So that's the way the cooky crumbles with the 'Grumwalt gang'!"

From "One Man's Beat," Grand Rapids *Telegram:*
". . . On our block, swapping holiday baked goods is becoming more complicated, now the Fimmisters have gone macrobiotic, the Tuggleses low-carb, the Woodses high-protein, and the Wellmans vegetarian-kosher. My wife wants to know how you make a macrobiotic low-carb high-protein vegetarian-kosher Christmas cooky. . . ."

Dear Aloise,
I just had to pass this great "tip" along! The next time you make any raisin-spice cookies, add some chopped dates too, and you'll find they stay moist and chewy and just delicious twice as long!

Doreen

Dear Doreen:
You're a real live doll! I tried it and you're right! I love you!

Aloise

DECEMBER 5   One year ago on this day, Stephanie ("Fats") Stumflug read in the paper that basil is just as good as mistletoe for getting kissed under. In Italy, it said, they call it "Kiss-Me-Quick," and wearing a sprig is considered a cordial invitation.

Stephanie didn't have any fresh basil, so she just hung the kitchen spice jar of it around her neck and it worked fine.

"Of course I had to tell everybody what it was for," she reported, "but what the heck."

Stephanie has always had a hard time keeping her mind on her cooking, especially vegetables, because she'd rather think about fruitcakes and fudge. The only holiday-type vegetable she can ever think to make is broccoli cooked as usual, seasoned with melted butter, salt and pepper, then jazzed up with pimento strips. She likes it because it matches the holly.

DECEMBER 6   Let us now celebrate the anniversary of Good St. Nicholas, who died on this day, A.D. 342, or else was born on this day, the book didn't make it quite clear.

Even as an infant, St. Nicholas was so good that he wouldn't suck on Wednesdays or Fridays, which were fast days then. Later, he became the patron saint of children, sailors, robbers, and virgins, most particularly virgins; and the way of it was this:

A nobleman in the town of Patera had three daughters and not much hope of marrying them off, for his fortunes had taken a terrible turn for the worse. Being something of a rotter, he had just about decided to sell them to a house of ill-repute, when word of his intention reached Archbishop Nicholas (he wasn't a saint yet) and perturbed him greatly.

Luckily, Nicholas had a great deal of money; and so, one moonlit night, he went by stealth to the nobleman's house and tossed a sack of gold through the open window, then vanished. This served as the eldest daughter's marriage portion, and the nobleman was thus able to unload her in holy matrimony.

Later, he did the same thing for the second daughter and later still for the third. (Doing it all at once would have been too hard on his pitching arm, because gold is heavy.)

But before he actually tossed the last sackful in, the nobleman—who had been dying of curiosity as to the identity of his unknown benefactor—caught him in the act.

"Oh, Nicholas! Servant of God!" he cried. "Why seek to hide thyself?" But Nicholas pledged him to secrecy, and understandably. There were probably many unmarried daughters in the town, and like the charity mailing list today, you get on one of them and you're on them all.

Anyway, that's why he is the patron saint of virgins.

DECEMBER 7   MS. AESOP'S FABLES (No. 8)
       An Ass decided one autumn to do his Christmas shopping early. He got new trousers for the Pig and a cigarette lighter for the Dog and a rear assembly for the Worm (who had recently lost his in a lawn mower), and a nice big megaphone for the Owl, who was getting weak in the hoot.

A couple of weeks before Christmas, he saw his friends at a party. He found that the Pig had gained thirty pounds, and the Dog had quit smoking, and the Worm had meanwhile grown himself a new rear end, and the Owl was very excited about a new transistorized megaphone which he had made a down payment on that very day.

Moral: He who shops early shops twice.

DECEMBER 8   From *Living Through Christmas* by Stella Trowbridge Hinky:

Christmas Shopping Rule No. 1: When you find a great little item that would suit several people on your list, *get* some, one for each, and all in the Fire Engine Red if that's the best color. No point getting them all different for variety's sake and then wondering who to stick with the purple one. Because you'll lose your nerve and end up with it yourself.

Christmas Shopping Rule No. 2: When you find something that looks about right, but you're not sure, get it anyway, instead of muttering, "Well, I'll think about it . . ." which gets you nowhere but tired. Even if you decide it's wrong, other gift times are coming around the bend. And other people.

Christmas Shopping Rule No. 3: Almost anyone can use another flashlight, flower pot, oven timer, timepiece, notebook, collapsible canvas traveling bag, pair of scissors, pencil sharpener, address book, dictionary, jar of caviar, dollar bill.

Just this one Christmas, One-Hoss wishes people would stop trying to spruce him up. He doesn't want an Aran Isle fisherman's cap or a Spanish beret or anything with leather on the elbows; he wants a new posthole digger.

DECEMBER 9   It is now sixteen days till Christmas and time to panic.

The fact is, so many objects are manufactured just to give to somebody else. Did anyone in her right mind ever buy herself a jeweled pancake turner? Or a set of crayfish forks? Or hurricane-lamp cozies? Or washcloths with sequins on them?

There is also the Phlugerhaggen. A phlugerhaggen is a sort

of non-thing, or thing-plus, which does or is whatever its builder wants it to do or be; and there is many a Phluger-haggen around at Christmastime. (The winner in a recent Phlugerhaggen exhibit in Elmira, New York, was a wonderful creation that incorporated a bathtub, a 1915 gas engine, a steam whistle, a toilet, and a pair of walking shoes. It brushes the tub, plunges the toilet, blows the whistle, rings bells, and sweeps the ground in front of where its feet walk, while the water in the tub cools the gasoline engine.)

". . . My only enduring gift principle is the $5 cake of soap. Best of breed. Better the $20 coin purse than the $20 handbag. Better the $10 handkerchief than the $10 shirt. . . ."
                                        —Albert Wooky

DECEMBER 10   From *Santa Claus Is Coming To Town & I'm Leaving,* by Shirley Shimmelfenner, chap. 22

". . . So there I was working my head off, Christmas coming, and suddenly I realized I was spending most of the time trying to make the house look like nobody lived in it and the kitchen look like nobody cooked in it. So I decided, Nuts to that, you expect to see some bodies around a battlefield. . . ."

BARLEY SHIMMELFENNER

(To bake along with a roast or serve with any cold meat)

2 tablespoons butter
1 cup barley, rinsed and
   drained
1 celery stalk, chopped
1½ teaspoons parsley, chopped

1½ teaspoons salt
¼ teaspoon pepper
2 cups chicken stock (made
   from bouillon cubes)

First she melts the butter in a skillet and sautés the barley briefly, not enough to brown it, then adds everything else and heats it to boiling. At that point she pours it into a casserole dish, starts to cover it, notices the dish doesn't have a lid, and mutters some basic English to herself while she hunts up the aluminum foil. When it eventually appears, she covers the casserole with that and bakes it for an hour at 350°. Serves six to eight and it's a nice change from spuds.

DECEMBER 11   A Personal Letter.
                 ". . . You ask me [*my friend wrote*]
why I don't send Christmas cards, and I suppose the answer
is that I've gotten self-conscious about it—can't decide what
sort of statement about myself I want to make. Because every
card seems to make one. If it's all jolly ho-ho-ho, don't you
look a trifle insensitive, these days? And foreign language
cards always seem to say *Look who's been where*, don't they?
And if it's a card sponsored by some terribly worthy cause,
then it's *Oh, what a good girl am I*. . . . Only in that case
it would be better to send a fat check straight to the Cause,
wouldn't it, and skip the cards. I don't know. . . .

"Not that I haven't sent cards, some years. Once, I know
my cards indicated that I was color-blind and broke, which
wasn't so that year, but I'd bought them from an old
Christmas-card peddler who was. And another time, all they
said was that I was in a hurry when I picked them out, because I meant to check #184A, Snowbound English Village,
and hit the #185, Andy Warhol Soup Cans, by mistake.
"And I do like to receive them, though under deep hyp-
nosis I might reveal that any name-engraved Christmas card
that comes without one personal note on it gives me the same
warm good feeling as any piece of mail marked OCCU-
PANT. . . ."

DECEMBER 12   Make fome Rofewater for lytle giftf!
                 ". . . The fcent of inflammable Spirit
of Rofes is ravifhingly fweet; if only two drops of it are
mixed with a glafs of Water, they impart to the Water fo
high a perfume, that it exceeds the very beft Rofewater."
        —From *Toilet of Flora* (15th Century)

DECEMBER 13   And make fome feafoning falt alfo!

FEAFONING FALT

Altogether in the blender mix ½ teaspoon each of

dill seed	dried thyme
celery salt	marjoram
onion powder	garlic salt

and one teaspoon each of

dry mustard	paprika

plus six tablespoons of plain table salt. Then make a green salad with a vinegar-and-oil dressing and some of your product and see how you like it. Perhaps you'll want a little oregano, or curry, or more garlic or paprika. Then you can quadruple the recipe, to pack in dime-store shakers. Tie one to a can of good olive oil for a nice lytle prefent!

DECEMBER 14   One-Hoss says things have sure changed. He can remember when he got 100 Christmas stickers and tags for 29 cents. Now it's four for a dollar. This year he's giving stickers and tags.

DECEMBER 15   Now begin the halcyon days.

These be the seven days before and after the winter solstice—a time of such calm and tranquillity (or so said the ancients) that the halcyon, who was of the kingfisher family, would nest upon the sea.

But what has happened to the halcyon days? It was on this day, in 1975, that Mumu Harbottle went to see Dr. Neitzelgrinder about a persistent ringing in her ears.

"H'mmmm," said Dr. N. thoughtfully, after he'd looked her over. "It can't be the oven timer, way down here, and it's too early for sleigh bells. It's probably nerves. What's bugging you, Mumu?"

"Christmas, I guess," she said unhappily.

"Can't get your shopping done? Trying to take too much on?" asked the good doctor.

"Well, yes, but mainly it's—Oh, it's just the whole big commercial mess," Mumu said. "The canned carols—'Silent Night' in the Ladies' Room at the dime store! And those awful Santa Clauses, two per block. What's the matter with little kids, are they feebleminded that they can't figure it out by the time they're two years old? And buying overpriced stuff for people who don't need it. And sending a bunch of cards to people you hardly know when you ought to be writing a decent letter to somebody you *do* know. . . ."

"Then why don't you do that?" asked the doctor mildly.

"Because I'm so frantic at this point I couldn't write a decent note to the mailman," Mumu snapped. "Excuse me, Doctor. But that's something else. My temper. It's starting to go. And the kids. Gimme, gimme, gimme . . ."

The doctor nodded.

"And the whole mechanized Christmas-tipping routine," Mumu said bitterly. "We'd like to give the janitor someth—"

"Maintenance man," the doctor corrected.

"Okay, maintenance man. We'd like to give him something. And the garbagem—"

"Sanitation engineer," the doctor corrected.

"All *right*," Mumu said impatiently. "And the switchboard girl, whatever you call *her*. But what does the Super bring up last night? A list of what we're *supposed* to give everybody. Twenty dollars here. Ten dollars there. Twenty-five dollars there. About as spontaneous as a forced march."

"Have a cooky," said Dr. Neitzelgrinder, opening a shortening can beautiful with contact-paper daisies. "The scrub lady brought me s—"

"Maintenance woman," Mumu said.

"Right!" said the doctor. ". . . Darned good, aren't they? Really crisp."

They chewed awhile.

"Well, now, I'll tell you, Mumu," the doctor said. "You put too big a load on Christmas, it's not going to blow a fuse, *you* are. It's funny, everybody expects Christmas to change something. Going to make everything and everybody different. Well, it hasn't. Not in a couple of thousand years, it hasn't. Christmas is like old age. Just makes everybody more so. If you're miserable at Christmas, you're going to be more so, just because it *is* Christmas. If you're happy, you're going to be happier. What we've got is a big jolly commercial carnival with overtones."

"That's just what I said," said Mumu. "Commercial."

"But why is commercial a dirty word?" asked the good doctor. "This country of ours is commercial, among other things. If it weren't, we'd never have come up with mass production to spread things around so more of us can have decent comforts."

"Yes, but—" Mumu began. The doctor held up a finger.

"And the fact that certain people have such lavish ones that they're indecent doesn't change the fact. You listen to me, Mumu," he continued, and Mumu thought, *O, boy, here we go again.* "Decent comforts is what the whole world's been after since Og spread out a bearskin in the first cave, and the only thing wrong with decent comforts is that the whole world doesn't have 'em. And—shut up, Mumu—trying to see that they get 'em is the devout endeavor of some of the best brains we've got. Wouldn't you admit that that involves a good deal of what we call the Christmas spirit?"

"Well, yes," said Mumu. "But I—"

"And, meanwhile," said the doctor comfortably, settling back, "Christmas is still a time when you remind people that you love 'em or like 'em, isn't it? Or at least that you don't hate 'em. Or that you *thought* about 'em. Isn't it? And what in the heck is the matter with that?"

Mumu couldn't think of anything, and she noticed that the ringing in her ears had stopped, when she got up to go. "Thank you, Doctor," she said, as he handed her some more cookies to eat on the way home.

"Merry Crispness!" she said.

"Ho ho ho!" he said.

MERRY CRISPNESS COOKIES

(Very crisp with a smooth semishortbread texture)

1 cup butter	1 egg
1 cup sugar	2 teaspoons cream or canned
3 cups flour	milk
½ teaspoon salt	1 teaspoon vanilla
1½ teaspoons baking powder	

Cream the butter and sugar, and add the sifted dry ingredients. Then beat the egg, cream, and vanilla together and add them.

Maybe you'll need to chill it before you roll it. Then roll it thin, about ⅛ inch thick, put a walnut half on each if you like, sprinkle them with sugar, and bake on a greased cooky sheet about ten minutes, till they're gilt-edged. They'll stay crisp a good while in a closed can decorated with contact-paper daisies.

LITTLE CHRISTMAS THIMBLE CAKES

½ cup butter	1 cup unsifted flour
⅓ cup confectioners' sugar,	¼ teaspoon salt
preferably sifted	¾ cup finely chopped pecans
1 egg, separated	
½ teaspoon vanilla	jams, jellies, marmalade . . .

Cream the butter and sugar, add the egg yolk and vanilla, then the flour and salt. (Put the egg white in a little dish for dipping, later.) Mix it well. If it's hard to handle, chill it.

Then shape it into ¾-inch balls, dip them in the egg white, and roll them in the chopped nuts.

Now we come to the thimble part: Put the balls on an ungreased baking sheet and, with a thimble, poke a little crater in each. Bake for five minutes at 350°. Then take them out and repoke them—the craters tend to level out—and bake about six minutes longer, till they're set. After they've cooled on racks, fill the centers with the jams and jellies. (If you're storing these, store them unfilled, or things will get pretty sticky.)

CURLED-UP CANDY COOKIES

(These give a lot of expression to a cooky plate.)

¾ cup unblanched almonds, grated or ground fine
½ cup butter
½ cup sugar
1 tablespoon each flour
                  heavy cream
                  milk

Put it all in a saucepan over low heat and stir it till the butter melts. Then whisk it a bit till it's smooth, and drop the batter by the teaspoonful onto a well-oiled and floured cooky sheet —only three per sheet, because they spread like mad and, also, you have to roll each one while it's malleable, and they cool fast. Bake at 350° about eight minutes till the centers bubble a little and they're deep gold. Take them out, let them cool a few seconds, then quickly roll each one around a broom handle or a wooden spoon handle. Reoil and flour the cooky sheet each time or you may be sorry.

PEANUT-BUTTER POKIES

Liberate two egg whites from two eggs and slip them into a bowl. Mix with 1½ cups of peanut butter and 1 cup of white sugar. Drop by the teaspoonful onto a greased cooky sheet, press gently with the tines of a fork, and bake eight to ten minutes at 350°.

DECEMBER 16   On this day in 1770, Beethoven was born. On this day in 1773, the Boston Tea Party was held in Boston Harbor.

And on this morning in 1975, a good brisk morning with a red winter sunrise, Dr. Neitzelgrinder woke up hungry for pork chops.—Hungry, specifically, for Mrs. Neitzelgrinder's pork chops. She has always said he married her for her pork chops, an allegation he denies but not very hard. And so she quit playing with holly sprigs and styrofoam balls and the grandchildren's Christmas stockings long enough to fix him a fine winter dinner, featuring her special pork chops and her special cranberries with almonds.

MRS. NEITZELGRINDER'S PORK CHOPS
for 6

She gets six good-sized pork chops, at least an inch thick, and a little thicker doesn't hurt. She also finds a brown paper grocery sack and in it she puts

¼ cup flour
½ teaspoon garlic salt
½ teaspoon celery salt
½ teaspoon seasoned salt
1 teaspoon paprika

Now she drops the chops into it, bounces them around a bit, and then browns them slowly in a couple of tablespoons of fat.

While they brown, she's slicing a green pepper into six rings, and three cored but unpeeled red apples into six thick chunks. On each chop—when they're browned—she puts a pepper ring and an apple slice.

Now. In a cup, she mixes

½ cup water
1 tablespoon brown sugar
2 tablespoons Worcestershire sauce

and pours it over all the chops, then puts the lid on the skillet and simmers it for forty minutes.

(What he generally gets with this is scalloped potatoes out of a box. No point spoiling the man.)

As for the cranberry arrangement, she generally makes it in the morning, to give it time to get cold.

MRS. N.'S
CRANBERRIES WITH ALMONDS

½ cup almonds, blanched and skinned*

2 cups sugar

1 cup water

4 cups cranberries

⅓ cup orange marmalade

juice of two lemons

She puts the sugar and water in a saucepan and lets them boil five minutes. Then she adds the cranberries and lets them cook for another five. When the skins burst, she takes the pan off the burner and adds the marmalade and the lemon juice. After it has cooled, she adds the cold almonds and then chills the whole thing.

DECEMBER 17   And on this splendid day in 1903, Orville Wright soared 120 feet high in the world's first power-driven heavier-than-air airplane! To commemorate it, make some

HIGH-RISE POPOVERS

(No one knows who started the unfounded rumor that popovers are risky or in any way a test of cooksmanship. These popovers can be easily made by anyone who is bright enough to blow her nose.)

Set the oven at 450°. Grease six custard cups with vegetable shortening (not oil), including the outside of the cup rims. Set them on a cooky sheet.

In a bowl, dump

- 1 cup unsifted flour
- ½ teaspoon salt
- 2 eggs (just break them over the bowl and drop them in so they're staring at you with their big yellow eyes)
- 1 cup milk

Beat this with an egg beater till it's just mixed—about fifteen seconds. Now fill the cups half full and set the cooky sheet in the 450° oven. Let them bake for twenty-five minutes. Then,

* If they're not already that way, she pours boiling water over them and lets them stand about five minutes. Then, with just a little pinch, the almonds squirt out, sometimes all over the kitchen. So she retrieves them, pours cold water on them, and lets them chill a couple of hours before she adds them to the cranberries. Finds they're crisper that way.

without opening the oven, lower the temperature to 400° and bake another thirty—fifty-five in all. That's it. You will have six splendid popovers, so golden brown and exuberantly puffed up that it's almost embarrassing.

DECEMBER 18   A Good Christmas Punch.
                        is what One-Hoss says he'll give the next department-store clerk who directs him to the Suburban Swingers' Boutique when he asks the way to Women's Underwear.

He also has a recipe for a ripsnorter that he says don't take much doing, once the derned cloves are stuck in the oranges.

HOT POT PUNCH
Christmas spirits for 15 people

5 oranges	**a fifth of apple brandy**
plenty of whole cloves	**½ gallon apple cider**
	cinnamon sticks, one per cup

Stud the oranges with cloves and roast them in a 350° oven half an hour, till they ooze a little and change color. Then put them in a metal pot, maybe the jam kettle. (One-Hoss used a glass punch bowl once, and he might as well have hit it with a pipe wrench.)

Heat the brandy—just put the bottle in hot water up to its neck over a low flame. Pour the apple cider into some big saucepan and heat it, too.

Then dim the lights, pour the hot brandy over the oranges, and light it. Whoosh! Put the fire out in a couple of minutes, after the flames have licked up the orange oils, and add the hot cider. Serve it by the big cupful, a cinnamon stick in each.

From Mrs. Beeton's *All About Everything*, 1869:

RUMFUSTIAN, a drink
greatly approved

Ingredients: 12 eggs, 1 quart strong beer, 1 pint
               gin, 1 bottle of sherry, 1 stick of

cinnamon, 1 nutmeg, 12 lumps of
sugar, peel of 1 lemon

Mode: Beat the eggs into a froth, and whisk
them into the beer; to this add the gin:
meanwhile, boil a bottle of sherry with
the other ingredients, and as soon as
they boil, mix both together. Serve
quite hot.

One-Hoss says this'll grow hair on sidewalks.

DECEMBER 19   "Without the door let sorrow lie
And if for cold it hap to die,
We'll bury it in a Christmas-pie
And evermore be merry!"
—Old Christmas carol

". . . Old English cookery-books always style the
crust of a pie 'the coffin.' . . ."   —R. Chambers

A CHRISTMAS APRICOT PIE

2 cups dried apricots	½ cup light brown sugar
1 cup orange juice	¼ teaspoon salt
1 tablespoon cornstarch	butter
pastry for a 2-crust pie	

Soak the apricots in the orange juice for two hours and line
an eight-inch pie pan with pastry at the same time, so it can
chill while the apricots soak. After two hours, drain the fruit
but save ⅔ of the juice. Put the liquid in the top of a double
boiler, and blend in

1 tablespoon cornstarch
½ cup light brown sugar
¼ teaspoon salt

and let it cook till thick, stirring most of the time. Now spread
the apricots around in the coffin, pour the syrup over them,
and dot with butter. Cover it with a lattice top or a plain slit
top—plenty of slits so the juice can bubble through—and
bake for twelve minutes at 400°. Reduce the heat to 325°

and bake another fifteen or twenty minutes, till the pastry looks pretty.

DECEMBER 20   On this bleak day in 1820, the sovereign State of Missouri leveled a Bachelor Tax. All unmarried men from the ages of twenty-one to fifty were liable for a special tax of one dollar per year.

Scholars of the period believe it was the husbands' lobby that got the bill through. They couldn't stand the thought of all those carefree unattached lads watching TV football the day before Christmas when they should have been messing with Christmas-tree lights.

DECEMBER 21   *A Dissertation on Camels.*
The Camel has not had an easy time of it, and it is no wonder he is bad-tempered. To begin with, he never liked his basic design and tried to get it changed. He wanted horns, according to Aesop—the kind of horns the buffalo had, or maybe a nice set of antlers, and so he took the matter up with Jupiter.

However, Jupiter not only refused to give him the horns he asked for, he cropped his ears short for being so impudent as to ask. The moral, Aesop says, is that *by asking too much we may lose the little that we had before.* Or, to put it another way, *Ask and ye shall receive, something else.*

It isn't true, by the way, that the Camel stores water in his hump. His hump isn't a reservoir, it is a pantry, for storing food. Mostly fat, the hump weighs about eighty pounds. When the Camel has little to eat, he lives off his hump which—naturally—shrinks. If things get tough enough, his hump can even slip off his back and hang to one side, so he loses his figure altogether—a development not calculated to sweeten the temper either. The moral here is *Keep your hump plump.* But of course the Camel is not always in a position to do so.

Carrying the Wise Men was really the high point for the Camel. Things have gone pretty much downhill ever since.

A good day to make a Scripture Cake.

THE FAMOUS OLD SCRIPTURE CAKE

(If you know your Bible well, this will pose no problems. If you don't know it quite that well, the translation is on pages 274-275.)

¾ cup Genesis 18:8
1½ cup Jeremiah 6:20
5 Isaiah 10:14 (separated)
3 cups sifted Leviticus 24:5
3 teaspoons 2 Kings 2:20
3 teaspoons Amos 4:5
1 teaspoon Exodus 3:23

¼ teaspoon each 2 Chronicles 9:9
½ cup Judges 4:19
¾ cup chopped Genesis 43:11
¾ cup finely cut Jeremiah 24:5
¾ cup 2 Samuel 16:1
whole Genesis 43:11

Cream Genesis 18 with Jeremiah 6. Beat in yolks of Isaiah 10, one at a time. Sift together Leviticus 24, 2 Kings 2, Amos 4, Exodus 30, and 2 Chronicles 9.

Blend into creamed mixture alternately with Judges 4. Beat whites of Isaiah 10 till stiff; fold in. Fold in chopped Genesis 43, Jeremiah 24, and 2 Samuel 16. Turn into ten-inch tube pan that has been greased and dusted with Leviticus 24.

Bake at 325° till it is golden brown or Gabriel blows his trumpet, whichever happens first. Usually it takes an hour and ten minutes. After fifteen minutes, remove it from the pan and have it completely cooled when you drizzle over it some Burnt Jeremiah Syrup.

BURNT JEREMIAH SYRUP

1½ cups Jeremiah 6:20
½ cup Genesis 24:45
¼ cup Genesis 18:8

Melt Jeremiah 6 in heavy skillet over low heat. Keep cooking it till it is a deep gold, then add the Genesis 24. Cook till smooth and remove from the heat. Add Genesis 18 and stir till it melts, then cool. After drizzling this on the cake, you can decorate it with whole Genesis.

DECEMBER 22   Now it is the first day of winter.

And now beginneth the sign of persistent CAPRICORNUS (controlling the Knees) that continueth through January 19, a favorable time to

pull teeth (if any be left now)

     bake a Christmas pudding
     execute the Christmas turkey
     start a romance
     continue one.

And Capricorn accomplisheth all duties, for in Capricorn the Desire to be well thought of nearly equaleth the desire to follow the Heart.

DECEMBER 23   A day to give a passing thought to Christmas Dinner.

". . . Since childhood, I have viewed with distinctly bridled enthusiasm the general custom of cooking and serving a large Christmas dinner. All I ever saw of my mother on that day was the bow on her apron."

                     —Albert Wooky

A GOOD CHRISTMAS DINNER

Oyster Stew
or
Clam Chowder
or
Vegetable Soup
or
whatever soup the family likes best

A Platter of Cold Sliced Meat and Thin-Sliced
Bread-and-Butter

Celery Stalks and Carrot Strips

A large tray of samplings from all edible gifts (and freeze the rest), including Mrs. Finnery's Blue Ribbon Cranberry Cake and the girl across the street's home-salted Cashews, and some of those foil-wrapped Cheese Wedges, compliments Dierdorff & Sons Insurance, and some of Mrs. Diddlehopper's Dream Puffs

Champagne

DECEMBER 24 "Just for a few hours on Christmas Eve and Christmas Day the stupid, harsh mechanism of the world runs down, and we permit ourselves to live according to untrammeled good sense, the unconquerable efficiency of good will. We grant ourselves the complete and selfish pleasure of loving others better than ourselves. How odd it seems, how unnaturally happy we are! . . ."

—Christopher Morley

Wrapping gifts on Christmas Eve, you will find that big brown grocery sacks, cut up, make cheerful packages when tied with bright yarn. As it grows later, small brown grocery sacks will prove handy, as is. Drop the present in, and tie it with the yarn. Newspapers aren't bad either, and when you run out of yarn, there may be some calico around, or an old printed shirt, to cut with pinking shears into ribbon.

DECEMBER 25 Now riseth the hillock of crumpled Tissue and emptie Boxes; now appeareth the bright welter: the Gift Glorious & the Gift Poopy, the rich-packed Pudding & the Toasts & the bright Sugar-plums. Yet through it all, the listening Ear heareth the sound of the Christmas Promise.

"Then let us all rejoice amain,
On Christmas-day, on Christmas-day,
Then let us all rejoice amain,
On Christmas-day in the morning!"
—Old English Christmas carol

DECEMBER 26 Aspects excellent for cooking the Christmas ham (or turkey) that wasn't cooked yesterday. A good thing to serve with it is

MAGGI COBB'S V. GOOD FRIED FRUIT

(V. festive too, and it can be ready well in advance, right up to adding the brandy)

A 1-pound can each of
   peach halves
   pear halves
   pineapple rings
An 11-ounce can of
   mandarin oranges

1 cup seedless grapes, canned
   or fresh
1 6-ounce jar maraschino
   cherries
2 pared apples cut in wedges
3 sliced bananas

    ¼ pound butter
    ⅓ cup brown sugar
    ½ teaspoon cinnamon
    ½ lemon
    ⅓ cup brandy

Drain all the fruit and use the syrup for something else if you can think of something. Melt the butter in a skillet over low heat and add all the fruit. Sprinkle it with the brown sugar and cinnamon; squeeze the half-lemon over it. Cook till the apples are just tender. Before serving, turn up the heat and add the brandy. Stir till blended, and serve quite hot.

DECEMBER 27   Now drink a friendly toast to the memory of Dr. Crawford Williamson Long, who administered the first ether for childbirth, during the delivery of his second child, Fanny.

DECEMBER 28   One day can bring what the whole year hath not.
                       —Old proverb

And perhaps this is the day for it: a letter or a new love or a check or an idea or a kick in the teeth or even a double rainbow.

DECEMBER 29   A True Account of a Curious Happening! It was early in the seventeenth century that Kepler published his Laws of Planetary Motion. They were, of course, the wonder of the age, at least to the comparatively few people educated enough to understand them.

Lord Orrery, in the north of England, was one of these. In fact, he became so fascinated by Kepler's picture of the universe that he hired an ingenious jeweler to build for him a mechanical model of it in miniature to place with all honor in his front hall.

There it stood, in its extraordinary shining complexity—a brass sun in the middle, the planets gravely revolving about it, four little moons revolving about Jupiter, one little moon revolving punctually around the earth, all exquisitely timed with a watchmaker's precision.

One morning, an atheist friend of Lord Orrery dropped by. Seeing it for the first time, he stood watching in awed fascination. Then he asked, "Who in the world made that for you?"

Lord Orrery said, "Nobody."

"Oh, come on, tell me," said his friend.

"That's right—nobody made it," Lord Orrery said. "It just happened. I came down one morning and there it was."

"Quit pulling my leg," his friend said with irritation.

And Lord Orrery said, "All right then, I'll make you a deal. If you will tell me who or what made the infinitely more intricate, mysterious, and beautiful universe we're living in, I'll tell you who made this one."

And for the first time, it is said, his atheist friend was without a ready answer.

GOD ISN'T DEAD, HE JUST DOESN'T LIKE BEING ON BUMPER STICKERS

DECEMBER 30 A good day to resolve to keep last January 2's Resolutions for the entire rest of the year.

DECEMBER 31 11:59 P.M. The neighbors went out for New Year's Eve. The kids went out. Even the tide went out, and it doesn't look like it wants to come back.

But your scribe goeth not out. (She did that once.) Your scribe sitteth in a new Christmas bathrobe by an old Christmas fire that will go out when the Old Year does. Listening to the wild bells ring out in Times Square and in the little church down the road, which were to ring out the thousand years of war and ring in the thousand years of peace but have not done so yet. Thinking the long thoughts that go with Old Year's Night. Viewing (as always) the Pandora's Box of a

new year, unfailingly packed with Mischiefs of many kinds,
yet also (like nuts in a cake) stuck therein with Pleasures &
Goodnesses great & small; and also Hope therein, like a moth
atremble, struggling to get her wings free.

And so your scribe now thinketh of the folk dear to her &
of the folk who would be if she but knew them. Hopeth for
them no troubles that cannot be in some good fashion coped
with; wisheth them all (pray it be not too bold a wish) much
joy in the year to come & the years thereafter. *Farewell.*

THE SCRIPTURE CAKE

GENESIS 18:8—"And he took *butter*, and milk, and the calf
which he had dressed, and set it before them."

JEREMIAH 6:20—"To what purpose cometh there to me
frankincense from Sheba, and the *sweet cane* from a far
country?"

ISAIAH 10:14—"And my hand hath found as a nest the riches
of the peoples; and as one gathereth *eggs* that are for-
saken, have I gathered all the earth."

LEVITICUS 24:5—"And thou shalt take *fine flour*, and bake
twelve cakes thereof."

2 KINGS 2:20—"And he said, Bring me a new cruse, and put
salt therein."

AMOS 4:5—"And offer a sacrifice of thanksgiving of that
which is *leavened*, and proclaim free will offerings and
publish them."

EXODUS 30:23—"Take thou also, unto thee the chief spices:
of flowering myrrh five hundred shekels, and of *sweet
cinnamon* half so much."

2 CHRONICLES 9:9—"And she gave the king a hundred and
twenty talents of gold, and *spices* in great abundance."

JUDGES 4:19—"And he said unto her, Give me, I pray thee,
a little water to drink; for I am thirsty. And she opened
a bottle of *milk* and gave him drink."

GENESIS 43:11—"Carry down the man a present, a little balm,
and a little honey, spicery and myrrh, nuts and *almonds.*"

JEREMIAH 24:5—"Thus saith Jehovah, God of Israel: Like
these good *figs*, so will I regard the captives of Judah,

whom I have sent out of this place into the land of the Chaldeans, for good."

SAMUEL 16:1—"And when David was a little past the top of the ascent, behold, Ziba, the servant of Mephibosheth met him, with a couple of asses saddled, and upon them two hundred loaves of bread, and a hundred clusters of *raisins*."

GENESIS 24:45—"And before I had done speaking in my heart, behold Rebekah came forth with her pitcher on her shoulder; and she went down to the *fountain*, and drew: and I said unto her, Let me drink, I pray thee."

MANY THANKS

All the people quoted in this book are real, though some are real only to me. That is, it was necessary to make some of them up, in order to be sure someone would say what I didn't feel quite comfortable saying myself. Accordingly, if they are not identified as they appear, or on this page or the following pages, that is probably the sort of people they are, and you are not likely to run into them anywhere again.

As for the others, I have identified them here if they seemed to need it, or if I could. (If I couldn't, it was because these writers were quoted in old old books, with no source given. Too bad.) If they seem to me familiar enough, I didn't bother to identify them. Identifying William Shakespeare, for instance, demands either innocence or effrontery, and at this point I haven't much of either.

But I want to thank everyone from whom I have quoted.

AMORY, CLEVELAND. Besides being the founder of the Hunt the Hunters Club, he is a social historian and writer, author of *Home Town, The Last Resorts, Man Kind?, The Proper Bostonians, Who Killed Society*, and *Vanity Fair*.

AUBREY, JOHN (1626–97). An English antiquary, folklorist, and gossip who delighted in the trivia of other people's lives, especially famous people, and preserved a lot of it in his *Miscellanies and Brief Lives*.

AUDEN, W. H. English-born and American-naturalized poet and playwright; author of *Poems, The Dance of Death, The Double Man,* and other books.

BAKER, JERRY. A popular garden writer, author of *Plants Are Like People,* which he seems to believe, and *Jerry Baker's Back to Nature Almanac.*

BEEBE, CHARLES WILLIAM (1877–1962). American explorer, naturalist, and writer of many books, including *The Arcturus Adventure, Half-Mile Down,* and *Book of Bays.*

BEETON, MRS. (nee Isabella Mary Mayson, 1836–65). English writer on cookery and housekeeping whose literary output was as voluminous as her life was short. Educated at Heidelberg, she became an accomplished pianist and gave it up in 1856 to marry the publisher Samuel Orchard Beeton. (Marrying a publisher is helpful to a writer, though not essential.) Her *Household Management,* published in several parts in 1859–60 and covering all branches of the domestic arts, made her name a household word. She died at age twenty-nine after the birth of her fourth son.

BOYD, LOU. American syndicated columnist.

BRILLAT-SAVARIN, ANTHELME (1755–1826). French gastronome and writer. A minor politician, his passion was food—eating it, preparing it, thinking about it. He wrote his *Physiologie du Goût* in 1825, an elegant and witty compendium on the art of dining.

BYRNE, SITA. A Ceylonese woman who worked with the poor in Hong Kong, Korea, Japan, and Southeast Asia for the Lutheran World Federation.

CANNON, POPPY. Knowledgeable U.S. author of many cookbooks.

CAPON, ROBERT FARRAR. Episcopal minister as well as Professor of Dogmatic Theology and Instructor in Greek at The George Mercer Jr. Memorial School of Theology. Author of *Bed and Board, An Offering of Uncles,* and *The Supper of the Lamb.*

CATO, MARCUS PORCIUS. The Roman statesman who lived from 234 to 149 B.C. and didn't like the Carthaginians. His every speech ended with "As for the rest, I vote that Carthage should be destroyed," and he deserves most of the credit for bringing on the Third Punic War. We probably wouldn't know about his hangovers if it weren't for Plutarch and his *Parallel Lives.*

CHAMBERS, R. Scottish publisher and bookseller, born in 1802.

He wrote voluminously on Scottish traditions, history, and biography. Singlehanded, he wrote *The Book of Days*—two immense volumes—working so hard on it that he lost his health and died in 1871.

CLAIBORNE, CRAIG. Food authority and author of several cookbooks. The lines quoted are from his *Kitchen Primer*.

CLAIBORNE, ROBERT. Free-lance writer for U.S. newspapers and magazines.

CLAYTON, BERNARD, JR. A former *Time-Life* war correspondent, now writer and editor attached to the School of Business at Indiana University, and author of a purely excellent and comprehensive bread book, *The Complete Book of Breads* (1973).

CORBITT, HELEN. Restaurant consultant to Neiman-Marcus and author of several books, including *Helen Corbitt's Cookbook, Helen Corbitt's Potluck, Helen Corbitt Cooks for Looks,* and *Helen Corbitt Cooks for Company.*

CORMAN, AVERY. U.S. advertising man; author of *Oh, God!*

DE LA MARE, WALTER JOHN (1873–1956). English poet and novelist who wrote many books, including *Songs of Childhood* and *Poems for Children.*

DE POMIANE, EDOUARD. French author of several charming cookbooks, among them one called *Cooking in Ten Minutes.*

DE VRIES, PETER. American author of *The Tents of Wickedness, Through the Fields of Clover, The Vale of Laughter,* and a number of other remarkable and remarkably funny books.

DILLARD, ANNIE. Poet (*Tickets for a Prayer Wheel*) and author of *Pilgrim at Tinker Creek;* also contributing editor to *Harper's.*

"ELIZABETH." Pen name of the Countess von Arnim, author of some delightful turn-of-the-century novels, including *Elizabeth and Her German Garden, Introduction to Sally,* and *The Father.* Born Mary Annette Beauchamp, she first married Count von Arnim and, next, a brother of Bertrand Russell.

FIRTH, GRACE. Missouri-born author of *A Natural Year,* a charming and fact-filled around-the-year book mainly concerned with how to live off the outdoors and like it (1972).

FROST, ROBERT. American poet. The quote is from a letter to *The Amherst Student,* published March 25, 1935.

FULLER, R. BUCKMINSTER. Designer and builder who developed, among other things, the geodesic dome, which is made of adjoining tetrahedrons, which are solids bounded by four plane triangular faces. He also wrote two good books: *Ideas and Integrities: A Spontaneous Autobiographical Disclosure* (1963) and *I Seem to Be a Verb* (1970).

FULLER, THOMAS (1608–1661). English clergyman, historian, and author of several books, including *History of the Holy Warre* and *History of the Worthies of England.* The remark about the guts and the heart quoted here is probably the shortest thing he ever said.

GILLIES, MARY DAVIS. Author of *The New How to Keep House* (1968).

GUNTHER, MAX. Free-lance writer, well versed in bugs.

HATT, CONGER T. I have been unable to track down his publisher, but I agree with a great deal that he says.

HAZELTON, NIKA. A good cook and writer on things culinary. The quote is from her *The Picnic Book* (1969).

HERTER, GEORGE LEONARD AND BERTHE. Authors of numerous books, all written, illustrated, and published by themselves in Waseca, Minnesota. Their works include *George the Housewife,* and three volumes of *Bull Cook and Authentic Historical Recipes and Practices.* They also run a thriving mail-order business in outdoor gear.

HIGGINS, ANNE. The quote is from her story "Maria at the Dentist," published in *Ms.,* April 1974.

HILLS, L. RUST. A man who writes and says quotable things. Author of several books, including *How To Be Good, or, The Somewhat Tricky Business of Attaining Moral Virtue in a Society That's Not Just Corrupt but Corrupting, Without Being Completely Out-of-it* (1976).

HOFFER, ERIC. The longshoreman-philosopher who wrote *The True Believer* and *The Passionate State of Mind.*

HOPKINS, GERARD MANLEY (1844–1899). Brilliant English Jesuit priest and poet, remembered for his God-haunted poems, not his sermons. Yet when he died, few of his obituaries mentioned that he was a poet.

KENNELLY, ARDYTH. Contemporary American novelist who knows and wrote about early Mormon days in Utah. Author of *The Peaceable Kingdom, The Spur, Good Morning, Young Lady, Up Home,* and *Marry Me, Carry Me.*

LAMB, CHARLES (1775–1834). English essayist who wrote, among other things, *Tales from Shakespeare* and *Essays of Elia.* These are fighting words from a very gentle man. But then, the people couldn't talk back.

LESLIE, FRANK. English journalist and artist whose real name was Henry Carter. In the mid-nineteenth century he came to the United States, changed his name for reasons of his own, and founded *Frank Leslie's Illustrated Newspaper,* a cozy and edifying sheet that contained something for everybody, as well as *Frank Leslie's Illustrated Family Almanacs.*

LEWIS, C. S. (1898–1963). English writer and Christian apologist; author of *Perelandra, Out of the Silent Planet, The Screwtape Letters,* and a number of other good books.

LYDGATE, JOHN. English monk and court poet who was born a couple of decades after Chaucer and wrote the same sort of thing Chaucer did but not so well.

LYND, ROBERT (1879–1949). Irish author of *It's a Fine World,* from which this quotation came.

MC CABE, CHARLES. New York–born newspaperman and professional Irishman, columnist for the San Francisco *Chronicle.*

MILLER, ELISABETH S. An early U.S. writer on the domestic arts. Author of *In the Kitchen* (1875).

MORE, SIR THOMAS. Well-known English writer and statesman who was beheaded at the age of fifty-seven because he wouldn't acknowledge Henry VIII as head of the English church.

MORLEY, CHRISTOPHER (1890–1957). Author of numerous novels, plays, poems, and casual pieces, who helped William Rose Benét found *Saturday Review of Literature* in 1924.

MORTON, J.B. Long-time columnist for the *Daily Express,* London.

MOSER, ROBERT. U.S. doctor and columnist, former editor of the A.M.A. *Journal.*

OLIVER, RAYMOND. Chef, writer, TV performer, and owner of Le Grand Vefours, a three-star Michelin restaurant in Paris.

PASCAL, BLAISE (1623–1662). An incredible and short-lived genius, mathematically, philosophically, and every which way. His *Pensées* were published after his death, and the quote is one of them.

PIRSIG, ROBERT. Author of the remarkable book *Zen and the Art of Motorcycle Maintenance* (William Morrow & Co., 1974). He studied chemistry, philosophy, and journalism at the University of Minnesota, and Oriental philosophy at Benares Hindu University in India.

PLATH, SYLVIA. American poet who wrote *The Colossus, Ariel, Uncollected Poems,* and *The Bell Jar.*

PLATT, JOHN RADER. American physicist and able writer. The quote is from *A Science Reader* (1962).

RAPP, LYNN AND JOEL. Authors of *Mother Earth's Hassle-Free Indoor Plant Book.*

RIVERS, JOAN. U.S. stand-up comedienne. It's always specified whether a comic stands up or sits down or lies down. Apparently it makes a difference in the quality of the work.

RUML, BEARDSLEY (1894–1960). Basically, a businessman but quite good at thinking. Chiefly remembered for inventing the pay-as-you-go Federal Income Tax plan.

RYSKIND, MORRIS. American playwright and collaborator of George Kaufman, George and Ira Gershwin, and Irving Berlin.

SAGAN, CARL. Director of the Laboratory for Planetary Studies and Professor of Astronomy and Space Sciences, Cornell University.

ST. JOHN, ADELA ROGERS. Contemporary California-born reporter and writer. The quote is from her most recent book, *Some Are Born Great.*

SCHOENSTEIN, RALPH. Columnist and free-lance writer. Author of *My Year in the White House Doghouse, I Hear America Mating,* and other funny books.

SCOTT-MAXWELL, FLORIDA. Writer and analytical psychologist. Author of several books, including *Towards Relationships, Many Women,* and *The Measure of My Days,* from the last of which the quoted lines were taken.

SHAND, P. MORTON. Self-termed gastrosopher; author of *A Book of Food*.

SHAPLEY, HARLOW. American astrophysicist, writer, and long-time director of Mt. Wilson Observatory. Among many other things, he figured out the size of our galaxy and the sun's position in it.

SHERATON, MIMI. A knowledgeable cook and writer. Author of *The Seducer's Cookbook*.

SZASZ, THOMAS STEPHEN. Contemporary Hungarian-born psychiatrist and author of several books, including *Pain and Pleasure*, *The Myth of Mental Illness*, and *The Second Sin*, from which the quoted lines were taken.

TAYLOR, JOHN (1580–1653). He was called "The Water Poet" because he wrote in the odd moments between collecting taxes from the barges on the Thames. When he wasn't doing either one, he was taking odd trips to write about, and he ended up keeping a pub.

TAYLOR, ROBERT LEWIS. U.S. free-lance writer.

VALÉRY, PAUL AMBROISE (1871–1945). French poet and philosopher.

VONNEGUT, KURT, JR. Indianapolis-born author of a number of good books, including *Player Piano* (1952) and *Wampeters Foma & Granfalloons* (1974).

WHITE, E. B. Contemporary American satirist, humorist, philosopher, and poet. The quote is from *The Second Tree from the Corner*.

WHITEHORN, KATHARINE. Author of *Never On Sundays* and other books; columnist for the London *Observer*.

WILLETT, SARAH. All I know of Sarah Willett is that she wrote to me several years ago about her mother's pastry rule, and I am grateful to her.

WILLIAMS, TENNESSEE. Mississippi-born playwright; author of *The Glass Menagerie*, *A Streetcar Named Desire*, *Cat on a Hot Tin Roof*, and other plays.

WILLIAMSON, DERECK. Columnist, free-lance writer, and author of *The Complete Book of Pitfalls*. Ordinarily a pleasant man, he becomes dangerous when the *c* in his first name is omitted.

INDEX